WYOMING

WYOMING

Nathaniel Burt

Photography by Don Pitcher

ODYSSEY GUIDES
Hong Kong

ACKNOWLEDGEMENTS

It would be impossible to thank all the people in Wyoming—friends and strangers—who were helpful in my months of touring and writing. Some of those are mentioned in the text, such as the hospitable Ulrichs of fossil fame. Others were kind strangers. My largest single debt is to my indefatigable editor Barry Parr, whose *San Francisco* guide preceded this one under the Compass imprint. Other friends, especially those in Sheridan, will recognize themselves and their works in the text; likewise inspirational Bob Spoonhunter of St. Stephen's on the Wind River Indian Reservation. I am deeply grateful to all these, and many others, for hospitality and information. Margot Holiday, also of Sheridan, was particularly kind and informative, as were a number of people at the University of Wyoming in Laramie. I remain grateful to Gene Gressley there for kindnesses past and present. And always thanks to the encouragement and help along the way of my publishers Christopher and Tobias.

Compass American Guides wishes to thank Don Pitcher, author of *Berkeley Inside/Out* (Heyday Books) and *Wyoming Handbook* (Moon Publications), for his editorial contributions regarding museums, and for his essays on the 1988 Yellowstone fires and Buffalo Bill Cody; point man Barry Parr for his insights, knowledge and caring concern; and Chuck Reher of the University of Wyoming's Deparetment of Anthropology for his helpful advice and assistance. The publisher thanks Peggy Cross for her geology piece on pp. 314-315; Peter Zimmerman for the Big Nose George Curry/Parrott article on pp.178-179, with pen-and-ink drawing by Harry S. Robins; and Cynthia Vincent for her meticulous proofreading. Finally, thanks to Anne Hikido for carrying the baton at the end.

Compass acknowledges the following institutions and individuals for the use of their photographs: American Heritage Center, University of Wyoming, Laramie, pp. 20, 77, 98, 118, 128, 154, 158 and 286-287; Buffalo Bill Historical Center, Cody, pp. 21, 27, 74 (photo by Robert Weiglein), 163, 189-192, 197-199, and 285; Wyoming State Museum, Cheyenne, pp. 32, 45 and 267; Donna Davis, p. 78; Kansas State Historical Society, Topeka, p. 82; Horace Albright Museum, Yellowstone National Park, pp. 150, 204, 227, and 232; Powell Museum, pp. 171-172, and 185; Thermopolis Museum, p. 175; Jackson Hole Museum and Teton County Historical Society, pp. 232, 254-255, and 258; Martin Vidak, p. 272; Dr George Gill, p. 278; Green River Musuem, p. 313 (photo by E.O. Beaman, U.S. Geological Survey); Mike McClure, p. 340, and Mark Theken, p. 248.

The Publisher also wishes to thank all of the great writers, artists, photographers, and explorers whose work and exploits accompany the following text.

First published in Great Britain in 1991

Distribution in the United Kingdom, Ireland, Europe and certain Commonwealth countries by Hodder and Stoughton, Mill Road, Dunton Green, Sevenoaks, Kent TN13 2YA.

British Library Cataloging in Publication Data has been applied for.

Contributing Editors: Barry Parr, Peter Zimmerman
Designer: David Hurst
Map Design: Bob Race

ISBN: 962-217-192-3

Proudced by Twin Age Ltd
Printed in Hong Kong

To my father and my son,
both full of Wyoming experiences.

CONTENTS

An Old French-Canadian Trapper. *From a drawing by Paxson*

AUTHOR'S PREFACE

THIS GUIDE TO WYOMING IS WRITTEN NOT SO MUCH FOR readers seeking minute details of the state's activities, nightlife, and wildlife, but for those who want an overall panorama of its geography, its oddities and beauties, its settlements and countryside. The book is fashioned around a continuous tour through every principal region of the state— though no one is really expected to take such a long trip in its entirety.

Wyoming is a state of vast spaces. This guide is designed to take you through the most exciting of these spaces, by car, *in the right direction*; for in Wyoming it is rather important to be going toward an exciting view, particularly mountains, rather than away from it. Obviously, travelers cannot design their itineraries with just this in mind, but they should be aware of this peculiarity of Western driving, and try to take advantage of it.

Wyoming is fundamentally *not* an urban or cultivated state. Rolling farmlands and quaint old villages are not its specialty. This guide takes you through all the major towns and cities, but they are not necessarily what the traveler should come to see. Wyoming's towns are for use rather than for show. It is in the empty areas beyond where Wyoming's beauties and curiosities usually lie.

Not to be left out are the great stories about Wyoming's colorful past. The state is saturated with myths, some true, others doubtful, but all an integral part of Wyoming's personality. To ignore them is to dismiss a basic part of the Wyoming character. So take the stories as repeated in this work (not designed for college credit) with the same grain of salt as you would the tales of any Wyoming old-timer.

MAPS

INTRODUCTION

WYOMING: "HIGH, WIDE AND HANDSOME," THE STATE that has a bucking horse on its license plate, where it is boasted that one of its native rivers, the Powder, is "a mile wide, an inch deep, and runs uphill all the way;" the state where the myth of the cowboy was born. . . .

Bucking horses are not exclusive to Wyoming, and rodeos, where horses buck in public, are native to the West from California to Kansas, Washington to Texas. Cattle roam all over this wide region. Indians, sagebrush, mountains, forests, and wide open spaces are commonplace all over the Far West. Just the same, Wyoming *is* special, and most certainly, high, wide, and in its various contrary ways, superbly handsome.

To see it properly one has to get off the main drag, which in this case is preeminently Interstate 80. This over-traveled route goes right across the bottom of the state along what was historically known as the Overland Trail. For a lot of the way it is pretty dreary—unmitigated brown badlands. Unfortunately, the vast majority of motorists who go through the state see this and judge Wyoming by it. In this way Wyoming is like its exact opposite, the country's most densely inhabited state, New Jersey, with its industrialized turnpike between Trenton and Newark, by which most people misjudge that state. It ain't necessarily so. As soon as you get off this Western version of the New Jersey Turnpike, things improve. The purpose of this book is to guide the traveler away from Interstate 80, and on to better things.

The beauties of Wyoming are largely scenic. The permanent rancher-farmer settlement of the state goes back barely more than a hundred years. Wyoming is still predominantly uninhabited; it is, after a brief spurt of oil boom-and-bust influx and exodus, the least populated state of the Union. Lots of Wyoming natives like it that way. There are few real historic antiquities, like the Indian and Spanish remains of the Southwest. There are few quaint mining ghost towns, like those of Colorado. There are no big urban centers like Denver and Salt Lake City, no striking man-made silhouettes. Wide-open spaces, mountains, forests and lakes, antelope and elk, buffalo and bear, hot springs, and waterfalls—these are what the traveler comes to see.

Wyoming is closely linked with its sister states Montana and Colorado, but differs from both in one special way. Unlike either of them, Wyoming is not sharply divided into an eastern section entirely plains and a western section almost entirely mountains. Wyoming is pretty consistently a mixture of both. It is basically a flat oblong, like a table with protrusions up under its tablecloth, an abstract rectangle drawn by engineers, 250 miles (400 km) north and south, 350 miles (560 km) east and west. This perfunctory piece of geometry should by rights have no special character at all.

Strangely enough, however, the obscure gentlemen who drew the lines managed to include an oddly homogeneous enclave: a plateau, seldom much less than 4,000 feet high (1,200 m), punctuated all over by various self-contained mountain ranges. There are not many places in Wyoming from which one can't see a mountain (the midpoint of Interstate 80 being one notable exception). From most of the mountains, in turn, one gets expansive views of plains or wide valleys.

The essential and typical beauty of Wyoming, then, is that of open spaces culminating in mountain ranges. A bare, hard Spanish rather than a fertile green Anglo-French beauty, a world that either exhilarates or depresses, sets the spirit soaring or seems forbidding and oppressive. Not cozy. There are numberless cozy pockets, but if you're to take Wyoming as a whole, it is spaciousness you have to take.

It is over this spaciousness that Indians, emigrants, cowboys, and soldiers moved and made Wyoming's history. If such spaciousness, relieved and exalted by mountains, exhilarates you, this is certainly the place for you. If not, roads lead on to virgin forests and indigo lakes; but all form the basis of these sagebrush rangelands where the cows and the cowboys work, and "the deer and the antelope play."

THE LAND AND SEASONS

Despite the prevailing uniformity of mountains and plains, the landscape of Wyoming is rather complicated. This basic contrast occurs all over the state, but there are huge areas of nothing but plains, and also of nothing but mountains. Sweetwater County is nothing but more-or-less open semidesert. The northwest corner is mostly nothing but peaks and forests. The contrast between the two is extreme. None of the state is real desert, such as one finds in the Southwest, but the Great Divide Basin certainly comes close. Nobody lives there. No rivers go through it. There are no good roads into it. Some of the mountain country, on the other hand, is pretty forbidding in just the opposite way. The summits of the Wind River Mountains are sprinkled with glaciers. Some forests in the Absarokas are so thick you can barely get through them, and people have been lost there for good.

Summer is glorious in the mountains—brilliant skies and wonderful cloud effects, riotous wildflowers from June into August. September, too, is glorious, with turning aspens and pellucid atmospheres. Of course a few little snowstorms may come up. Steady long rains are unusual except in the spring, but thunderstorms abound in summer. On the plains, summer can get pretty dry and hot. Mosquitoes and flies are common in wet, wooded places. June to September is the usual tourist summer season. January to April is for winter sports. Fall is for hunters. The rest of the year is for natives.

Since Wyoming is up high and up north, winters are rough. Below-zero temperatures, deep snows, and deadly blizzards can appear at any time from November to June. In mountain areas, six feet (two meters) or more of snow settle for the winter. Skiers rejoice in all this. On the plains, winds of 60 mph or more (100 kph) drive along blizzards that can and do kill people. One of these killed a hundred immigrants in the old covered wagon days. In the Red Desert, stock can be wintered because the wind is so fierce it keeps the range comparatively free of that extra-dry snow. In the summer the desert is too hot to handle, yet when night falls it can go down to freezing. Which gives you some idea of Wyoming's climate.

Wyoming, then, is a place for extremes; extremes of open bareness, extremes of mountain fastness, of summer heats and winter freezes. You don't fool around with Wyoming. It is exalting, but dangerous. Lightning strikes, bears disembowel, floods wreck, snows bury, dust storms obliterate, fires rage, all almost as a matter of routine. On the other hand the air and altitude invigorate and intoxicate, the vastness and beauty uplift, the oddities and grandeur intrigue and awe. It's not dull, not humdrum, not "average." It is, for residents of most of the rest of the country, no place like home.

■ THE PEOPLE

This all affects the people who inhabit the landscape, the people who put up with the summer heats and winter freezes. As anywhere, there are all sorts, but nowhere are extremes of personality more evident and tolerated. A democracy of people who are all individuals, rather than all just equal. The ethnic composition is also varied: Native American Indians, Central European farm workers and miners, Spanish speakers from the south, Chinese (perhaps a few descended from the days of railroad building), a few blacks, even some descendants of British aristocrats, and Basque sheepherders. Basically, however, the state is dominated by emigrants

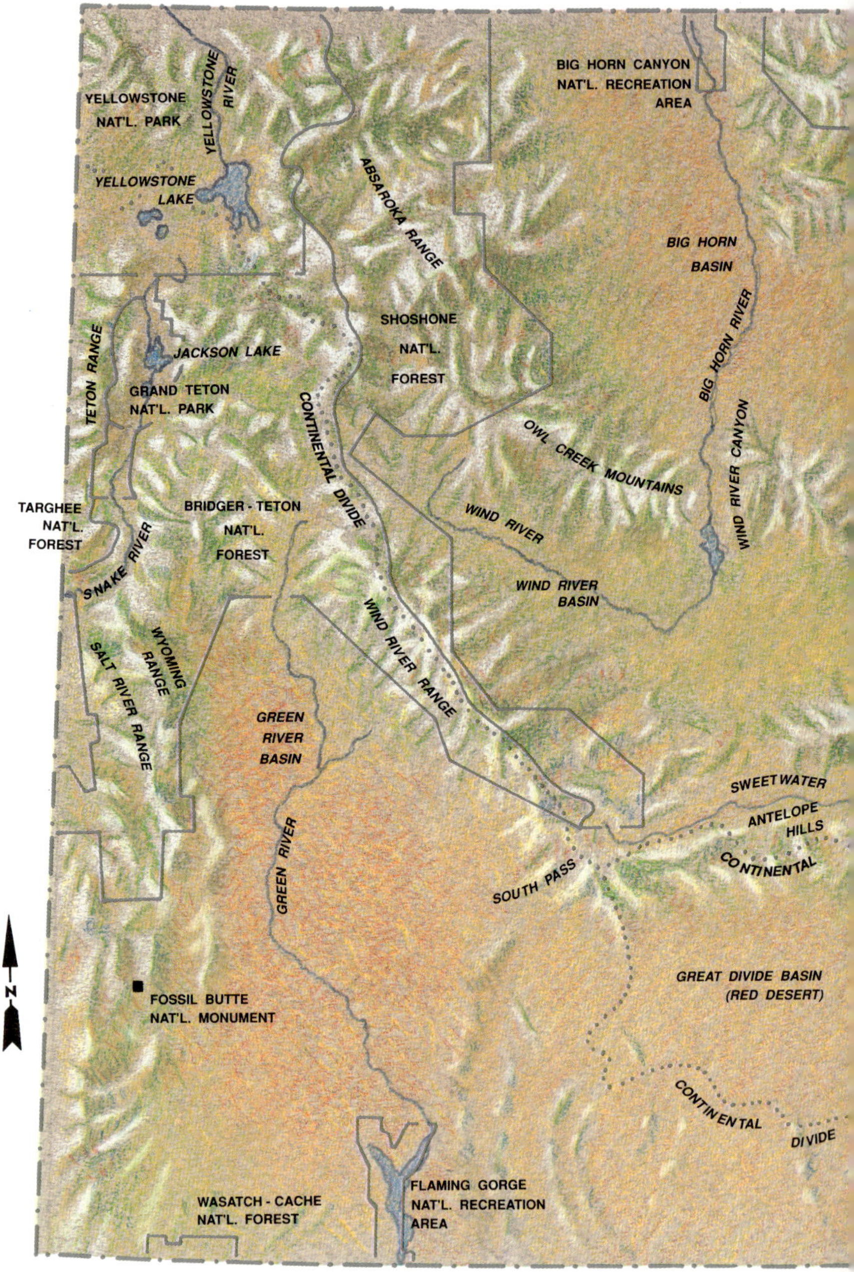
YELLOWSTONE NAT'L. PARK
YELLOWSTONE RIVER
YELLOWSTONE LAKE
ABSAROKA RANGE
BIG HORN CANYON NAT'L. RECREATION AREA
BIG HORN BASIN
BIG HORN RIVER
SHOSHONE NAT'L. FOREST
TETON RANGE
JACKSON LAKE
GRAND TETON NAT'L. PARK
CONTINENTAL DIVIDE
OWL CREEK MOUNTAINS
WIND RIVER CANYON
TARGHEE NAT'L. FOREST
BRIDGER - TETON NAT'L. FOREST
WIND RIVER
SNAKE RIVER
WIND RIVER BASIN
WYOMING RANGE
SALT RIVER RANGE
WIND RIVER RANGE
GREEN RIVER BASIN
SWEETWATER
ANTELOPE HILLS
CONTINENTAL
SOUTH PASS
GREEN RIVER
N
GREAT DIVIDE BASIN (RED DESERT)
FOSSIL BUTTE NAT'L. MONUMENT
CONTINENTAL DIVIDE
FLAMING GORGE NAT'L. RECREATION AREA
WASATCH - CACHE NAT'L. FOREST

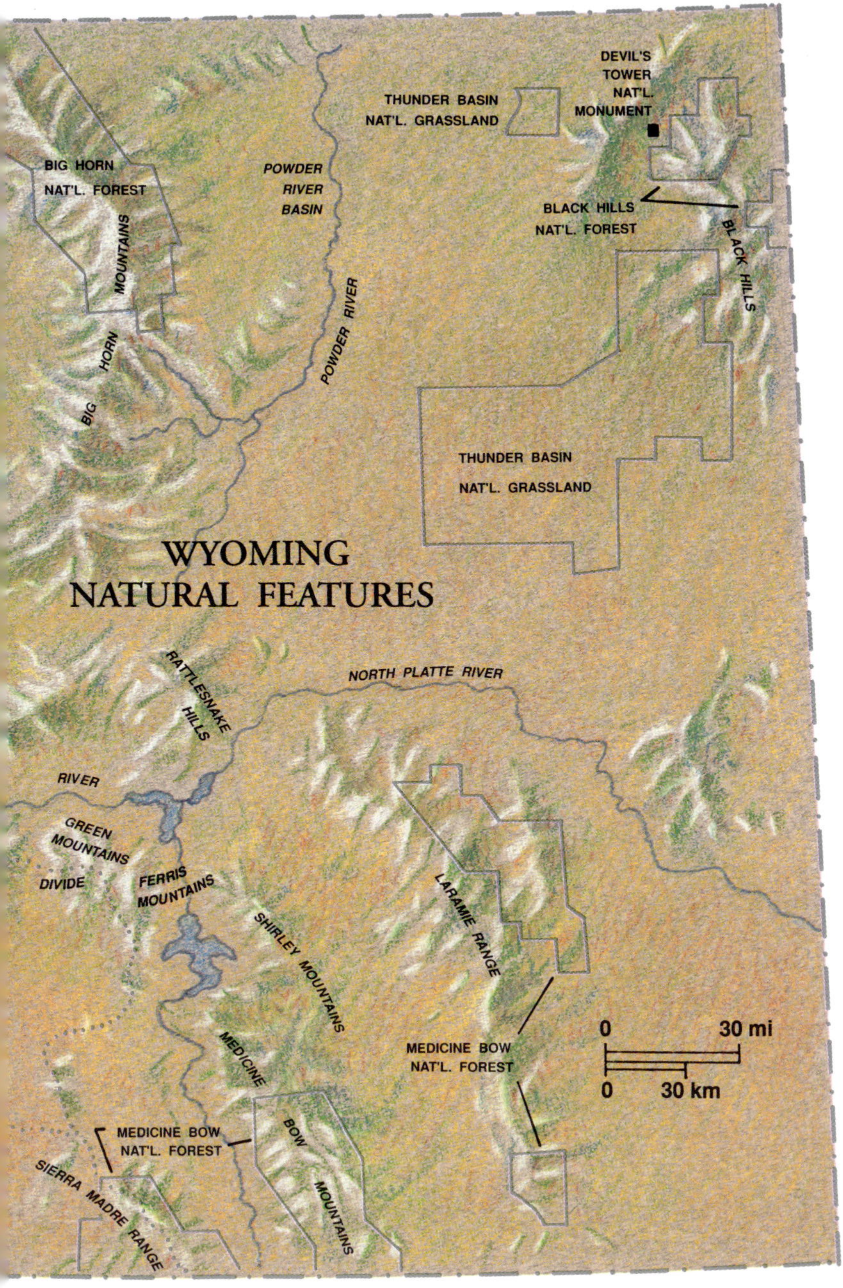
WYOMING
NATURAL FEATURES
DEVIL'S TOWER NAT'L. MONUMENT
THUNDER BASIN NAT'L. GRASSLAND
BIG HORN NAT'L. FOREST
POWDER RIVER BASIN
BIG HORN MOUNTAINS
BLACK HILLS NAT'L. FOREST
BLACK HILLS
POWDER RIVER
THUNDER BASIN NAT'L. GRASSLAND
NORTH PLATTE RIVER
RATTLESNAKE HILLS
RIVER
GREEN MOUNTAINS
DIVIDE
FERRIS MOUNTAINS
SHIRLEY MOUNTAINS
LARAMIE RANGE
MEDICINE BOW NAT'L. FOREST
MEDICINE BOW MOUNTAINS
MEDICINE BOW NAT'L. FOREST
SIERRA MADRE RANGE
0 30 mi
0 30 km

from the Midwest and the South, with British (English, Scotch-Irish) and northern European (Dutch, Scandinavian, German) backgrounds.

The archetypical Wyoming citizen is characterized by the various meanings of the word "ornery." This can mean obstinate, cantankerous, obstructionist, resentful, and revengeful, or independent, individualistic, non-conformist, and strong-minded. Even in the late twentieth century, specimens of this character abound outside the radius of Better Business bureaus.

In any case, this orneriness is usually covered with a somewhat superficial facade of smiling politeness, or even joviality. Over the years, outsiders (particularly Easterners used to the snarls of city dwellers), have fallen in love with the good, sweet, innocent, loveable, open-handed sons and daughters of the West, only to find out later that there's hard rock underneath. Things like loyalty, respect, consideration, and instant handy response to emergencies and disaster are embedded in the rock, too. Just don't believe everything a citizen tells you.

■ Wyoming History: Boom and Bust

Part of Wyoming's character and orneriness comes from its thoroughly outrageous and pretty recent history. It has been really settled only since the Civil War, and it has never really settled down. Throughout the state's past, people have learned to expect the worst. Usually they've been right. On the other hand, like the landscape, it has not been dull. The year of 1990 proudly marks the centennial of the state. Considering what's happened there, it's a wonder that it has survived.

The story of Wyoming from its very beginnings has been one of boom and bust, so its history and its economy are constantly parallel. Each boom has brought with it a new wave of immigrants.

The first boom took place before recorded history. Sometime, perhaps in the late seventeenth or early eighteenth centuries, the North American Plains Indians discovered the horse. The horse was also an immigrant. The Spaniards brought him (and her) to the New World, hitherto horseless, and so impressed and intimidated the natives with their horsemanship that they conquered all of Central and South America in no time at all. The descendants of these horses gradually worked their way northward, either as wild strays or brought by settlers across the Rio Grande. When, where, and how the red men of the north met and mastered them is another story, but their mastery was complete. For a century or more, these horseback Indians developed one of the most successful non-agrarian civilizations in the world.

The West was teeming with another four-footed friend—the bison, popularly (though incorrectly) called the buffalo. Men on horseback with primitive but effective weapons—bow and arrow, spears, and knives—could hunt buffalo for food, clothes, and shelter (teepees). In summer you hunted. In winter you holed up in your teepee or camp. No fences, no boundary lines or landed property, no towns or taxes, no lawyers. Rival tribes engaged in summer battles, often man-to-man, often based on ritual horse-stealing. Scalps were taken. Prisoners were very painfully tortured. A chief badge of honor, usually posthumous, was impassive bravery under torture. But it was all sort of fun in a grim way. Prestige, first access to buffalo grazing grounds, above all *face*—this is what one fought for. Not for King and Country, not for walled-off territory or gold or religions or dynastic disputes. It was a nice boom while it lasted, and might possibly have gone on forever.

Not only the horse, but also some of the horse's Indian masters were immigrants. It's possible that all the plains dwellers first met by the white men were interlopers, and not direct descendants of the prehistoric inhabitants who left all sorts of artifacts, from arrowheads to awe-inspiring murals on cliffs and in caves. The Sioux, the most active, warlike, prominent tribe with which Wyoming had to deal, were definitely outsiders. Originating down the Mississippi, they gradually moved north on foot or by river into Minnesota in the early eighteenth century. Along the way they adopted the horse and became what has been called the finest natural cavalry in the world. They drove the Crows off the Powder River and into the Big Horn Basin, and ended up with control of an area stretching from the Dakotas and the Black Hills to the Big Horn Mountains.

The next boom was based on beaver skins. Trappers from French Canada first began to penetrate the Far West in the mid-eighteenth century. Sieur de la Verendrye actually saw either the Black Hills or the Big Horns, and recorded the fact. Beginning in the early nineteenth century, those supreme adventurers, the early trappers, pushed farther and farther into the vast, remote, beaver-inhabited areas of the Rockies. Wyoming became the central theater of the new thriving business, under the sponsorship of distant capitalists, notably John Jacob Astor, one of the earliest and most successful of these money-men. A big golden statue of a beaver should dominate the lobby of the Waldorf-Astoria on Park Avenue in New York, because that's where the seed money came from. The beaver dams of Wyoming and of its forested neighbors made many other fortunes.

Annual rendezvous of these woodsmen and their backers took place in western parts of Wyoming until suddenly, after 1840, the boom collapsed. Gentlemen in London gave up beaver hats and took to wearing silk toppers. The beaver trade was doomed. Astor, of course, went on to higher things. The poor trappers found themselves unemployed.

Fortunately for many of them, a third Wyoming boom occurred just in time. Drawn by hopes of free land in Oregon, gold in California, and freedom in Utah from persecution back east, great mass migrations across the continent began in the 1840s. The ex-trappers were there to act as guides, hunters, and shopkeepers along the new emigrant trails. Between 1845 and 1865, hundreds of thousands of farmers, Mormons escaping persecution, and gold seekers crept across Wyoming, first up the North Platte River and along the Sweetwater that ran into it from the west, then over the comparatively low and easy South Pass, and then south and west into what are now Utah and Idaho. This was the Oregon Trail, also called by other names. A pass safer from Indian attack later developed closer to the present south Wyoming border: the Overland Trail.

This invasion brought a sudden, hectic sort of prosperity to the region, along with devastation and danger. Indians who resented this intrusion on their hunting grounds

Painting by George Catlin shows how Indians used wolf skins to approach bison more closely. (Courtesy, American Heritage Center, University of Wyoming)

took out their irritation on these unwelcome tourists. The army came to protect the immigrants, fought the Indians, and stayed to establish permanent forts. Buffalo were slaughtered as only nineteenth-century Americans could slaughter game. Soon, like the beaver, the bison was on the road to extinction. (Buffalo Bill alone killed over 4,000 buffalo to provide meat for the later railroad workers).

Famed guide Kit Carson about 1850. (Courtesy, Buffalo Bill Historical Center, Cody, Wyoming)

Trappers had brought guns into the Indian world. Indians quickly adopted them. Indians didn't make guns or powder. Traders eagerly supplied them. They also eagerly supplied whiskey, which proved disastrous to many Indians who had never tasted it before. The Indian warfare tactics of lightning surprise attack and mysterious disappearance were terribly effective at first, but not in the end.

Like the buffalo and beaver booms before it, the immigrant boom also suddenly collapsed. Came a fourth boom: the railroad. The westward edge of the country's first transcontinental railway struck Wyoming in 1867. The covered wagon became obsolete. With the railroad came a horde of adventurers: gunmen, gamblers, whores, shady entrepreneurs, and—at last—real, solid, permanent settlers. All along the route of the old Overland Trail, now the Union Pacific Railroad, towns exploded into existence virtually overnight as the tracks crept west. Cheyenne, Laramie, Rawlins, Rock Springs, and other towns suddenly sprang up to the sound of gunfire and the roars of lynch mobs. Wyoming was settled, so to speak.

This boom, too, was short-lived. The golden spike joining the transcontinental railroad, east and west, was driven on May 10, 1869. Construction was over, the effect was permanent. The presence of railroads right in Wyoming now created the fifth and most characteristic of all Wyoming booms: cattle.

The end of the Civil War had brought prosperity to cattle owners in Texas. Cattle drives from Texas to the new railheads in Kansas for shipment to the new stockyards in Kansas City and Chicago had become regular yearly epics. Gradually, Texas longhorns were driven farther north into Wyoming for rich summer feeding and fall shipment east on the new Union Pacific. Starting in the early 1870s, for a short and vivid period of less than two decades, the seemingly endless richness of grass in the eastern half of Wyoming nurtured a cattleman's paradise. Younger sons of English titled families, hard-bitten Texans, and restless farm boys from farther east all flocked to Wyoming to try their luck with cows. On those extremely open ranges, the state reached the climax of its earlier history and created its final heroic embodiment: the cowboy.

Cowboys had worked long before in Mexico and the Southwest, as well as Texas, but they were more or less peons. The cowboy as he developed very quickly in Wyoming was English-speaking and restively independent. The heady glamour and high living of the cattle barons rubbed off on their cowhands, who were pretty glamorous and certainly high living, too. The great cattle spreads, with their lavish, often baronial ranch headquarters and surrounding wilderness of far horizons, as well as the dash of young horsemen in their chaps and spurs and sombreros, all seemed to adventurous and impressionable young visitors from the East like a sun-baked version of Camelot. Theodore Roosevelt, Owen Wister, Frederic Remington, and many others were smitten by this brand-new chivalry, and survived to tell about it. It was to them, and pretty soon to most Americans of the time, *romantic.*

So it was in the area from the Big Horns to the Black Hills—eastern Wyoming, southeast Montana, and the western Dakotas—that this myth of the American cowboy was really created. Of course, this is rather unfair to the American Southwest, where it all started, and to the cattle kingdoms of Texas in particular. But this didn't stop the public at the turn of the century from identifying the Wyoming cowboy, the horseman of the plains, with those earlier heroes of the frontier: Cooper's Natty Bumpo, the Indian scout, and the real-life Buffalo Bill, also of Wyoming. To the present day, that glamour of the horseman pervades the psychology of the state—as attested by its license plate.

But this significant boom also came a cropper. Success brought the disasters of overcrowding and overgrazing. The big owners got careless, spending less and less time on their ranches. Finally, the desperate blizzard in the winter of 1887-88, with the terrible loss of cattle, brought the boom to its end. Many of the big cattlemen were ruined. Homesteaders began to invade the cattle range. Overgrazing by sheep ruined the rangeland for cattle. All through the next two decades at the turn of the century, cattlemen fought "grangers" (homesteaders) and sheepmen in a series of violent and bloody engagements. Cowboys out of a job turned into outlaws, and the equally picturesque figures of such lawbreakers as Butch Cassidy and the more sinister Tom Horn continued the tradition founded by earlier robbers of stage coaches.

No sooner had the cattle and sheep boom simmered down and adjusted itself to normal living than still another boom-and-bust cycle struck the state: oil. This one was neither as glamorous nor as specifically Wyoming as the earlier cycles. It produced a few high-placed villains rather than figures of romance, even if they did become national figures.

Oil spouts in many places in the West, but Wyoming was one of the first states to take advantage of it. The center of the boom was the town of Casper on the North Platte River, in mid-state. The oil business started in 1890, when the first well was drilled up on Salt Creek—just as the country's first oil boom in Pennsylvania began to die down. It didn't amount to much; too far from transportation, for one thing. But beginning in the early twentieth century, a frenzy of exploitation and prosperity struck Casper and its fields. As frantic real estate promoters got to work, the town doubled in size. The demands of the First World War brought the boom to its crest, continuing through the Roaring Twenties. But the Depression and scandals attached to the Teapot Dome drillings brought it to an end. For a while, Wyoming was in the headlines, and "Teapot Dome" was a byword.

When this boom collapsed, Casper lost half its population. But then came another war, another boom. And since then the pattern of oil boom and bust has continued regularly. In the seventies, it was boom time once more. But then came the eighties and another collapse of oil prices. In the 1980 census, Casper had outstripped Cheyenne as the state's largest city.

There have been other booms. Hard coal mining had a boom in the area of Newcastle near the Black Hills. Copper had a wild fling in the Sierra Madre, based on the mushroom city of Encampment. There was a short spree of gold mining in South Pass City, now a ghost town. There was a boom of dry farming at the turn of the century

The crossroads settlement of Shoshoni, a boomtown just a few years ago,
seems ready to blow away with the next wind.

when homesteaders, lured by free land, broke the soil of the grasslands and watched their soil and savings blow away in the wind.

The latest boom is tourism. Millions of travelers a year have been going through Jackson Hole and Yellowstone for the last couple of decades. At this writing, tourism is the only industry that can be called booming in Wyoming. The problem now is how to control this flood without stopping it, and how to preserve the things that have caused it—the scenery and character of Wyoming. Hard-headed stockmen and businessmen find themselves facing the issues of conservation and environmentalism, preserving natural beauty and wildlife, not as a matter of morality, but of money. Will the tourist business destroy the tourist business?

Not necessarily so. Stock, farming, some mining, and oil all still go on as regular, regulated businesses. Nobody shoots people because of the conflicts over these businesses anymore. But looking back over the socio-economic history of Wyoming, almost anyone should be able to draw a few conclusions and learn a bit of common sense. But then—people in Wyoming are ornery.

Sinclair's oil refinery, one of several in Wyoming, by sunset's glow.

■ The Myth Creators

No one can really claim that Wyoming is an important center of the arts. No nationally famous, native Wyoming artist, like, say, John Steinbeck in California, has made his or her home state the scene of a classic work of imagination. Famous abstract expressionist artist Jackson Pollock was born in Cody, but he sure enough didn't work there. (However, if Idaho can go around claiming poet Ezra Pound, who left the town of Moscow, Idaho, as an infant to grow up in Philadelphia, and who never returned. . . .)

This does not mean that Wyoming is artless, or that the arts haven't been important in at least creating an *image* of the state. In fact, it's possible to claim, perhaps, that few other states of the Union have been so influentially presented and characterized by artists of national fame. The fact that these artists were by no means native doesn't alter their impact.

Two writers and three artists in particular have almost created the image of the state. Their works have spelled "Wyoming" to millions of Americans. By its wild success at the turn of the century, it was one novel—*The Virginian*, by the very Philadelphian Owen Wister (1860-1938)—that created and established once and for all the character of the cowboy-as-hero, and Wyoming as his proper setting. Like its counterpart *Uncle Tom's Cabin*, it may not be a model of academic literature, though it is in fact very well written. It certainly can be accused of being melodramatic and sentimental, like Uncle Tom. But as a myth-creator in America, like Uncle Tom and the more academically revered *Scarlet Letter* and *Huckleberry Finn*, *The Virginian* is a regional epic. There are other more grubby, graphic, and authentic pictures of the West and the cowboy, but certainly never one that has so captured the national fancy and fixed the national stereotype. The handsome, polite, handy, soft-spoken and laconic, humorously menacing ("When you call me like that, *smile*"), deadly marksman who has ridden through almost a full century of print and film was first introduced to the world at large by the enormous success of Wister.

No one could have been a less obvious person to have done that. Wister was a neurotic, class-bound, talented, but frustrated intellectual and well-born gentleman who wanted to be a serious musical composer. He once played his compositions for Franz Liszt in Germany. His mother was the daughter of the beautiful, scandalous, and intellectual Fanny Kemble, last of England's greatest theatrical family. She had shocked the Victorians by very publicly deserting her raffish husband, planter Pierce Butler, and then—even worse!—publishing poems about her unhappiness. *Not* done, par-

Owen Wister, author of The Virginian. *(Courtesy, Buffalo Bill Historical Center, Cody, Wyoming)*

ticularly in Philadelphia. Fanny's daughter, Owen's mother, was a beautiful, intellectual snob, one of the intimates of Henry James. Owen's father was a stuffy German doctor from one of Philadelphia's most prestigious medical families. The supercilious put-downs of his mother, and his father's insistence that he give up music and become a proper Philadelphia lawyer, drove young Owen to a nervous breakdown. His doctor advised him to go West as a cure. It worked. He began writing Western short stories, and finally, *The Virginian.* It sold from the beginning, and over the years, *millions* of copies. It was dramatized in a Broadway hit, and later a long-lasting TV serial. *The Virginian* is certainly the ancestor of the pulp novel and the Hollywood Western. Owen Wister never really wrote anything else popular.

Horse packer Jeff Benkowsky dries out after a summer squall in the Bridger-Teton National Forest's Teton Wilderness.

One of Wister's best friends at Harvard had been the equally frustrated New Yorker, Theodore Roosevelt. He, too, had suffered from all sorts of youthful traumas. He, too, went West to find himself. In the process he, too, became not only a profuse and popular writer about the West, but also, almost incidentally, one of the country's most flamboyant presidents. It was certainly on the basis of his Western experience, and in his character as former cowboy, ranchman, and then Rough Rider, that he developed into a national idol.

Between the two of them, in fiction and non-fiction, Wister and Roosevelt presented a view of the Wyoming-Dakota plains and its cowboys that really, along with the equally horsey exploits and showmanship of contemporary Buffalo Bill, put the area, and the state, on the map.

Both Wister and T.R. were active big-game hunters and lovers of the wilderness, and both popularized and presented the beauty of Wyoming's mountains and forests, as well as the glamour of its plains. Roosevelt in particular, from his position as president, can be considered the most prominent and publicized founder of the conservation movement. Devils Tower in the Black Hills of Wyoming, created as the country's first National Monument by Roosevelt in 1906, could be considered his monument as America's first (and perhaps last) true presidential nature-lover.

The third member of this trio of friends who (so to speak) "created" the cowboy was the artist Frederic Remington. He was a native of upstate New York, and an accomplished realist painter who specialized in the American outdoors and its men of action. Among these were cowboys, very much in action. As painter and sculptor, he captured them in violent cinematic exuberance, and in the process made his fortune, became a cult, and ruined his reputation among "serious art lovers." It was all very much like Wister, who was also sneered at by all right-thinking, serious, literary critics. Cowboy art.

But Wister and Remington certainly had and have their rewards: the creation between them in prose and paint of the archetypical image of the wild, wild West. An image pretty definitely framed by the plains and ringed by the mountains of the Wyoming grasslands and badlands.

Two other artists, Thomas Moran and William Henry Jackson, also did much to open the eyes of their countrymen to Wyoming glories. With his vivid first paintings of the amazingly colorful scenery of Yellowstone, Moran became a pioneer in what has continued to be a never-ending vein of profitable landscape art. He did not spe-

(preceding page) A silver moon gleams over the jagged Tetons.

cialize in Wyoming. He also painted the Grand Canyon and other such miniatures. Few have improved upon them.

As staff artist on the first Hayden survey of Yellowstone in 1872, Moran was joined by Jackson, the staff photographer. They became bosom friends, and between them they first brought the wonders of the place to the attention of the public; more to the point, to the attention of Congress, which on the basis of their eye-opening revelations of beauty, created Yellowstone National Park. Thus began the whole amazing process of governmental preservation of nature. It would be hard to think of two visual artists who had a more overwhelming effect on political events.

In 1877, Jackson came back to the area and took the first pictures of Jackson Lake, spread at the feet of Mt. Moran in the Tetons. Mount Moran had been named after the artist by Hayden on his later expedition to Jackson Hole. Moran never saw his mountain. (Jackson Lake is *not* named after W.H. Jackson, though it should have been. David Jackson, after whom the valley and the lake are named, has more then enough honor done him. Perhaps a simple ceremony by the Park Service of rededicating the lake to the later Jackson would be sufficient; with photographs, of course.)

Ever since Jackson, Wyoming has been increasingly overrun by photographers as well as landscape artists. One of the most famous of American photographs is Ansel Adams' picture of the Tetons from the northeast over the Snake River and Deadman's Bar.

The most famous non-fiction writing about Wyoming, and among the very earliest, was that by Francis Parkman, infatuated Bostonian, whose *The California and Oregon Trail* is the most vivid first-hand account of the Sioux and of Wyoming before settlement really began. His rigorous expedition of 1846, based from Fort Laramie when it was just a trading post, ruined his health, but started him on his long career as an American historian.

During this same period, adventurers such as Parkman, visual interpreters like George Catlin, the German-Swiss Karl Bodmer, accompanying his patron the Prince of Wied, and especially Alfred Miller, who traveled with the English Sir William Drummond Stewart, left an unforgettable record of the world of plains, distant mountains, trappers, Indians, and the game they pursued, notably the buffalo. Two later, more academically accomplished artists—Albert Bierstadt and Worthington Whittredge—celebrated the landscape of Wyoming and of the West in general.

■ WYOMING WRITERS

Most of the people mentioned so far didn't actually live in the state as settled natives, though Owen Wister spent many summers there. Culture *in* Wyoming, not just works *about* it, presents no very grandiose panorama, but it has existed, not without both national reputations and Wyoming flavor. One could say without much argument that writing in the state of a literary sort began with the humorist Bill Nye. He was actually a very professional newspaperman and columnist, but his writings became enormously popular in book form. As with Wister, Nye began his career in Wyoming, and his works became best-sellers. He wandered out West with the new railroad and came to roost in the brand-new, raucous town of Laramie. He was postmaster there and eventually started his own newspaper. He called it the *Boomerang*, after his pet mule, and as such it exists to this day. Not many university towns have a newspaper named for a mule. He wrote an awful lot, much in the vein of the early Mark Twain (also a newspaperman in the old West), and generally in that same tone of satiric exaggeration that was the trademark of early Western writing. A lot of it—and there was indeed a lot of it—is tedious now, but he was enormously popular then, and is sometimes very funny still. He left Wyoming in 1887 and went to New York, fame, and riches; however, he emerged from Wyoming as its first literary lion, and the frontier gave him his style and subject matter.

Humorist and newspaper publisher Bill Nye in1880. (Courtesy, Wyoming State Museum)

Nye came and went. One of the really truly indigenous writers was the cowboy-artist-writer Will James. He flourished in the 1920s and 1930s in both Wyoming and Montana under the editorship of Max Perkins at Scribner's. As such he belonged in the same stable as Fitzgerald and Hemingway, but couldn't have been more different. He wrote in authentic cowboy vernacular, un-reformed as it was spoke, and illustrated his books with his own vivid drawings of riders and horses, using himself as a model. His handsome books—*Cowboys North and South* (1924), *Cow Country* (1927), *All in the Day's Riding* (1933), and others—give a far more unvarnished and genuine view of cowboy life than Wister did. His most famous work is the self-illustrated children's book *Smoky* (1926). They were immensely popular (like those of Nye) at the time, but don't seem to be as well remembered now as they ought to be.

Somewhat less indigenous than James, but certainly closely identified with the state, have been various writers settled in Jackson Hole. Struthers Burt (born in Baltimore in 1881 but a native of Philadelphia), his wife Katharine Newlin Burt (born in New York in 1882), and son Nathaniel (actually born in Jackson Hole) have written 60 books over a period of 70 years, some definitely centered on Wyoming; notably Struthers Burt's *Diary of a Dude Wrangler* (1924) and his *Powder River* (1938). All three Burts were also published by Scribner's and edited by Perkins. Famous naturalists, like Olaus Murie and his wife Margaret (*Wapiti Wilderness* and others), the Craighead brothers, and many more have centered their prestigious careers in the Hole. The humorist, Donald Hough, settled into Jackson bars before the Second World War and wrote amusingly about what he saw from that point of view.

Writers identified with the southeast of the state have made a national impression, notably Mary O'Hara with her *My Friend Flicka* (1941), and Thurman Arnold with his New Deal sarcasm in the *Folklore of Capitalism* (1937). But there still has not been a writer who holds the position of local champion comparable to, say, A.B. Guthrie of Montana with his novels *The Big Sky* and *The Way West*; although Emerson Hough's *The Covered Wagon* (1922), an immensely popular emigrant epic, was made into a movie in Wyoming, its setting.

■ Wyoming Artists

As for art and artists in Wyoming, again the list may not be prestigious, but it *is* really characteristic of Wyoming. Will James, of course, was an artist as well as a writer. Jackson Hole has been as full of active painters (notably landscapist Conrad Schwiering) as it has been of movie makers; but once again nobody quite like Charles M. Russell in Montana has emerged on the national consciousness.

The state does have one center of genuinely national reputation: the Buffalo Bill Historical Center in Cody. No less than four separate museums celebrate various historical and esthetic qualities of Cody himself and of the state and region where he flourished. The Whitney Gallery of Western Art is one of the most prestigious of its kind in the country. Remington, Russell, and others are magnificently represented, but there is no special concentration here on Wyoming natives as such.

The most distinguished of Wyoming's resident artists is the once-neglected but increasingly appreciated Bill (christened Emil) Gollings. Born in Idaho in 1878, and schooled in Chicago, Gollings came west after eighth grade to work as a cowhand and horse wrangler. After a return to Chicago and art school, he settled in Sheridan in the 1920s. There he was patronized by art lovers, like Bradford Brinton, and received commissions for works at the capitol in Cheyenne. His art is only gradually emerging from the incubus of "cowboy art," for unlike many such artists he can be appreciated purely as a master of form and color, as well as a dynamic realist in the vein of a John Sloan or George Bellows.

Another such artist was Archie Teater of a slightly later period. He, too, was a ranch boy who somehow got to New York, studied under Thomas Benton, and became for a while a modestly well-known member of the school of American native realism—so overwhelmingly popular in the 1930s, when represented by Grant Wood, John Steuart Curry, and Benton himself. This movement was eclipsed after World War II by the overwhelmingly popular new school of abstract expressionism, as represented by Wyoming-born Jackson Pollock. Teater settled in Jackson and became a local lion; but like Will James, he too seems to have been perhaps undeservedly lost in the shuffle of artistic fashion. Wyoming at least hasn't done much to save the reputations of her truly indigenous talents.

■ Other Wyoming Arts

As for Wyoming music, it's hard to pin down anything as specifically "Wyoming." The indigenous cowboy songs originated throughout the West and were sung all over it; though some do have references to Wyoming, such as "Goodbye Old Paint, I'm Leaving Cheyenne," with its slow, loping rhythm. There has always been a sort of cheap, sentimental, commercial output of songs, like "In the Gloaming of Wyoming" and "Home on the Range."

Of an entirely different sort has been the growth of serious music in Wyoming, most notably the annual season of the Grand Teton Festival in Jackson Hole. A splendid symphony orchestra, famous soloists, a rich series of chamber music performances, and big, enthusiastic audiences make this one of the important musical events of the

West. Even a few works by Wyoming composers are performed, off and on. But it can't be said that either serious or popular music has come to roost in the state with any special local accent.

One would not naturally suppose that such a recent settlement would produce a native architecture. There are no seventeenth or eighteenth-century Spanish adobes or ancient Indian cliff dwellings. Teepees were native alright, but impermanent. The true native architecture of later immigration was the log cabin, and if anything can be called typical of Wyoming, that's it. Of course, it's typical of most northwestern states, too. But in all rural and some small urban settings close to timber, a style of residential log cabin developed that was certainly characteristic: cabins with low, broad roofs (originally sod), lazy windows (that is, sliding horizontally, not sash windows), and usually with a porch out front. Many examples can still be found in less up-to-date rural areas, even in towns like Jackson and Pinedale. This style of architecture remains obligatory for dude ranches. Many handsome ranch houses and summer places, some palatial, were built of logs, and still are. It's an appropriate, beautiful, cozy, and certainly *local* product, as opposed to the Californication of more modern mountain villas and town subdivisions.

Time claims a log cabin in the Wind River Indian Reservation

■ SPACES

Despite all the influx of summer trippers and winter snow lovers, despite the persistence, waxing and waning, of oil and uranium, mining and logging, cattle and sheep, beets and alfalfa, the real secret of Wyoming's fascination is still basically *emptiness*. There are square miles and miles and miles of Wyoming where nobody lives at all. You can drive, for instance, from Jackson Hole into Colorado and beyond, via Rock Springs (the only sizable settlement), and not see more than a ranch house, a filling station or two, for hundreds of miles. To some, who find the urbanization of some parts of the country claustrophobic, this openness just by itself gives a wonderful feeling of release and relief. Just to go along seeing nothing is a pleasure. When in fact this nothingness is mostly varied by tantalizing distant heights and penetrated by awesome valleys, the appetite for elbow room is spiced by more definite pleasures. There is always that lure of distances: What's in them thar hills? What's down that there river? This call of distance was certainly one of the subconscious motivations of old-time explorers of the region.

On the other hand, for those who like lots of busywork and objects of interest close about them, a corresponding agoraphobia (fear of openness) can prevail. For them, the densely packed mountain-forest areas are the goal, and the wider, open spaces just a way to get there.

To appreciate the state of Wyoming you should ideally be receptive to both the horizontal of plain and the vertical of mountain. As said before, the essence of Wyoming scenery is the combination of both—mountains seen over a vast distance, coming closer and closer, and finally revealing their contrasts of lower forests and higher glaciers. The Tetons, for instance, wouldn't be properly visible without the flats at their feet, nor the flats be as beautiful without the interruption of the swath of riverbed and cottonwoods down the middle of them. And even at its worst and most unrelievedly desert, the state at its high altitude responds wonderfully to weather and times of day. What can seem utterly dreary in drizzle, or hard and mean at blazing noontime, can become a fairy-tale under cumulus clouds and blue sky, or as evening comes on. Above all, those clouds build up magnificently in midsummer, and though storms may be scary, they are certainly grand.

Though Wyoming is amazingly cohesive, the geometrical boundaries of the only rectangular state of the Union (except Colorado) do cut across some natural sub-areas, notably the Black Hills and the midwestern plains. However, it is remarkable how many self-contained regions the state embraces. Moving generally from southeast to northwest, and back again, you can broadly distinguish at least 16 such areas. Each is dealt with in a separate chapter of the book:

Chapter I: OLD WYOMING—a southeast corner of old settlement;
Chapter II: STAGECOACH CORRIDOR—an eastern border of plains and rangelands spilling west from Nebraska and the Dakotas;
Chapter III: BLACK HILLS—a northeast corner of low mountains, the western extension of the Black Hills;
Chapter IV: THUNDER BASIN—a corridor of plains south from Montana to the North Platte River;
Chapter V: OREGON TRAIL ROUTE—another corridor of plains going west from the bend of the North Platte and its mountains toward the Wind River Basin;
Chapter VI: BIG HORN BASIN—the Big Horn Basin, west of the Big Horn Mountains;
Chapter VII: POWDER RIVER BASIN—the Powder River Basin, east of the Big Horns;
Chapter VIII: ABSAROKAS—the Cody area and the Absaroka Range;
Chapter IX: YELLOWSTONE—Yellowstone National Park;
Chapter X: JACKSON HOLE—Grand Teton National Park and Jackson Hole;
Chapter XI: INDIAN LAND—the Wind River Basin, east of the Wind River Mountains;
Chapter XII: TRAPPER LAND—the Green River Basin, west of the Wind Rivers;
Chapter XIII: STAR VALLEY—Star Valley and the western border;
Chapter XIV: FOSSIL COUNTRY—the southwest corner;
Chapter XV: GREAT BASIN—Sweetwater County and the Great Divide Basin; and
Chapter XVI: COPPER COUNTRY—the Sierra Madre Mountains.

This guide is based on the assumption that you are driving an automobile, since nowadays the vast majority of the travelers to the state come by car. Except for a few bottlenecks, like the approaches to Yellowstone, the highways of Wyoming are as wide open as the landscape, smooth, well-paved, and pretty empty. For those who just like driving, they can be a special pleasure. Much of Wyoming is visible from these highways. Some areas are not and must be seen on horse or foot; but wide-open or secluded, the state is always worth exploring. There are some queer corners of the state, and some pretty queer things have happened in them, but some wonderful things, too, in Wonderful Wyoming.

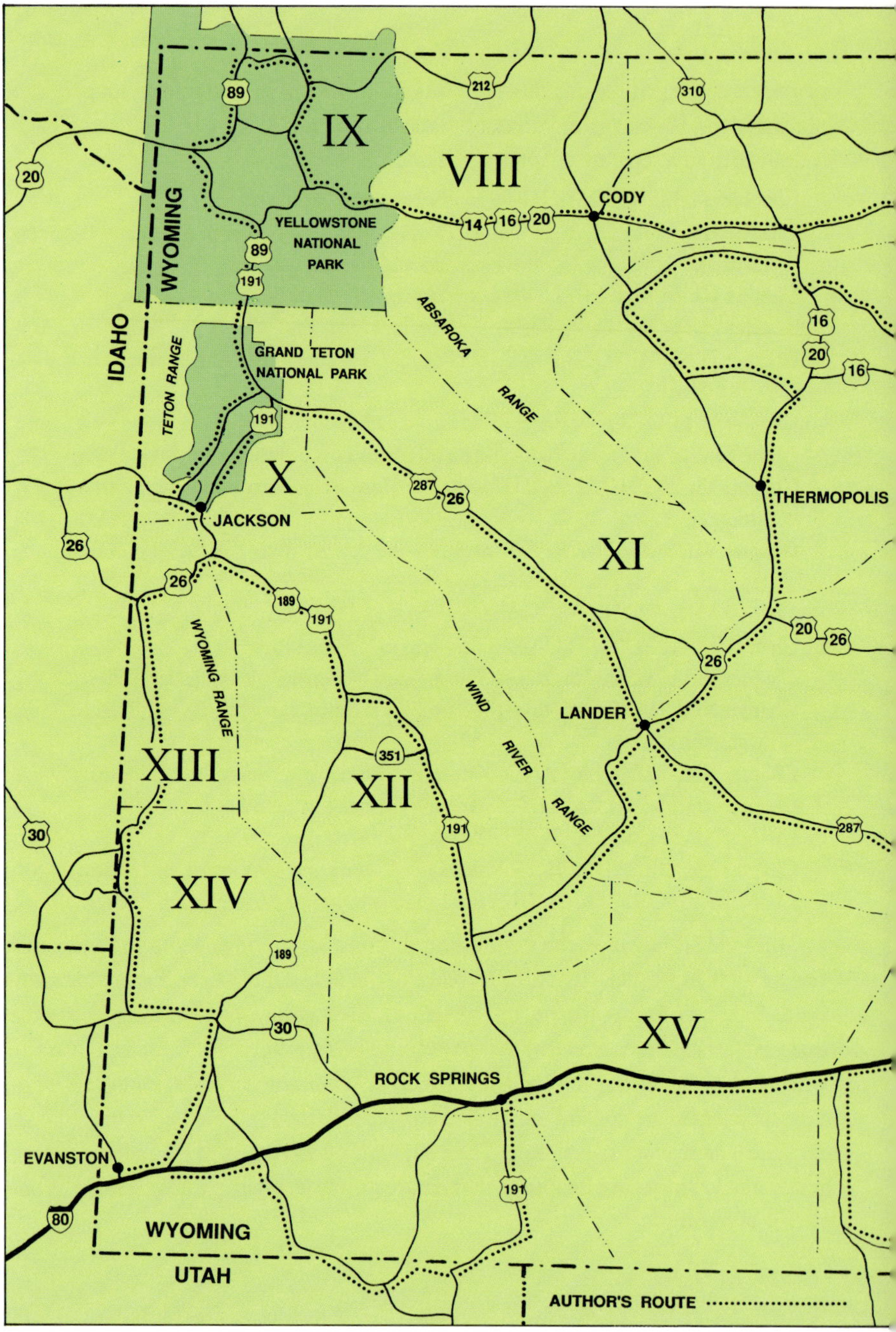
IX
VIII
X
XI
XII
XIII
XIV
XV
YELLOWSTONE NATIONAL PARK
GRAND TETON NATIONAL PARK
WYOMING
IDAHO
UTAH
TETON RANGE
ABSAROKA RANGE
WIND RIVER RANGE
WYOMING RANGE
CODY
JACKSON
THERMOPOLIS
LANDER
ROCK SPRINGS
EVANSTON
89
20
212
310
14
16
191
287
26
189
351
30
80
AUTHOR'S ROUTE

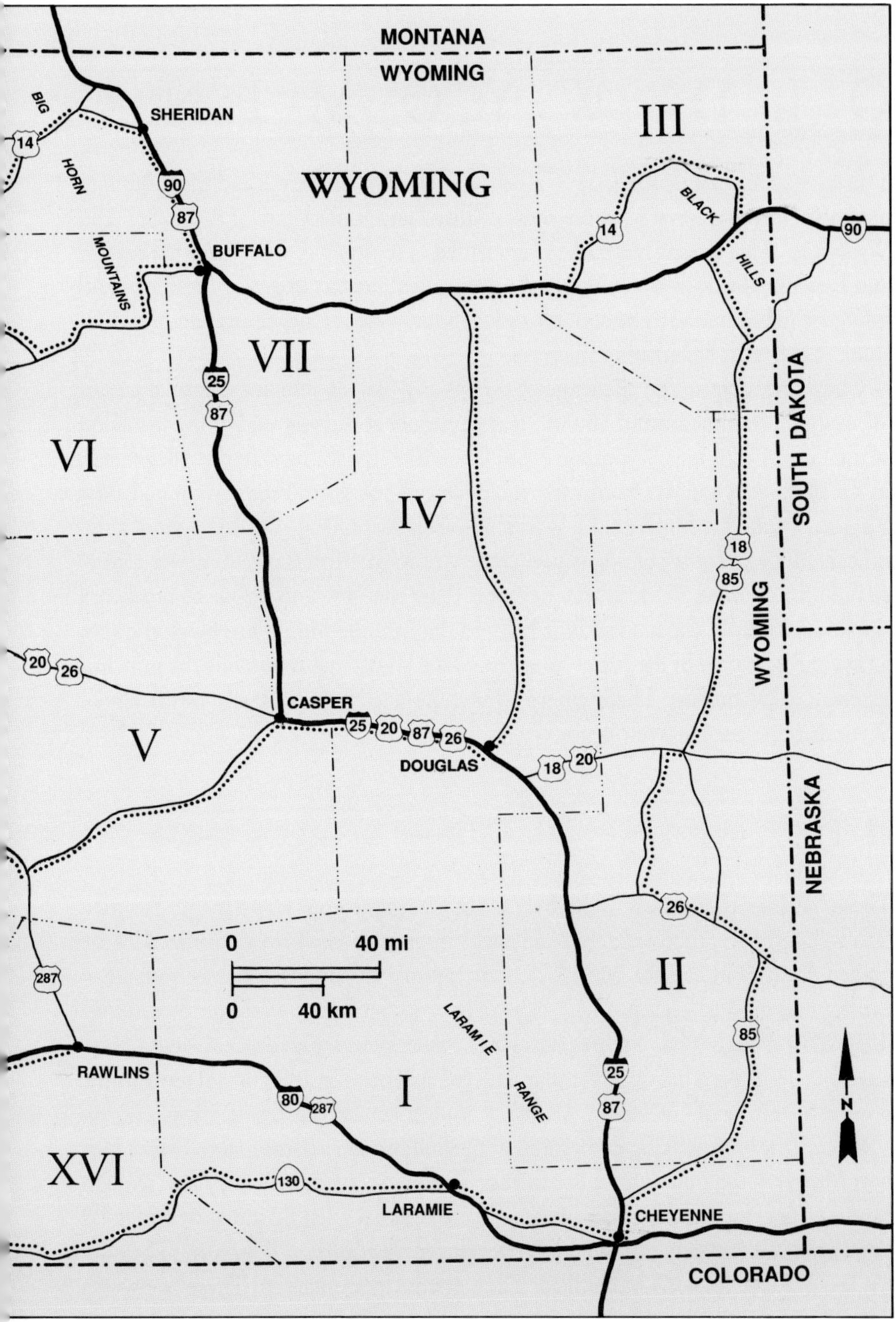
MONTANA
WYOMING
WYOMING
III
SHERIDAN
BIG
HORN
MOUNTAINS
14
90
87
BUFFALO
BLACK
HILLS
14
90
VII
25
87
VI
IV
SOUTH DAKOTA
18
85
WYOMING
20
26
CASPER
25
20
87
26
DOUGLAS
18
20
V
NEBRASKA
26
0
40 mi
0
40 km
II
287
LARAMIE
RANGE
85
25
87
RAWLINS
80
287
I
XVI
130
LARAMIE
CHEYENNE
COLORADO
N

OLD WYOMING

THE SOUTHEASTERN CORNER OF WYOMING, including Cheyenne and the mountain territories to the west of it, is the most civilized and settled part of the state: "Old Wyoming." That doesn't mean it's so very settled or so very old. Cheyenne, the capital, and Laramie, the university city, are the preeminent centers of power (political) and influence (educational). The country roundabout, west of Cheyenne and Laramie, is some of the most beautiful in the state.

Cheyenne, despite the challenge of the oil-city Casper, remains the chief city of Wyoming, hovering around 50,000. It is physically at the very end of the intrusion of the Great Plains into Wyoming. From Cheyenne straight back to the Alleghenies, it's flat all the way, and you won't strike mountains till you get to Pennsylvania and West Virginia. From Pine Bluffs on the Wyoming-Nebraska border—the first sight of a significant ridge of some stature as you come westward—Interstate 80 drives arrow-straight for 40 miles (64 km) to Cheyenne. After that the land begins to break and ripple significantly, the road sways a bit, and the Laramie Mountains block the way. Cheyenne is another of the many "gateways to the West," and is certainly the principal gateway to Wyoming. That's where—psychologically, if not really physically—Wyoming and the Far West begin.

■ THE CAPITOL

There's nothing particularly Wild West about Cheyenne now. It's no longer Frontier. It's a well-settled, spruce, staid, but still rather impressive small city dominated by the golden dome of its **capitol**. Most U.S. state capitols are supposed to pay homage to the big one in Washington, D.C., especially to its St. Peter-like dome. Wyoming's doesn't, for though it has a dome, it's a small, rather pretty, gilded one. Construction started in 1886, even before Wyoming achieved statehood in 1890. It still remains the dominant feature of Cheyenne.

Perhaps the most striking decorations of the building are a **memorial to Esther Hobart Morris** of the now extinct South Pass City, who served as the very first woman Justice of the Peace in the whole universe in 1870, and a splendid statue by native Ed Fraughton of a wickedly bucking horse, designated ***The Spirit of Wyoming.*** (The rider has lost one stirrup—will he be piled? The suspense is permanent.) These two works of art define Wyoming as both the cowboy state, where men are men, and the Equality State, where women are office holders. Women had the vote here before anywhere else in the United States. Nellie Tayloe Ross, whose elegant portrait greets visitors to the governor's office, reigned as the first woman state governor in the nation, elected in 1924. (There has not, incidentally, been another one in Wyoming since, but Thyra Thompson was Secretary of State from 1962 to 1986, and the position now seems to be traditionally feminine.)

The interior of the capitol is an odd blend of sophistication and wildlife, formality and informality—just like Wyoming itself. Architecturally it's very imposing and chaste. The office doors of high dignitaries, however, use nicknames: "Mike" Sullivan, Governor; "Stan" Smith, Treasurer. You'll find some stuffed animals—a bison, a wildcat, an elk—as well as some newer, tasteful, and elegant decorations in the dome, and murals in the legislative chambers. The paintings in the Senate Chamber—especially those by Emil Gollings, Wyoming's best, if least-known, native painter—are of particularly high quality. Like the striking statues front and back, Wyoming art is not to be sneezed at, however neglected.

Plaques on the downstairs walls of the central rotunda commemorate the state's earlier great patrician-politicians, names which are still remembered all over Wyoming: Joseph M. Carey, Francis E. Warren, and John B. Kendrick. All three were big cattlemen of the plains areas. Between the three of them they held some office or other almost continuously from 1869 to 1933.

Carey Street (once called Ferguson) was the Fifth Avenue of Cheyenne when the city had settled down, about 1880, as the state's metropolis. Cattle grandees and other such personages built splendid late Victorian Italianate villas side by side near the Cheyenne Club, where they entertained lavishly. At dances, champagne flowed, the halls were wreathed with flowers, and the local belles wore gowns shipped out for the occasion from New York on the railroad. Even the haughty wives of senior officers at the fort were impressed. The villas on Carey Street are now all gone—liquidated by "progress"—and the street itself is a wasteland of parking lots interspersed with large institutional structures. But the memory lingers on. A very New York woman recently described how she drove impulsively up from Denver to Cheyenne hoping to see cow ponies hitched to rails along the streets. Instead, to her disgust, she saw "nothing but Mercedes." Cheyenne probably hasn't seen a cow pony hitched to a rail since the early twentieth century.

ESTHER HOBART MORRIS
PROPONENT OF THE LEGISLATIVE ACT WHICH
IN 1869 GAVE DISTINCTION TO THE TERRITORY OF
WYOMING
AS THE 1ST GOVERNMENT IN THE WORLD TO GRANT
WOMEN EQUAL RIGHTS

■ The Founding of Cheyenne

State capitols are intended to be, and sometimes are, an index of the state's general atmosphere. Cheyenne's capitol is comparatively modest and discreet; but these are most certainly not the characteristics of Wyoming as a whole. One thing for sure, the capitol is no proper memorial to the city's exceedingly raucous beginnings in 1867. Cheyenne owes its birth to the swift progress of the Union Pacific (U.P.), the eastern arm of the first transcontinental railroad. The town site was picked by Major General Grenville M. Dodge, a planning engineer of the U.P., who was prospecting for a proper railroad route across the mountains. He camped first on Crow Creek in 1865, and as chief engineer chose this campsite in 1867 for a railroad-building terminal town. Dodge named it for the Cheyenne Indians, who ranged in this area, and who actually attacked him during his prospecting. (The name is a French trapper adaptation of the Indian

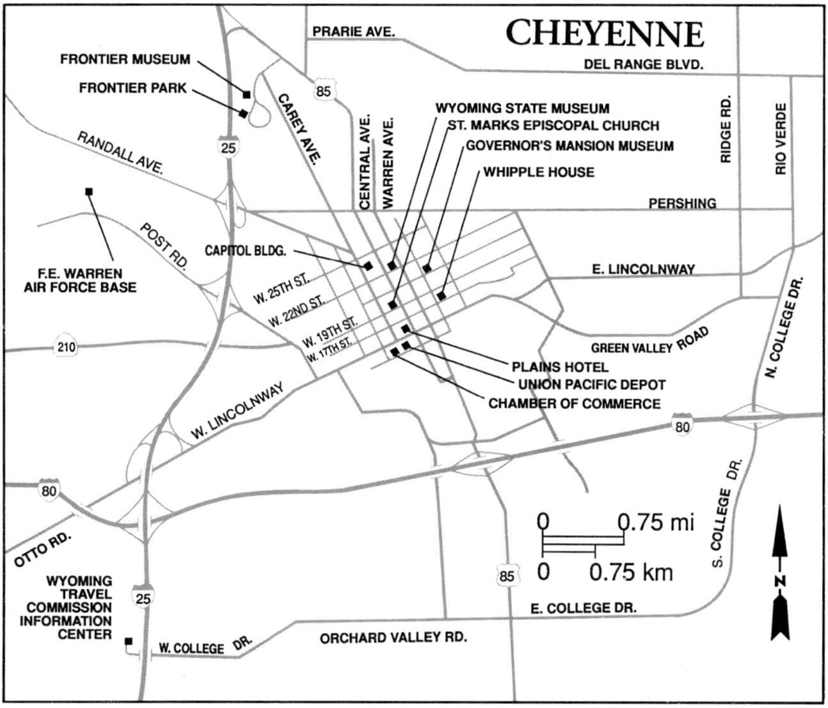

(opposite) Esther Hobart Morris, the nation's first woman justice of the peace, guards the entrance to the state capitol in Cheyenne.

"She-en-na," a good deal closer to the original than some adaptations. It's now pronounced *shy-ANN.*)

Soon afterward, the army established Fort D.A. Russell, later Fort Warren, northwest of the town. Then came the raffish population preceding the first train westward, known as "Hell-on-Wheels" for its unsavory passengers. Speculators, gamblers, shopkeepers, craftsmen, whores, and preachers soon made up the motley citizenship. A charter was adopted in that same year of 1867, and H.M. Hook, owner of the Pilgrim House Hotel, was elected mayor. That charter was accepted by the Dakota Territorial Legislature, which then controlled the area, and Cheyenne was in business.

The town business was fraught with peculiar difficulties. For instance, the new transcontinental telegraph, one of the town's principal lifelines, was constantly disrupted by buffalo. Herds used the poles as scratching posts; they could rub a pole out of the ground in a few hours. Preventive spikes were no good. The buffalo loved the spikes and thirty or more scratch-hungry animals would line up at any pole between Omaha and Cheyenne.

The lid blew off when the first train arrived on November 13. It came piled high with the "rubbish of a mushroom city"—frames for shacks, boards, furniture, and more derelicts. When the locomotive came to a wheezing stop, a guard jumped off his van and shouted "Gentlemen, here's Julesburg!" Julesburg was, of course, some 150 miles east. That month, the population hit 4,000. Lots that sold originally for $150 were now going for $2,500, and the place was littered with an unsightly and disorganized mess of some 3,000 shacks, "a standing insult to every wind that blew." But life certainly went on regardless. John Hardy, aptly named, and John Shaughnessy, fought a 126-round prize fight on the same day that the first public school entered the official planning stage.

By the summer of 1868, the town was in full swing. There were 300 businesses that catered to trappers, hunters, trainmen, engineers, and a whole transitory population of card sharpers, promoters, professional gunmen, and unattached

(but easily attachable) ladies. Cheyenne soon was ranked with that far eastern Colorado railroad station, Julesburg, in its bad reputation. As of 1868, the undoubtedly appalled founder, General Dodge, said it was the "gambling center of the world." At the same time, the Reverend J.W. Cook organized an Episcopal congregation and built perhaps the first Protestant church in Wyoming; other denominations followed fast. The local cemetery was considered as essential as the post office. Both came second to the saloons. "Hell must have been raked to furnish the inhabitants," noted one critic, "and to Hell they must return after graduating here." Vigilante justice was the only partially effective law, and when the log cabin jail got too full, prisoners were told to get out of town. Or else. Colonel Luke Murrin, first mayor of incorporated Cheyenne, added 25 cents to each fine he imposed for his own liquid use and pleasure. Law was "such dry work," he found.

But already dreams of capitalization were budding, even as early as 1867, although there was nothing yet to be capital of. Wyoming hadn't even become a territory. By 1868, however, Laramie County was organized. Wyoming Territory, approved by Congress in 1868, began to function in 1869. Brigadier General John A. Campbell, assistant secretary of war under Ulysses Grant, was named governor. Cheyenne, the largest and just about the only town in the new Territory, was now at last a capital.

In the 1870s and 1880s, Cheyenne also became the cow capital of the state. The coming of the railroad meant that cattle could be shipped east directly from Wyoming. In the southeast corner, but particularly up in the Big Horn and Powder River grasslands, the flamboyant era of the cattle boom began. Cheyenne was where the cowboys celebrated after driving their herds to the railhead. The big ranchers celebrated at the elegant Cheyenne Club. Here they sat in winter, "sipping rich wine, playing Boston, and settling cattle policy for the West." The Wyoming Stock Growers' Association ruled the range, and those younger sons of titled English families came down from their big ranch houses to disport themselves.

When the Black Hills gold fields officially opened in 1875, Cheyenne also became the outfitting center for miners. Stages left for the boom in Deadwood, carrying thousands of passengers and enriching scores of holdup men on the way.

Over the years, population doubled and tripled. Settled down to some 3,000 by the 1880s, it reached 16,000 by the late 1890s. Cheyenne was one of the first cities in the country to have electric lights, as of 1882. Streets were paved in the 1890s. Newspapers flourished. (As soon as a western town started, a couple of rival editors would begin to fight it out. In this case it was the *Wyoming Eagle* versus the *Wyoming State Tribune-Leader.*)

(opposite) Cheyenne in 1867 was a wild and woolly town. (Courtesy, Wyoming State Museum)

Deputy sheriffs and rodeo queens brighten up Cheyenne Frontier Days festivities (above). Frontier Days means more than buckin' horses and parades; for many, the best memories come from the carnival (opposite).

POP CORN
COLD DRINKS
Caramel APPLES
COLD Drinks
TAKE

The blizzard of 1887-88, followed by the end of the Black Hills gold rush, brought hard times to Wyoming, but by then Cheyenne was thoroughly established. The cattlemen in the south survived the blizzard; many to the north did not. To this day, Cheyenne remains Wyoming's "cow capital" and center for cattle organizations, policy makers, politicians, and shipping companies—with the focus on politics. From 1890 on, this was where the state's leaders got together, and where native politicians could graduate from local law-making to national prestige. Today, Wyoming's two senators and one representative wield influence out of all proportion to numbers, and often go on to still higher things—as witnessed by the appointment under George Bush of Wyoming's Rep. Dick Cheney as Secretary of Defense. This kind of thing is not uncharacteristic. Cheyenne is where the power gathers. Rustlers and gunmen, like the notorious Tom Horn, are no longer executed there as celebrities. The clamor of Hell-on-Wheels is long gone, but the stakes can still be pretty high in Cheyenne. All the paths of glory in the state lead there—and on to Washington.

■ Sights and Sites

After decades of devotion to progress (and its consequent destruction of the past), Cheyenne is now (as of Wyoming's centennial) full of nostalgia for the great days of the 1880s, when the city was built up on the debris of Hell-on-Wheels. The façade of this boom town still remains pretty well intact along the central blocks of 16th Street—"main street"—the city's business center. Rows of handsome buildings from that period face one another, or look across a plaza at the grandiose Union Pacific Depot, still extant if not exactly functional (no passengers). The **Plains Hotel** at the corner of 16th and Central dates from 1910 and remains one of the few fine old hostelries left functioning in the state. It still flourishes, flamboyantly and atmospherically, as a focus of downtown life.

The glorious town houses of the cattle barons have pretty much disappeared, but the massive churches that they once surrounded still stand on the way north toward the capitol, notably the Gothic Catholic St. Mary's Cathedral, the Romanesque redstone Methodist Church, and St. Mark's Episcopal Church of 1886 (on the site of Reverend Cook's original of 1868). One remnant of Cheyenne's former residential elegance is the fine old **Whipple House**, built in 1883 at 300 E. 17th Street. It has been beautifully restored and turned into one of the most sophisticated restaurants in the Far

West. Otherwise, this once "best part of town" is notable only for scattered big government buildings and banks. The more prosperous residential section doesn't begin until about 20th Street, closer to the capitol.

Near the capitol itself is the **Governor's Mansion**, an imposing, porticoed, 1905 affair (the governor doesn't live there anymore). The fine, big **Wyoming State Museum** stands at 24th and Central. It is a recapitulation on a rather grand scale of all the things you see in the local museums of every town in the state—old days of trappers, cattle, mining, even some pre-historic aboriginal items, and of course lots about Indians. It lacks the quirky local color that makes the lesser museums so amusing, nostalgic, and evocative.

The **Cheyenne Frontier Days Old West Museum**, at the northwest end of Carey Avenue in Frontier Park, portrays the growth of that annual extravaganza from a small, local, bucking-bronc affair to the great civic event that it is now, full of parades, beauty queens, dignitaries—and still, basically, bucking horses. Though most contestants are nationally famous professionals, there's still plenty of Wyoming and Cheyenne feeling about Cheyenne Frontier Days. Though every other town in the state has rodeos and similar events, this is unquestionably Wyoming's biggest celebration, and it really packs them into Cheyenne in the last week of July. The museum also has old carriages, miscellaneous railroad exhibits, and Indian relics.

West of town, beyond the barricade of Interstate 25, lies huge **Fort Warren**. It's now very actively devoted to missiles, which are supposedly dotted around the nearby prairies. The base is not hermetically sealed, and weekly tours are given, for which one checks at the main east gate. There are also missile tours, but for the most part these are restricted to VIPs. It does no harm to ask, however.

A **Cheyenne Area Visitors Council** office occupies one of the more interesting red brick Victorian survivors at 301 16th Street, downtown, where you can get details on these buildings as well as the many other things to see and do around town. But whether you see a Mercedes or not, you certainly won't see a cow pony hitched to a rail.

Cheyenne Frontier Days: Bullrider and horseshoer Clint Dimit (top); bareback rider Ty Skiver of Big Piney savors a shiner after being kicked by a bronc (left); Bob "Bulldancer" Romer, rodeo clown for more than two decades (right).

Cousins Arlette Corbin and Bobbie Griffy (top). Frank Edward Neal, who was a 15-year-old bucking bronc rider in 1914, returns to Frontier Days 75 years later (bottom).

West to Laramie

There are two ways for the motorist to get from Cheyenne to Laramie: Interstate 80 and Happy Jack Road.

Though the 46-mile (74-km) route on the Interstate over the pass to Laramie may lack any special interest, there are two curious detours off it. The first goes south to the railroad ghost town of **Sherman**, once a busy Union Pacific depot. When the railroad line was moved south, the town was deserted. Nearby is a forlorn memorial, the **Ames Monument**, erected in honor of Oakes and Oliver Ames, two New England capitalists who backed the Union Pacific via the Credit Mobilier. The monument, a stern rock pyramid, was designed by famous architect H.H. Richardson, and the portrait plaques of the Ameses by the famous sculptor Augustus St. Gaudens; and nobody cares. The noses of the Ameses have been shot off by hunters. *Sic transit gloria mundi.*

The second detour—to the north, a few miles west of the Sherman exit—leads to a natural phenomenon called by the Indians the **Vedauwoo** (VEE-dawoo), an appropriately weird name for a weird spectacle. These are forbidding towers of great gray rocks, round or square, piled on top of one another as if by giant human hands, looking like sinister temples, or strewn about at random like elephants turned to stone. The Indians quite probably felt the area was haunted by earthbound spirits. The surrounding landscape is, by contrast, a pastoral one of open meadows, aspen or pine groves, and hidden ponds. Under the shade of the principal Vedauwoo is an extensive camping and picnic area, shady and picturesque. All this is on a plateau of around 8,000 feet (2,400 m) in altitude, on top of which are piled the Vedauwoo, and farther north, Pole Mountain and its companions—bare on the east side, forested to the west. Though these are pretty mild mountains, they would be the first that a west-bound traveler on Interstate 80 would see since leaving the very different ones far to the east—by now a welcome change from endless plains.

This plateau ends at Sherman Hill, the high point on Interstate 80, where the descent to Laramie begins. At this summit of 8,640 feet (2,633 m) stands a towering black **bust of Lincoln** on a pedestal, commemorating the bygone Lincoln Highway, old Route 30. Sherman Hill was also the highest point on the first transcontinental railroad of 1868. A campground and big visitor platform are there too; high, but totally viewless.

■ HAPPY JACK ROAD

A far more ingratiating parallel route, **Happy Jack Road**, travels west in a more intimate way. Beautifully engineered and maintained for smooth-sailing through unspoiled scenery, it's a typical specimen of Wyoming's secondary highways, the glory of the state's road system. These Happy Surprises occur all over the state, and will of course be noted.

To reach Happy Jack Road from Interstate 80, take the Interstate 25 exit (toward Casper) to Missile Drive, one of the entrances to the Warren Air Force Base. The road curves around the south side of the base, near a new base housing development, and heads west out of Cheyenne. The road is immediately out on the range. Western cities often end in that abrupt way, except along main routes cluttered with commercial crud—the usual Strip—and even sizable roads like this suddenly find themselves in wide-open spaces. Antelope pose on hills right outside of the city.

On this highway, it's wide-open alright. Nothing there but cows and those antelope, once you get past the high fences that guard Fort Warren to the north. For some 15 miles (25 km), the road grandly swoops and curves toward the mountains. At last the endless plains have ended and you have something definite to look forward to. After a scattered, bare bit of semi-suburbia, and then more range, the road curls up onto an open plateau, interrupted by copses of evergreens and increasing projections of odd rock formations.

Soon you pass through **Curt Gowdy State Park**, named after a well known Wyoming sports broadcaster. This is centered about a pretty reservoir in a valley to the south, with campsites and a marina. Then Happy Jack crosses into **Medicine Bow National Forest**, which surrounds the scattered, modest peaks of the Sherman Mountains—Twin Mountain and Green Mountain on the east edge, Pole Mountain and others farther west. These protuberances are all on top of the plateau of the Laramies and within one of the four separate sections of the Medicine Bow National Forest.

The surrounding country, totally uninhabited, is fenced off in places for private cattle range, and has some well-known camping and picnic sites—Blair, Wallis, the Vedauwoo, Pole Mountain (with a small stream through it), and Tie City. The latter was once a camp for tie-hackers, lumbermen who cut railroad ties. Shortly after Tie City, Happy Jack turns south and is devoured by Interstate 80.

Two picturesque, gravel Forest Service roads connect Happy Jack to Interstate 80, southward. One takes off before you get to the first outcropping of the Shermans, and

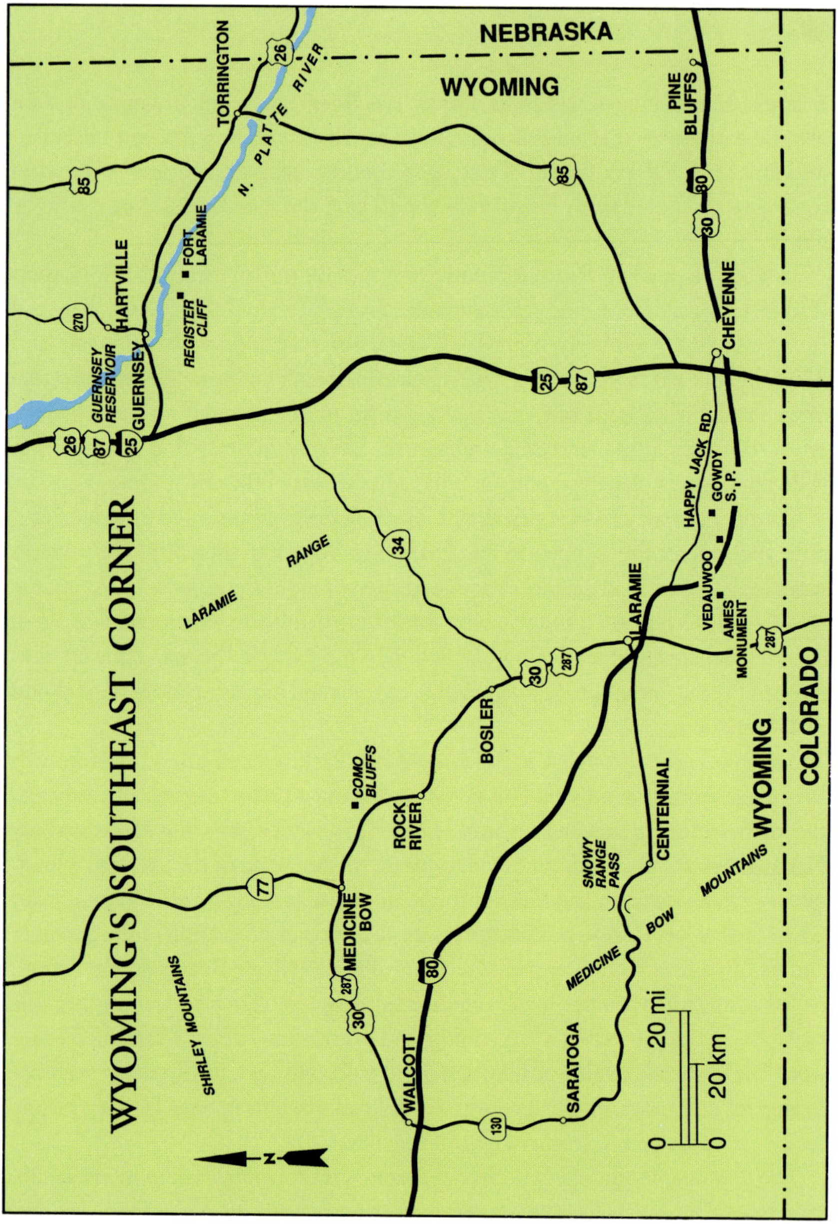
WYOMING'S SOUTHEAST CORNER
NEBRASKA
WYOMING
COLORADO
WYOMING
TORRINGTON
N. PLATTE RIVER
PINE BLUFFS
HARTVILLE
FORT LARAMIE
REGISTER CLIFF
GUERNSEY RESERVOIR
GUERNSEY
CHEYENNE
HAPPY JACK RD.
GOWDY S.P.
VEDAUWOO
AMES MONUMENT
LARAMIE
LARAMIE RANGE
BOSLER
COMO BLUFFS
ROCK RIVER
MEDICINE BOW
CENTENNIAL
SNOWY RANGE PASS
MEDICINE BOW MOUNTAINS
SHIRLEY MOUNTAINS
WALCOTT
SARATOGA
26
85
80
30
270
25
87
34
287
77
130
20 mi
20 km
0
0
N

wanders eight slow but rewarding miles (13 km) through open country, rangeland and copses interspersed all along the way with an amazing assortment of those Vedauwoo rock formations, which make the pleasant meadows seem like an African veldt, with herds of stone hippos grazing. Eventually you reach the big Vedauwoo campground, just north of Interstate 80.

The other even more scenic Blair-Willis Road takes off from Happy Jack beyond the first of the Sherman Mountains, and goes all the way up to Sherman Hill on Interstate 80, where Happy Jack ends. It has weird rock formations and more exciting wooded scenery than the parallel road from Happy Jack to the Vedauwoos.

As for Happy Jack, he was Jack Hollingsworth, who had a ranch in the 1880s in the foothills beyond Cheyenne, and hauled wood. He was always singing at his work, and the road past his adobe shack was much traveled, so he became a local character.

In the same decade, there was a short-lived gold boom in the area. A Professor Aughey announced a discovery which he named Carbonite Belle. This would, he claimed, outshine the Comstock Lode. Eager Cheyenne businessmen prepared to invest $500,000, only to discover the Professor had salted the area with specimens of ore.

The Vedauwoo rise up like some bizarre, sculpted dreamscape.

■ Laramie of the Past

Laramie, with a population of around 25,000, is the second largest city of the southwest corner and the third largest in Wyoming. It lies west of the Laramie range, on the Laramie plains, and along the Laramie River. One may wonder who Laramie was to be so thoroughly memorialized. In fact, nobody much. He was a French trapper, Jacques la Ramie or Ramée, who was killed somewhere along his river by the Indians about 1820. His trapper friends must have loved him, since they named everything in sight after him. Then from later days came Fort Laramie and the town and county of Laramie, all of which have no geographical connection.

As the seat of the University of Wyoming, the first (1887) and for a long while only college in the state, Laramie is the educational and intellectual center of Wyoming. (There are now two-year colleges scattered about in Riverton, Rock Springs, Cheyenne, Torrington, Powell, and Sheridan.) Of necessity, the university's practical side gets the emphasis—animal husbandry, geology, engineering, etc.—but the humanities make a showing. The library is famous for its coverage of Wyoming writing and mining records, as well as for its splendid rare book collection in the American Heritage Center.

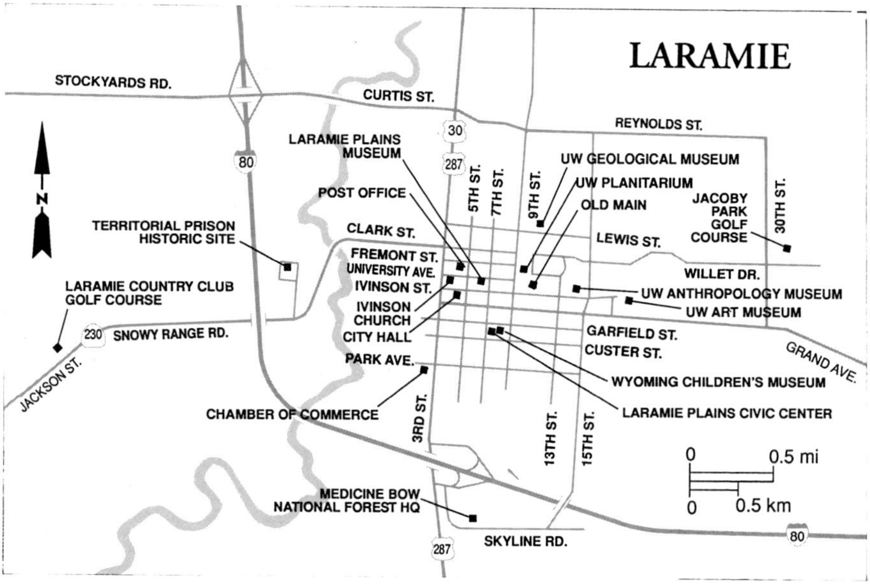

There is a comparatively new but burgeoning art gallery, and from the beginnings of both town and gown there have been resident writers.

When Old Main, a massive, Victorian, yellow-stone, semi-Gothic mass, was built in 1887 out on the flats, it gave the effect of being the only collegiate edifice within a thousand miles. Actually, nearby Colorado and Utah had gotten into the act, but Old Main was certainly one of a kind in Wyoming. Now it's flanked by a big bustling modern institution. This is not a campus full of Old World charm, but it does exude a certain progressive Western energy. There are about 10,000 students now.

Altogether, however, Laramie is quieter and prettier than most Wyoming, and indeed, most Western, cities. Though on the flats itself, it is ringed by mountains, near and far, and the street trees have had time to grow tall. But its early history is just as active as Cheyenne's. It, too, suffered from the perils of Hell-on-Wheels.

There had been some earlier settlement in this area along the Overland Trail in the 1860s. As at Cheyenne, a military post had been set up—Fort J. Buford (later Ft. Sanders)—to protect immigrant trains. The railroad and its passengers first arrived May 9, 1868, and of course all hell broke loose. There was the same outburst of business and mayhem. Law and order were imposed in that first May, when a vigilante group lynched a desperado called The Kid. This was a mistake. The Kid's friends terrorized the town that summer; and in the fall, the vigilantes grew to a formidable 500. They raided outlaw strongholds, such as the Belle of the West dance hall. In the ensuing battle, five were killed and fifteen wounded. Four outlaws who surrendered were hanged on as many telegraph poles. A young stranger who arrived in town at this moment recorded his astonishment at this quadruple example of civic virtue. Many outlaws headed west with Hell-on-Wheels. A committee of the righteous took over in December. Albany County was created in 1868, with Laramie as its seat. Unfortunately, residual outlaws, under a mask of respectability, took over the reform committee. Things returned to normal and went to pot. Dakota Territory revoked the town's charter, dissolved the committee, and put the town under the jurisdiction of federal courts until 1874. By then, Wyoming was its own territory.

Things quieted down and women emerged as a force in town. Women were impaneled on a state grand jury as early as 1870. This first fruit of female emancipation received worldwide attention. No less a worthy than King William of Prussia cabled his congratulations to President Grant on such evidence of human progress, and newspaper correspondents gathered to witness the jury at work. Heavy veils masked the women jurors' faces to protect their privacy. A jingle made the rounds: *"Baby, baby, don't get in a fury; your mamma's gone to sit on the jury."* This feminized jury convicted a man of manslaughter "following a duel in a hotel lobby."

■ BILL NYE AND OTHERS

It is characteristic of the town that Wyoming's first famous writer, Bill Nye, was a prominent early citizen. Born in Maine and reared in Wisconsin, he came to Wyoming in 1876 as a lawyer, though he never practiced. He served in the Territorial Legislature, and became postmaster and a justice of the peace. He began his literary career as a writer for the fledgling *Sentinel*, then started his own mule-inspired *Boomerang* in 1881. His style was widely copied all over the country, and by the time he finally left in 1885 he was famous. He went to New York and the *New York World*, and from 1881 till his death in 1896 published a series of books including *Bill Nye and the Boomerang* (1881), *Forty Liars and Other Lies* (1882), *Baled Hay* (1884), and many others. He belongs in the tradition of early Mark Twain, Josh Billings, and other poker-faced, tall-tale humorists of the period—the nation's first jokesters with a wholly American accent.

Since then, Laramie has continued to harbor the Muse, but never with the same early acclaim. Grace Raymond Hebard wrote on Wyoming history, and her close friend Agnes M. Wergeland composed music and poetic eulogies on Wyoming in Norwegian. As an undergraduate, Ted Olsen practiced his poetry and went on to a considerable reputation as prize-winning poet. He returned to Laramie in the 1920s as editor for the *Boomerang* before moving on to the *New York Herald Tribune.* Thurman Arnold, born in Laramie, became well-known as the author of *The Folklore of Capitalism* (1937) and as a legal figure of prominence (assistant attorney general of the United States). Olga Moore, too, went on to a respectable reputation as a novelist. Though none of these came close to the national fame of Nye, they and others from and in Laramie have kept the flag of Wyoming native literature flying.

■ THE UNIVERSITY

Laramie is still very much dominated by the **university campus**, which stretches along Grand Avenue from 30th to Ninth streets. It has the usual collegiate effect of an oasis, particularly surrounded by such dry, flat, open countryside. Almost all the buildings

Bill Nye

When Bill Nye resigned as postmaster of Laramie, he supposedly drafted the following letter to President Chester A. Arthur. It is a representative example of the Nye style.

Laramie, Oct. 1, 1883
To the President of the United States:

Sir:

I beg to leave at this time to officially tender my resignation as postmaster of this place, and in due form to deliver the great seal and key to the front door of this office. The safe combination is set on numbers 33, 66 and 99, though I do not at this moment remember which comes first, or how many times you revolve the knob or which direction you turn it at first to make it operate.

You will find the postal cards that have not been used under the distributing table and the coal down in the cellar. If the stove draws too hard, close the damper in the pipe and shut the general delivery window. Acting under the advice of General Hatton, a year ago, I removed the featherbed with which my predecessor, Deacon Hayford, had bolstered up his administration by stuffing the window, and substituted glass. Finding nothing in the book of instructions which made the featherbed a part of my official duties, I filed it away in an obscure place and burned it in effigy, also in the gloaming.

I need not say that I herewith transmit my resignation with great sorrow and genuine respect. We have toiled together month after month, asking no reward except the innate consciousness of rectitude and the salary fixed by law. Now we are to separate. Here the roads seem to fork, as it were, and you and I, and the cabinet, must leave each other.

You will find the key under the door-mat and you had better turn the cat out at night when you close the office. If she does not go readily, you can make it clearer to her mind by throwing the cancelling stamp at her. If Deacon Hayford does not pay his box rent, you might as well put his mail in the general delivery, and when Bob Read gets drunk and insists on a letter from one of his wives every day in the week, you can salute him through the box delivery with an old Queen Anne tomahawk, which you will find near the Etruscan water pail. Mr. President, as an official of the government, I now retire. . . ."

—Bill Nye

are built of the characteristic yellow stone of the area, which you see when you look east up the main streets toward the bluffs above town. The buildings are mostly early modern (1930-50), block-like constructions—handsome, solid, and by now looking pleasantly old-fashioned. There are huge, ornamental spruce trees, and lawns desperately kept green by sprinklers in summer—so you're sure to get wet on walks around campus at that time of year. **Old Main**, more than a century old, is reverently preserved in a sort of garden-corner of the grounds, at Ivinson and Ninth, with the biggest trees and greenest lawns on campus, and even some flowers. At the eastern end of the campus is a long, open alley culminating in the handsome, modern Fine Arts Center. Along the sides are fraternities (north) and sororities (south)—a pleasant promenade when the sun isn't too hot or the wind too cold, especially at sunset.

On campus there are at least four noteworthy sights. You can find them on a compact yellow map with numbers, available at the **University of Wyoming Visitor Center** at 1408 Ivinson, near 15th Street. The **Anthropology Building and Museum** is almost right across the street (14th and Ivinson). The **Geological Museum** is buried back across campus in the row of grandiose buildings devoted to Engineering, Agriculture, Mining, and the practical side of education. Both museums are small, but choice. The anthropology museum covers the known human history of the state. One thing it makes clear is just how very recent the presence of the horse is in Wyoming's history. The Indians that so wonderfully adapted their lives to horsemanship did so only in comparatively modern times—not long before the first appearances of French trapper-explorers in the mid-eighteenth century. In the thousands of years preceding, the native population wandered afoot, chipping spear points, driving bison over cliffs for food, and making pictographs and petroglyphs on high cliffs or rock recesses. The geological museum displays the more inordinately remote history of the state as left by prehistoric rocks and animals, and is dominated by an immense and gloriously terrifying Wyoming dinosaur skeleton.

The other two centers of university interest are the **American Heritage Center** in the Coe Library and the **University Art Museum** in the Fine Arts Center. The Coe Library is a spacious new building on the south-central side of campus. For the visitor, the principal attraction is upstairs (hard to find; ask at the front desk) where the American Heritage collection is at present situated. Besides an enormous reference collection of papers, notably mining archives, the Heritage Center possesses one of the state's most significant collections of Western art. It's now crowded into a passage that leads past a series of special rooms, culminating in the beautiful, panelled Rentschler Room.

Dominated by striking Western scenes, there are also beautiful Moran drawings and other gems of Western Americana, but above all a big collection of Gollings—perhaps the best in the state and the world. This underappreciated artist is finally gaining recognition, at least in his home state, and though the Heritage collection is terribly cramped for space, it gives you a more vivid impression of this colorful nativist than any other assemblage.

By contrast, the University Art Museum deliberately does not concentrate on Western art (which in this part of the country means Far Western cowboy art). Though it does have plenty of examples of this kind of thing among its 6,000 items, it prefers not to compete with Cody. The museum ranges over the entire spectrum of Western art in its broader meaning, concentrating considerably on twentieth-century American art. It has reasonable ambitions of becoming the most significant such general collection in the Rocky Mountain area, next to Denver; but like the American Heritage Center, it's desperately cramped for space. At present, unfortunately, especially for the casual visitor, the museum isn't really yet a true "museum"; that is, a place where a permanent collection of permanent worth is permanently exhibited. They have to use their entire present space in the fine arts center for rotating exhibits, which often do include objects from their big collection. As a result, a visitor may be stuck with an exhibit of Wyoming photographs and nothing else—splendid and interesting, but hardly a fair sample of the total eclectic holdings.

Archaeology, geology, heritage, and art will keep you busy and well-exercised as you pursue the various buildings from one end of the campus (paying homage to Old Main) to the other. Concerts and plays are performed in the arts center.

■ Laramie Town

The campus, like the capitol in Cheyenne, observes the usual odd Wyoming contradiction of ruggedness and sophistication. Here it's the contrast of the rough-hewn, native-stone, big academic structures, with the elegant fine arts center and its exhibitions, and the special treasures of the American Heritage Center. In town, somewhat of the same contrast exists. As you proceed down Ivinson Street westward, from its beginnings in the heart of the campus to its end on Third Street, you will pass some especially attractive residential blocks of greenery and nice-looking houses. At Sixth and Ivinson is the grand, turreted, late Victorian **Ivinson Mansion**, with grounds and a big coach house. Edward Ivinson was an Englishman, born in 1830 on St. Croix in the Virgin Islands, who made his way west and to Laramie. There he made his fortune, beginning with general merchandise and groceries, and spreading out in all directions, mostly in ties for the railroad. He flourished later as banker and real estate operator. He arrived at the very beginnings of the town in 1868, and died in 1928— at the age of 98. He and his English wife determinedly set the tone for Laramie's atmosphere of civility, still evident. He was involved in everything civic—treasurer of the university's first board of trustees, mayor of Laramie, a candidate for governor of the state in its second election of 1892 (unsuccessful—after all he wasn't a cattleman).

Ivinson was also senior warden of Laramie's St. Matthew's Cathedral. It is surely due to him as much as anyone, and to his constant beneficence, that the Episcopalian church has the odd universal spread and long-time preeminence (now much reduced) not only in Laramie, but all over Wyoming. In nearly every Wyoming town you can count on finding the three sacred edifices of the Catholics, the Latter day Saints, and the Episcopalians, usually huddled together in the center of a shady older section of town. Lutheran, Methodist, Presbyterian, and nowadays more free-wheeling sects flourish too, but none more centrally, solidly, and traditionally than those first three.

The Ivinson house, saved at the last moment from the wrecker's ball, as usual, is now a wonderfully full and all-embracing house museum, despite the misleading title of **Laramie Plains Museum**. The emphasis is on the Ivinsons and their devotion to good form and good taste, but it's not so much a preservation or even restoration of the original Ivinson glories, as it is a survey of all aspects of domestic life in the latter third of the nineteenth century in pioneer Wyoming. The house is full of old-fashioned oddities: quaint bathrooms, antique kitchen equipment, clothes, toys, handsome furniture, woodwork, lamps, even a nice shelf of books of the period, including quite a few Nyes. It's also full of ladies from all over the U.S. taking the tour.

Down Ivinson Street from the Ivinson house is the Ivinson church—**St. Matthew's Cathedral**—a beautiful example of Anglo-American neo-Gothic, very exotic on this site, with a charming if anachronistic garden-close next to it and a handsome neo-Gothic office beyond. Inside, the church is a model of its kind. Two big chancel windows memorialize Mr. and Mrs. Ivinson. The side chapel and high altar are especially handsome.

Unfortunately the surroundings are less than romantic. This part of town has been left to decay—broken sidewalks, no trees, dreary vacant lots, inappropriate commercial buildings—despite the fact that it is Laramie's civic center. City Hall is across the street

(opposite) The Ivinson Mansion houses a rich collection from early Wyoming.

LARAMIE
PLAINS
MUSEUM

and one block up from the cathedral. The handsome church of St. Laurence O'Toole (one can't help but wonder who he was) is one block over. The Masonic Hall is a neighbor, and the big Albany County Courthouse fills a nearby block. Yet the impression is that of a depressed neighborhood. Evidently, Laramie's civic pride ends at the university boundaries.

On the west side of town, the huge **Wyoming Territorial Prison**, built in 1872, is being restored. Concurrent with a program of anthropological excavations by the university, this is a notable example of the centennial urge to preserve and dig up. The restored Territorial Prison will be expanded into a large civic center full of various attractions. (Why not spruce up the present real civic center around city hall and the cathedral?)

■ Circle Tour: The Snowies, Saratoga, and Medicine Bow

This tour starts and ends in Laramie, and includes the first taste for the traveler from the east of **real** mountain scenery: the 12,000-foot (4,000-m) peaks of the Snowies. You climb above timberline going over Snowy Range Pass at 10,800 feet (3291 m) and pass right alongside glacial lakes (Mirror Lake, Lake Marie, Silver Lake), canyons, and gorgeous vistas. (The pass, incidentally, is very easy driving, though it's closed by snow from October or November through May.) On the lower slopes grow forests of evergreen and aspen, full of game. Streams flow through them, full of fish. Picnic places line the route, and winter sports flourish there.

The road to all of this, Wyoming State Highway 130, leaves Laramie to pass almost immediately through tawny rangeland, with the Snowies right ahead and other mountains southward. Before the start of the pass on the east side lies **Centennial**, which once had a population of thousands and now has about a hundred. Centennial is a picture-postcard of a small mining town. Its old buildings contain shops for tourists, and a museum down in the old depot. Though the whole town is visible at a glance from the road, it's worth a stop. This area was the scene of short-lived booms, most of them in the 1870s and 1880s. A platinum mine operated as late as the 1920s, but nothing operates now except for summer visitors and winter skiers.

The Snowies are an even more striking example of the Wyoming geological phenomenon of "range upon range." Like the portion of the Laramies between Cheyenne and Laramie, this part of the Medicine Bow Mountains consists of a great, rather flat plateau, out of which stick almost autonomous super-ranges—in this case, the Snowies. In fact, the Snowies are part of the Medicine Bows, but have a distinct character of their own.

The road from Snowy Range Pass comes down from these high mountains on the west side into the North Platte River Valley, fringed with mountains, and with bosky riverbanks down the middle. Handsome, rolling ranchland lies all about. The river is clear, rippling over stones and drifting through shallows before it takes off north through semidesert, then through mountains and dams to start its long curve around eastward and off to Nebraska, where it joins with the southern branch of the Platte, and ultimately, with the Missouri and Mississippi. Altogether a long, long way to go from its fresh beginnings, here.

Heading north, State Highway 130 takes you by magnificent ranches to **Saratoga**, a charming little spa and (across the river) village. Starting in 1878 as a trading post, it gradually became popular for its hot springs, particularly after a railroad was built south from the main line of the Union Pacific to serve nearby Encampment during the Sierra Madre mining boom. The springs were christened Saratoga in honor of the fashionable New York State spa and horse racing center, and since the turn of the century Wyoming's Saratoga has been a mildly active summer resort. There is a well-established and comfortable spa hotel, the Saratoga Inn, as well as other nice tourist facilities. Though the small town itself remains a rather run-down Western hamlet, there is good eating and shopping in the tiny "city center," and fishing along the river. It's a delightfully remote stopover for anyone going to or from nearby central Colorado, or for those poking around the environs of the Medicine Bows and Sierra Madre. Don't miss a meal at the nicely reconstructed Hotel Wolf in the town center. Handsome summer houses surround the spa's golf course on the east side of the river.

Driving north through increasingly flat, open plains to Walcott, you cross Interstate 80 and continue on old Route 30. This highway, curving back to Laramie, is the last, lost remains of the old Lincoln Highway in this corner of the state. It circles around the north end of the Medicine Bows along with the equally dispossessed Union Pacific. On the way east it passes by Hanna (coal and oil, of which there's quite a lot scattered about this northern part of Carbon County), and then through the vast, open valley of the Laramie Plains. To the south are the Medicine Bows, to the north the Shirley Mountains, the eastern-most edge of the chain of central belt ranges that starts in the west, where the Wind Rivers end. Far to the north, and bending around to the south

(following pages) Elk Mountain looms over an abandoned homestead.

and east, are the Laramies. You are never out of sight of some of these encircling ranges, but they are often far, far away, with nothing in between but enormous, wide rangelands.

The town of **Medicine Bow**, 37 miles (62 km) from Interstate 80, was once famous as the setting for the novel *The Virginian.* Medicine Bow, near the river so named by Indians because mountain birch from its banks became good medicine for making bows and arrows, is where Owen Wister himself in real life, and where the "I" of his book, got off the train and began the experiences that led to his writings at the turn of the century. His fictional hero, the Virginian, first appears in this town, and the climax of the story, the gun battle with the villain Trampas, took place there. A 1939 stone pyramid was erected in memory of Wister, and there are other mementos. Some may have forgotten, but Wyoming hasn't.

The most striking building in modern Medicine Bow is a big oblong of yellow stone, the **Virginian Hotel**, opened in 1911 on the expectation that the phenomenal success of the novel would bring it fame and fortune. Though the modern town of Medicine Bow is as derelict in its different way as the Wister town of the 1880s, the hotel is in fine shape. It's become a stylish hotel museum (on the National Register) with bedrooms ornately decorated in styles from 1880-1910. There is an especially fancy Owen Wister Suite, and downstairs a stately Owen Wister Dining Room, suitable for banquets. Actual eating takes place in an exceptionally cozy dining room and bar full of local characters, and probably not so unlike the Medicine Bow of 1880—except for us tourists, and much better food. Opposite, across the wide desolation of the almost deserted Lincoln Highway, is the former **U.P. Depot** made into a local museum. Next to it is the **Owen Wister log cabin**, moved from its original site on his ranch in Jackson Hole, but not yet fixed up for visitors. Trains don't stop at the station anymore, but they still go by—endless freight cars of coal or cattle, still with nostalgic train whistles. There is something altogether odd and remote about this memorial enclave alongside the railroad and the empty highway, its traffic siphoned away by thundering Interstate 80. One can't help wondering what epic events and discoveries will make *that* another such deserted monument to past transportation.

The other towns on the map along the 57 miles (95 km) to Laramie are equally marooned. Shortly beyond Medicine Bow is **Como Bluffs**, not even the pretense of a town, but the site of one of Earth's most famous treasure troves of dinosaur bones. This was the scene of the epic battle between the two world-famous dinosaur experts, Othniel C. Marsh (1831-92) and Edward Drinker Cope (1840-99)—representing the

Medicine Bow

Owen Wister gives a graphic and unflattering description of Medicine Bow at the beginning of *The Virginian* as it was in the 1880s. The "I" of the story, pretty obviously Wister himself, steps off the train as a rather haughty, very green dude, and meets the hero, the Virginian.

Enthralled with the first sight of his hero, he was less enthralled with Medicine Bow. "Town, as they called it, pleased me less. . . . But until our language stretches itself and takes in a word of closer fit, town will have to do. . . . I have seen and slept in many like it since. . . stark, dotted over a planet of treeless dust, like soiled packs of cards. . . . Houses, empty bottles, and garbage, they were forever of the same shapeless pattern. . . . They seemed to have been strewn here by the wind and to be waiting till the wind should come again and blow them away. Yet serenely above their forlornness swam a pure, quiet light such as the East never sees. . . . I took its dimensions, twenty-nine buildings in all—one coal chute, one water tank, the station, one store, two eating houses, one billiard hall, two tool-houses, one feed stable, and twelve others that for one reason and another I shall not name. . . . There they stood. . . amid a fringe of old tins while at their very doors began a world of crystal light."

Washing required "a trough. . . slippery with soapy water." A roller towel, dirty with use, was changed only at the beginning of the new day. But the pretty hotel keeper changed it especially for the Virginian. She evidently had her reward.

And eating? "Canned stuff it was—corned beef. And one of my table companions said the truth about it. 'When I slung my teeth over that. . . I thought I was chewing a hammock.' We had strange coffee and condensed milk." Sleeping was no better, but the narrator managed a clean night on top of a store counter.

The standard of living at Medicine Bow has skyrocketed in modern times, especially at the modern Virginian Hotel. But though the town itself has totally changed, it still has an air of forlornness, and still sits in the middle of the shining plains as something of an intrusion. There are now lots of trees on the few streets, but no more commercial buildings than there were a century ago; just different ones. A fine modern school and a pretty small church seem the most substantial buildings visible except, ironically, all those memorials to Wister: the hotel, the pyramid, the cabin moved from Jackson Hole, and the museum in the depot (a different depot from that of 1880) which celebrates Wister and *The Virginian*, among other things.

FOSSIL CABIN

Peabody Museum of Yale, in New Haven, Conn., and the Academy of Sciences in Philadelphia, respectively. They were led to their discoveries by two local men named Reed and Carlin, who worked for the Union Pacific. These two stumbled upon a lone line camp hut built entirely of huge dinosaur bones, and when the news percolated to the rival scientists, Reed became Marsh's man and Carlin was Cope's. The two scientists struggled over bones from the local quarry for decades, writing diatribes, wresting prize skeletons from one another more or less at gunpoint, blackening one another's reputations in the press, and sending their loot back to New Haven and Philadelphia. It was one of the classic scientific feuds of all time, but the battlefield is moribund now. There's nothing left on the quarry site itself, a mile or more north of the road, but the dinosaur-bone cabin is preserved alongside the road inside a stone hut as a paying tourist attraction.

The town of Rock River (on Rock Creek), some 20 miles (33 km) from Medicine Bow, still exists among its pleasant riverside groves of trees. Rock Creek was the scene of an attack in 1865 by Cheyennes on an immigrant train of 75 wagons. Among the victims was the Fletcher family. The mother was killed; the father, wounded, escaped with three sons, and two daughters were taken prisoner. Mary lived as a squaw for a year, returning to her family in 1866, but sister Lizzie became completely adapted to Indian ways and refused to return until 35 years later.

The now-vanished town of Rock Creek, then a railroad stop, was a lively place and starting point for a stage route up to Junction City, Montana—a 400-mile (660-km) trip. The railroad stop was abandoned around 1900 in favor of Rock River, and the stage was gone by then. Things have been pretty quiet since.

As for **Bosler**, it is now a memorial, both sad and funny, to the decline of the Lincoln Highway. It consists of a huddle of derelict buildings leaning together in vacant despair, labeled "Tourist Court," "DANCING," and other indications of roadside prosperity and whoopee. Nothing seems to remain of Bosler but these raffish mementos. The Medicine Bows, west, and the Laramies, east, loom in the distance over the great silent spaces. In about 20 miles (33 km), you're back in Laramie.

(opposite) Ethel Nash stands at the entrance to "the world's oldest building," built from dinosaur bones collected at nearby Como Bluff.

STAGECOACH CORRIDOR

THE LANDSCAPE AND HISTORICAL BACKGROUND of Wyoming's southeast corner make it the proper introduction to any overview of the whole state: mountains, cities, plains, rivers, history, wildlife, dinosaurs, sports, even some industry, and lots of ranching. The same can't really be said of the eastern border. It has its own very regional characteristics and lots of history; but to some extent, it's the least indigenous area of the state, an eastern frontier which is much more like the rougher parts of the true plains states, Nebraska and the Dakotas, than like Wyoming itself.

Due north from Cheyenne to the Black Hills, five smallish counties (including the southernmost Laramie County, covered in the last chapter) exhibit similar general characteristics: plains broken by ridges and penetrated by green cottonwood valleys, the rivers nearly all flowing west to east. This region has no true mountain ranges in it, but the Laramies loom large on its north-central edge, and there's a fringe of the Black Hills prominent in its northeast corner. Otherwise, it's generally wide open.

On the other hand, except for a brief intrusion around Torrington, there's none of the endless cultivation and gridiron road systems of the real, settled-down Midwest. The very names of the numberless creeks that cross the region are enough to establish its total Far West character: Horse, Bear, Rawhide, Lance, Sage, Lightning, Thunder, Beaver, Lodgepole, and Dogie (an orphan calf, but used sarcastically for cattle generally, as in the song lyric, *"Whoopie-ti-yi-yo, git along little dogies, you know that Wyoming will be your new home"*). The larger rivers are already familiar—the North Platte and Laramie, plus the Cheyenne farther north, nowhere near the city of the same name.

Historically, this region is famous as a way to other places. From south to north it was the route of the stagecoaches from Cheyenne to the Black Hills and Deadwood in South Dakota. From east to west, the Oregon Trail crossed it along the course of the North Platte. The Texas Trail, the cattle drive route from Texas to the Powder River, also went through the area. The immigrants started through as early as the 1840s and phased out during the 1860s. The cattle drives culminated in the 1870s and 1880s, along with the gold rush travelers. After that, there were coal and oil booms. The whole area had been a prime hunting area for generations of horse-mounted Indians, and there is evidence of hunting and camping even before that by mysterious aborigines.

TOWARD GOSHEN HOLE

You leave Cheyenne for the north on Interstate 25, but once out of the city, U.S. Route 85 takes off northeast, diagonally toward Goshen Hole and Torrington. Of all the routes so far suggested by this guide, the 30-mile (50-km) stretch through Laramie County is no doubt the closest to being really dull. It's a rather splendid sort of dullness: great, rolling range country rich in grass and hay, the delight of ranchers and wheat growers, but not very exciting scenically after a while. The charm palls. Just when you think enough is enough, the road turns north—and suddenly the landscape opens wide into the depression of **Goshen Hole**, a big basin named, as usual somewhat inaccurately, for a French trapper, Gosche (odd name for a Frenchman). Nebraska is now within spitting distance, 10 miles (17 km) east. Goshen Hole is "real West"—cottonwood river courses wriggling away, and grim, broken tablelands all around; a grandly spacious (if not exactly inviting) landscape, which you can see from the north at one of the Wyoming highway rest areas on the other side of the valley. Like so many other Wyoming landscapes, it requires early morning, clouds, or especially late afternoon or sunset, to bring it out.

Beyond the Hole the road continues straight up to **Torrington**, first penetrating a great, long, yellow wall of castle-tipped ridges, and then through a dull, flat, but irrigated green belt of farmland. By now you're deep into Goshen County, which has more cropland than any other in Wyoming—which isn't saying very much. Beets, alfalfa, potatoes, and even fruit are grown, especially along the fertile North Platte River. The low altitude (about 4,000 feet, or 1,200 m) helps this production. Torrington has been the center of Wyoming's considerable sugar beet industry for years, growing, storing, and processing them. Altogether a contrast to anything yet seen, and a determined invasion of the agricultural Midwest, with small surrounding villages connected by perpendicular roads. Torrington itself, with about 5,000 inhabitants, counts as one of the state's more prosperous and stable towns. But it's not Wild West.

THE GRATTAN MASSACRE

From Torrington, you're in a position to follow the immigrant route up the Platte River, a highway impregnated with Oregon Trail history and mementos, and increasingly beautiful scenery. From 1843 onward for two decades, hundreds of thousands of im-

THE HOMESTEADER'S MUSEUM, TORRINGTON

Located right at the crossroads of the Oregon Trail, the Cheyenne-to-Deadwood Stage Route, the Mormon Trail, and the Texas Cattle Trail, the Homesteader's Museum seems to sit atop history. It is housed in the old brick Union Pacific depot, built in 1926, the same year the Holly Sugar plant came to Torrington. Although the sugar plant still operates, the last train stopped at the depot in 1964. Today, the depot houses a small museum that focuses not on the Indians, mountain men, outlaws, and cowboys, but on the thousands of homesteaders who flocked to eastern Wyoming during the late nineteenth and early twentieth centuries. Displays include artifacts from the 4A Ranch and an interior reconstruction of a local homestead, plus a marvelous collection of old black-and-white photos. Outside is an 1824 Concord stagecoach—considered the Rolls Royce of travel at that time—an old homestead cabin, and a windmill.

—Don Pitcher

The famed Deadwood Coach used in Buffalo Bill's Wild West Show. A similar coach can be viewed in Lusk's Stagecoach Museum. Photo by Robert Weiglein. (Courtesy, Buffalo Bill Historical Center, Cody, Wyoming)

(opposite) Deep ruts of the Oregon Trail carve through the sandstone hillsides near Guernsey.

migrants made their way west along here. This was where the various widespread routes from the northeast concentrated to funnel all the traffic through to such western destinations as Oregon, Utah, Nevada, and California. Souvenirs of one kind or another are scattered all along this route, as well as other sites not visible nowadays, most of them bloodily reminiscent of Indian troubles. Just beyond Torrington, across the river, was a trading post and site of the so-called Rock Ranch battle of the early 1850s, in which Indians attacked an immigrant party. This kind of almost routine incident was made special by the fact that these particular immigrants had brought along their black slaves. Some of these were killed and buried under the floor of the post. Except for the presence of such partly black trapper-guides as Jim Beckwourth and Ed Rose, these may perhaps be the first African Americans of record in the Rocky Mountain Northwest, or at least in Wyoming.

Farther west was the site of the Grattan battle of August 19, 1854, one of the most significant, if *basically* most trivial, incidents of the entire history of the Indian troubles. Some Mormons, camped along the trail, accused several Miniconjous, a subgroup of the Sioux, of butchering a beef belonging to them. A friendly chief, Brave Bear of the Brulés, came to Fort Laramie to straighten things out and agreed to pay for the beef. But a hot-headed young recent graduate of West Point, Lieutenant John Grattan, wanted action. He insisted that the malefactors be arrested and, against all advice, set out with 28 men and two howitzers to bring the culprits in. He marched into a village of some 5,000 Oglalas, Brulés, and Miniconjous, and demanded the beef killers. Things were confused by the fact that Grattan's Indian interpreter seems to have been drunk. The Indians refused and made threats. Grattan lost his nerve and fired. He and all of his men died. Some of the Indians were killed, too, including, ironically, Brave Bear, the peacemaker. From then on, till after Gen. George A. Custer's death and the final end of the fighting, the war with the Sioux went on and on, sporadically. It really all began with Grattan, but no doubt would have happened inevitably. Now there are peaceful farms along the river. Laramie Peak is faintly visible to the west.

■ Fort Laramie

Twenty miles (33 km) due west along U.S. Route 26 from Torrington, you come to **Fort Laramie**—still another memorial to that unfortunate Frenchman. It began as a trading post of the Rocky Mountain Fur Company under Robert Campbell and William Sublette, and was originally called Fort William, after Sublette. In 1835, it was sold to a syndicate of trappers, who in turn sold it to the American Fur Company. They rebuilt and rechristened it Fort Laramie. The federal government finally purchased it in 1841. (For Wyoming, this is about the earliest permanent settlement—decades before the cities of Cheyenne and Laramie.) By the mid-forties, Fort Laramie was a major stop on the increasingly busy Oregon Trail. The Oglala Indians held rendezvous there when relations with Indians were comparatively peaceful. Later, when the situation was no longer peaceful, Fort Laramie was the permanent and prominent base of operations for U.S. troops.

A treaty with the Indians was signed at the fort as early as 1851, guaranteeing them a subsidy for not harassing immigrant trains. Other treaties were signed there in 1865, 1868, and 1876. But despite treaties, or because of them, things deteriorated steadily, climaxing in the vicious fighting of the late 1870s, and General Custer's death in Montana. The fort continued to be garrisoned long after that defeat, until 1890. It then fell into disrepair. The state eventually acquired it, and it now belongs to the National Park Service as a national historic site.

Fort Laramie, several miles south of the highway, is probably the most impressive

Fort Laramie, as painted by Alfred Jacob Miller in the late 1850s (courtesy, American Heritage Center, University of Wyoming)

(top) Mailboxes add color to a Wyoming roadside. (Photo by Donna Davis)
(bottom) Smitty's State Line Truckstop straddles the Wyoming-Nebraska line near Pine Bluffs, Wyoming.

A weathered old garage in the almost-ghost town of Jay Em.

display of past military might still existing in Wyoming. Other such forts, notably Fort Bridger, have their beauties and interests, but Laramie not only has more original buildings, but also more of the feeling of what it really must have been like *then*. For one thing, the surrounding country, though beautiful, is very austere and particularly evocative of immigrant trains and Indian attacks. For another, the huge extent of this military installation is evident immediately to the eye. There are almost a score of structures scattered about this wide, bleak area, so that you can easily survey what this oldest and most important of Wyoming posts was like.

Starting at the old **commissary**, now the large visitor's center and museum, a most rewarding tour leads along the row of buildings on the west side of the wide, empty, *hot* (in summer sun) **parade ground**. Here, in a line, are an **enlisted-men's bar** (where you can now get *cold* non-alcoholic drinks), **officer's houses**, **surgeon's quarters**, **powder magazine**, and, most handsome and evocative, a lovingly restored bachelor officers' quarters nicknamed **Old Bedlam**. This is the original two-story verandahed building, rescued from ruin in 1938 and restored. It dates from 1849, and as such is probably the oldest extant building in the state of Wyoming. It was at this building that Portugee Phillips appeared, nearly dead, on Christmas Eve, 1866, after his epic winter ride from beleaguered Fort Kearny. One of the parties that inspired the building's name was going on when Phillips staggered in. But that story belongs to the Powder River.

■ Oregon Trail Monuments

Pleasantly situated on the North Platte River, the town of **Guernsey** was named after the original promoter of the nearby Hartville-Sunrise mines. Damming of the Platte above town has made a reservoir complex and popular recreational area: the lower, smaller, more picturesquely mountain-ringed Guernsey Reservoir and, upstream, the larger, flatter Glendo. Small roads lead to boating, fishing, swimming, and camping.

From the very center of Guernsey, you can cross the river and follow marked gravel roads to two of the area's most curious relics of the great covered wagon trek. One is **Register Cliff**, where (like the more famous Independence Rock farther west) immigrants carved their names when they camped, one day's journey (11 miles, or 18 km) beyond the safety of Fort Laramie. The cliff, somewhat far back from the river, is a high, white, sheer landmark, and is indeed covered with names. Unfortunately, the first part of it you come upon is thick with modern carvings, though some go back to the 1880s. Farther along, protected by a high fence, are the older signatures of Oregon Trail days, distinguished by their large size and regular design. It's awesome and beautiful along the green riverside, but the later vandalism does take away some of the historical thrill.

Somehow more mind-boggling are the **Oregon Trail ruts**, worn in stone by thousands of wagon wheels clanking west. Oregon Trail National Monument preserves several hundred yards of the sunken road. You climb a short hill on foot from the parking space, and there is a deep, narrow gash in the white rock made by those thousands and thousands of covered wagons, traveling hundreds and hundreds of miles west a century and a half ago. It's hard to explain why it's so moving, but many people testify to this emotion. The site is beautiful too. If you can find your way to the top of the low, rough summit, you get a restful view up the romantically tree-bowered river, and westward to the Laramies.

■ Hartville and Northward

U.S. Route 26 goes west from Guernsey to be swallowed by Interstate 25; but back east, hardly more than a mile from Guernsey, Wyoming State Highway 270 takes off north across the railroad tracks to Hartville, and eventually on to Lusk. This road is another Happy Surprise, like Happy Jack Road: a nearly empty and masterfully graded, engineered, and paved road through scenery of red gorges and green rangeland, which hardly anyone seems to know about.

One of three such sites in Wyoming, Register Cliffs near Guernsey records the names of hundreds of Oregon Trail emigrants.

Hartville is more or less a ghost town now, but it was once the site of an important Indian village. Then, in 1889, a copper boom struck and faded, in that pattern so familiar all over the state.

There followed an iron boom. Finally, Hartville settled down as a rail depot when Wyoming's second railroad—the Chicago, Burlington, and Quincy, now the Burlington Northern—came through on its way west. At nearby **Sunrise**, one of the largest open-pit iron mines flourished for many years; but no more. Hartville was the scene of a rather remarkable event in 1902. The defunct White Swede, assisted by friends, sat in on a poker game. The cards were propitious and the corpse won enough money to pay for his own burial. The town lies in a gully of great, red, tree-spotted ridges, and seems to be pretty well decomposing. You see ruined cabins along the road as you go up through handsome wooded heights to a plateau ringed by forested ridges and punctuated by grassy buttes. A road shortly after Hartville goes west to Guernsey Reservoir; a second one 10 miles (16 km) farther takes you to Glendo. Wyoming State Highway 270 continues smoothly on to Manville, where you turn east. After nine miles (15 km) on U.S. Route 18/20, you're in Lusk.

Passengers on the new transcontinental railroad helped destroy the massive plains bison herds with their track-side "hunting." (Courtesy, Kansas State Historical Society, Topeka)

■ Spanish Diggings

An interesting sight you're not likely to see unless you take the trouble is called, wrongly, the Spanish Diggings, among the most curious remnants of prehistoric history in the United States. This is a series of hundreds of ancient stone quarries north of the Platte, west of Lusk. Early settlers believed the holes had been dug by Spaniards looking for gold, which is not the case. Rather, they were dug by the original inhabitants of Wyoming who lived centuries before the present-day Plains Indians. They may certainly have been ancestors, but had a different culture based on the extensive use of stone tools and pottery. They were given to pictographic (surface painting or drawing) or petroglyphic (incised in rock) murals in caves or on high cliffs, where Plains Indians never thought of going. These old quarries, worked for perhaps a good thousand years, produced material that was fashioned into artifacts that can be found as far away as the Ohio and Mississippi river valleys. The stone is identifiable as coming from Wyoming. It was Wyoming's first industry.

These mysterious quarries now are mostly on private land and can't be seen just at pleasure. However, an organization called Hell Gap Expeditions, based in the town of Fort Laramie, takes interested people on tours of the Spanish Diggings, and elsewhere in the region. The folks at the Conoco gas station at the junction of the road to the fort will tell you how and where to get in touch.

■ Lusk

With a population of about 2,000, **Lusk** owes its existence to the railroad (Chicago and Northwestern) and cattle shipping. It's also at the junction of U.S. routes 20 (east to west) and 85 (north to south), which also helps. Lusk is the county seat of Niobrara, which has the smallest population, some 3,000 people, of any county in the state. No doubt the population of cows exceeds that of humans. Lusk is also probably more remote than any other town of comparable size in the state, though there's a good deal of competition: it's about 70 miles (115 km) from Chadron, Nebraska, to the east; 60 miles (100 km) to Douglas, west; 80 miles (130 km) to Newcastle, north; and 70 miles (115 km) to Torrington, south. The town has the look of being well-organized, self-reliant, and sure of itself. Lusk had a big moment in 1918, when a Buck Creek Dome oil strike suddenly boosted the population to 10,000. Things then settled down, but nearby Lance Creek is still an oil-spouting area. Lusk is now a town where travelers can take refuge in spruce motels (notably a Best Western Pioneer Court) and restaurants. Annually in early July, a rather odd pageant celebrates one of the most odd stories that cling to the region. This particular legend concerns **Rawhide Butte**, that rugged height west along Route 85 as it comes up to Lusk from the south. It gets its name from an immigrant coming westward who swore he'd kill the first Injun he saw. The first he saw was an Indian maiden, and he shot her. She was suitably revenged when her relations caught him, skinned him alive, and stretched his skin to tan on top of Rawhide Butte. Hence the name and the pageant.

In fact the road below and particularly above Lusk is so full of old tales that a small book would be required to hold all of them. This was preeminently the stage route from Cheyenne to Deadwood in the Black Hills, and though soldiers were stationed at the old Hat Creek stage station, about 20 miles (33 km) north of Lusk, that did not seem to prevent all sorts of devilment.

In 1876 some Black Hills freighters were attacked by 500 Indians, and rescued (as if before the cameras) by cavalry in the nick of time. Hat Creek was a favorite locale

Stagecoach Museum, Lusk

The eastern Wyoming ranching town of Lusk has one of the state's nicer historical collections, the aptly named Stagecoach Museum. Climb up the steep narrow stairs to find the reason for this name, an old coach built by Abbott & Downing of Concord, New Hampshire, in the 1860s. Used for many years on the famed Cheyenne-Black Hills Stage and Express Line, the stagecoach is one of only two in the world; its sister is in the Smithsonian Institute. The difficult 300-mile (483-km) stage route passed through Indian territory, over treacherous river crossings, and past hideouts of notorious road agents. Drivers made the trip in three days and three nights, and station stops lasted just long enough to change horses—usually less than three minutes. First-class fare from Cheyenne to Custer was $20; third class (sitting on the top of the coach) was half that.

The museum also houses a treasure chest broken open during the Canyon Springs stage robbery of 1879 (it once contained gold bullion from the Black Hills destined for Cheyenne). Other attractions include an old buggy, a sulky, dray, covered wagons, Indian artifacts, a photo collection from Niobrara County's one-room schoolhouses, and a 31-star U.S. flag from 1876. Ask for directions to the still-standing Hat Creek Stage Station north of town.

for holdups. Stuttering Brown, who had been sent by the stage owners to stop this kind of thing, died at the Hat Creek Station after being shot by Persimmons Bill Chambers, who got his nickname from his birth in the unlikely (for a Western outlaw) state of South Carolina. Two men of the Tom Paris gang, operating along the road, were captured and taken to Cheyenne for trial. Court had just adjourned, so the criminals were taken right back toward Deadwood for another attempt. En route, a masked posse kidnapped them and strung them up on the nearest cottonwoods. The stage proceeded unmolested.

In August 1877, Boone May and a companion, guarding a passenger coach on a trip to Hat Creek, were attacked by road agents near Robbers Roost. May shot and killed one of the bandits, Frank Towle, whom he knew. When he got back to Cheyenne, he found that a reward of several thousand dollars had been posted for Towle, so he went back to the scene of the shooting, found Towle's corpse in the bushes, cut off his head, and returned to Cheyenne to collect his reward. But by that time, unfortunately, word had gotten around that Towle was no more. The reward offer had been withdrawn and May had made his return trip for nothing; and with a head on his hands.

However, Mrs. Thomas Durkin had no such difficulties. She took the stage to Deadwood right after the notorious murder of the entire Metz family, on the route in South Dakota, by that same Persimmons Chambers. Mrs. Durkin was carrying $10,000 in her handbag to Deadwood to finance her brother-in-law's new bank. Nobody stopped her.

The problem that faced Phatty Thompson could safely be called unique. In 1877, he decided that the dance hall girls in Deadwood were lonesome for pets. To fill that need, he gave the kids of Cheyenne 25 cents for each stray cat they brought him. Then he started north with a huge crate full of cats. En route his wagon toppled over, the crate broke, and the cats got loose on the range. Somehow he got them back into the crate ("cajoling with tasty morsels"), took them to Deadwood, and sold them all to the girls for $10 to $20 a head.

■ Newcastle

Tales like this by the dozens decorate the history of this especially lonely route; but by the time you get to **Newcastle** in Weston County, the mountains and forests have encroached from the north and east, and you come to a very different and more amiable world. Newcastle is definitely in the mountains, or at least steeply built on forested foothills. It was founded as a coal mining center, and named nostalgically for the great English coal port, Newcastle-upon-Tyne. It still has much of a Welsh or West Virginian character, and nearby is the extinct town of Cambria (the ancient name of Wales). The hard coal mined there from the 1880s for 40 years was the only such deposit being mined in the West. A polyglot population of Austrians, Italians, and Swedes survived in this so-very-untypical-of-Wyoming saloonless town, where the owners forbade the sale of hard liquor. That did not prevent an Italian barkeeper, though he sold only beer, from being fingered by the Black Hand. The town and mines closed down completely in 1928, and nothing is left in the canyons but ancient debris.

Newcastle still retains exactly the atmosphere of a somewhat aged Appalachian mining center. Its picturesque setting doesn't help downtown, but there are pretty residential sections tucked away in the surrounding hills. It is properly looked upon as the southern gateway to the Black Hills, coming from the west.

As soon as you leave (or rather, bypass) Newcastle, you are suddenly transported into another world—forest, mountains, deep valleys with rushing streams, fresher air, greener everything. First there's the dense ponderosa pine forest of the foothills. Then the road passes alongside a fantastic vision: the **Flying V**. This huge Tudor castle, set in a valley (Salt Creek Canyon), was called the Casino and was built as a memorial to the discovery and development of anthracite coal at **Cambria**. It still functions as a summer pleasance with a golf course and other amenities. A trail from it leads to the Cambrian ghost town.

By the time you reach Four Corners, which is that and nothing more, you are on a high, rather bare plateau—a "hole" ringed by mountains. Most significant of these, to the west, is isolated and rugged Inyan Kara, intimately associated with Custer. The nearby South Dakota Black Hills lie to the east. Turning northwest toward Sundance on Wyoming State Highway 585, you cross the line into Crook County, and into Wyoming's Black Hills.

B L A C K H I L L S

THE BLACK HILLS PROPER BELONG TO SOUTH DAKOTA, but Wyoming possesses a somewhat separate western enclave, surrounding and including the Bear Lodge Mountains. They are all part of the Black Hills National Forest. Around this forested and elevated core of hills, about 6,000 feet (2,000 m) high (which is pretty low for Wyoming hills), lies an area of foothills, canyons, streams, and open range that has its own special quality.

In general, this is also Wyoming's lowest corner. The lowest point of the state lies at the junction of Oak Creek and the Belle Fourche River, near where Montana, South Dakota, and Wyoming meet, an altitude of only 3,125 feet (953 m). Actually the atmosphere and vegetation here seem Eastern, with the only proliferation of oak trees found in the state, and also ponderosa pines rather than lodgepole. Even the highest points are below 7,000 feet (2,300 m), which is level ground in much of the state. Warren Peak, 6,656 feet (2,027 m), is the giant for this region, but by Wyoming's standards it's practically sea level. The *surface* of Yellowstone Lake is 7,731 feet (2,356 m) high.

The Black Hills form a delightfully green, watery, flowery, hilly contrast to the nearby enormous plains. This island of greenery is exceptional in the lineup of the easternmost Far Western states of Montana, Wyoming, Colorado, and New Mexico—all of which are pretty dry and flat in the east.

The tourist center of the area is Sundance, the destination of Wyoming State Highway 585 from Four Corners. Sundance lies in a valley between the Bear Lodges (north) and the Black Hills of South Dakota (east). Right back of town (south) is Sundance Mountain, from the top of which, after a stiff climb, one is said to be able to glimpse the Bighorns on a good day, 180 miles (300 km) west.

Sundance Mountain was the rendezvous of the Sioux and their allies in summer, when they held their annual Sundance religious ceremonies, interspersed with berry-picking, dancing, and gossip. One particular ritual, however, was no laughing matter. It was meant as a test of a young brave's courage and endurance. Medicine men would gather the brave's back skin, run a knife through the fold, and thread a line of rawhide through the wound. The thong would be fastened to a high scaffold. The brave would then let himself go, with his weight hanging from the thong and swing and swirl about until the rawhide tore through his flesh. The rest of the tribe would form a surrounding circle and dance and sing to help him keep up his courage. When he got through the

ordeal the medicine men would cleanse the wound and lead him to a special teepee to rest and recover.

In surprising contrast to this scene is the story of another sort of encampment in the Bear Lodges. In 1874, General Custer and his cavalry were sent on a massive expedition to survey the Black Hills. The idea, ostensibly, was to determine what the area was worth for its projected purchase from the Indians by the United States government. The less publicized purpose was to find out if there was any gold there. At the time, Custer's was the largest and best-equipped expedition ever sent into the northwest. There were over 1,000 men involved—ten companies of the Seventh Cavalry; 100 Indian scouts, guides, and interpreters; 110 wagons, 1,000 cavalry horses, 300 beefs, and a military band. They camped first on Soldier Creek near Newcastle. They then proceeded up to Inyan Kara, that semi-isolated promontory just north of the Weston County line and west of Wyoming State Highway 585. Custer climbed to the top and carved his name. Then he and his group camped on Spring Creek, a tributary of Sand Creek. The valley where they settled was a riot of wild flowers. Custer named it then and there "Floral Valley," and a sort of flower festival took place. The soldiers festooned their hats and horses with wreaths of flowers, and that military band climbed up on a ledge and played "Garry Owen," "The Mocking Bird," "The Blue Danube," and selections from *Il Trovatore.* Surely one of the more fetchingly bizarre episodes in the history of the Wild West; but somehow in key with at least the more amiable aspects of the Black Hills.

The mission was a secret and disastrous success. Horatio W. Ross, one of the two professional geologists on the expedition had (or so it is supposed) made the first authentic gold discovery in the Black Hills of South Dakota on July 30, 1874. When the news got back to Cheyenne, the rush was on.

This put the government in a difficult position. They had turned the area over to the Sioux in the treaty of 1868, which temporarily ended the war. Now, of course, they wanted it back. They decided to buy it back. They offered the Sioux either six million dollars, cash down, or a rental of four hundred thousand dollars a year. The Sioux demanded six *hundred* million (did the U.S. have that much money then?) and a promise that the government would feed and clothe them for seven future generations. After all, they had been there for seven past generations, so naturally the government should take care of the next seven. Much to the surprise of the Sioux, the government lost its temper and just decided to take the Black Hills. They ordered the wild bands to evacuate by January 31, 1876. The Indians paid no particular attention. They just went

(previous pages) The Belle Fourche wends its way through the Black Hills near Hulett.

to winter quarters and made excuses. Pretty soon the final phase of the war began, which resulted in the ultimate, ironic victory of the whites, after Custer's mortal defeat by the Indians at Little Bighorn in 1876—only two years after Floral Valley and *Il Trovatore.* No bands played at Little Bighorn, far to the west.

■ Sundance

With a population of about 1,000, **Sundance** is the only town of any prominence in Crook County. It is the county seat, and lies in a delightful mountain-shaded valley. The town has every reason to be a proper and pretty tourist center—choice scenery and nearby sights. But it isn't. There are very modest motels, and one nice enough restaurant, but otherwise nothing much but a wide, desolate main street with garages on one side and the county courthouse on the other. There is a **historic museum** connected with the court house complex. Mementos of Harry Longabaugh (known as the Sundance Kid for his imprisonment in the local jail) are extensively displayed. Otherwise, Sundance merely invites you to pass by.

The problem is that Interstate 90 zips along south of town, thus cutting Sundance and the Bear Lodges off from tourism. People thought that interstates would bring tourists. Instead they take them—onward.

A frontage road (old U.S. Route 14, kept paved for use by ranchers) heads east from town as a continuation of Sundance's main street. Though parallel to the interstate, it's prettier, and really part of the landscape. After some 11 miles (19 km), it meets **Wyoming State Highway 111** going due north. Here, once again, begins one of Wyoming's best Happy Surprises. The trip up toward Aladdin (which lies east of the main road), and then westward on **Wyoming State Highway 24**, around the edge of the Bear Lodge Mountains, is one of the loveliest in the state. The scenery really deserves the word "unique," at least for Wyoming. On the east side of the mountains, where tributary creeks of the Belle Fourche come down from darkly forested hills into sunny valleys, exists a pastoral world of meadows and glossy-leafed oak trees, farms, and small ranches exactly like some tucked-away New England or Appalachian beauty spot—only with an exotic Western accent. Far northward, out beyond, are glimpses of vast, distant plains.

The highway circles around the mountains, sometimes through Black Hills National Forest. After some 45 miles (75 km) from Sundance, it reaches the hamlet of **Hulett**,

(top) Wade Spracher and Rick Duran work the automatic stacker at Hulett's Neiman Sawmill, sorting ponderosa pine lumber. (bottom) Saddlemaker Carson Thomas at his Hulett shop, The Stockman. (opposite) Glen "Gabby" Solberg enjoys a fall afternoon at the Aladdin store.

ALADDIN, WYO.
1890
PACKAGE LIKKER
Coca-Cola
ICE
Marlboro

a quaint place alongside the meek, meandering Belle Fourche. Food (at the Little Wrangler Café) and gas are available there, the only places since Sundance.

Finally comes **Devils Tower**, 10 miles (17 km) farther south. This is the one certified famous sight of Crook County. You get exciting, far views of it sticking above the forests all along the highway before Hulett. (The name "Black Hills," incidentally, came from the Indians' description of the effect of such ponderosa pine forests from a distance.)

■ Devils Tower

This startling monument, which rises 1,250 feet (381 m) straight up over the valley of the now-tiny Belle Fourche, is the frozen core of a volcanic upsurge of lava, some 20 million years old. The volcano has melted away, but the core remains, a circular pylon of volcanic rock (phonolite) in long, vertical, geometrically edged prisms. Like anything in the Black Hills, this was sacred to the Indians. They called the phenomenon Bear Lodge, which gave the name to the whole surrounding range. Various rather charming legends accounted for the tower's odd looks. According to one, maidens were gathering flowers when they were attacked by bears. They climbed up a rock, the bears followed after. Gods made the rock grow higher and higher as the bears clawed their way up. The striations of the stone were caused by their claws. Eventually they fell off and were killed (a butte in South Dakota was supposed to be the corpse of such a bear). The girls braided ropes out of their flowers and got down safely. Another similar story, also involving bears and girls, had seven little maidens attacked by bears when they were playing. They, too, got up on a rock. This one shot up into the sky. Once again, bears clawed the rock, broke their claws, fell down. The children went soaring up into the sky and became stars, the constellation of the Pleiades, or Seven Sisters.

Devils Tower was the first national monument in the United States, created by Theodore Roosevelt in 1906. It stands as a natural memorial to his pioneering efforts as a conservationist. More recently, the climax of the movie about extraterrestrials, *Close Encounters of the Third Kind*, the Spielberg classic, was filmed at Devils Tower. Spaceship landings somehow seem appropriate for the Tower.

Nowadays this spectacle is inundated by crowds on a nice summer day. Tourists eagerly watch mountain climbers crawling up the impossible heights, no doubt hoping they'll fall off and cause some excitement. They don't. By now the ascent is an estab-

(opposite) An unusual apparition in the daytime, Devils Tower displays an even more distinctive aura at night.

lished science, and thousands go up, carefully guided. Roundabout the tower there are long, forested walks. Postcards and information are available in the buildings at the edge of the parking lot, but no food. As national monuments go, it's a rather low-key establishment. The eerie quality of the place comes off better early in the morning when the deer are about, and not so many people, or in the evening when the light enhances the always awe-inspiring shaft of this uncanny column.

■ Black Hills Exit

On the way to Moorcroft you pass **Keyhole State Park and reservoir**, another one of those many water-parks of which Wyoming is so full and so proud. These offer the local citizens, particularly those living on dry plains, a wonderful chance at refreshing summer recreation; but for the stranger, they are often not particularly scenic or secluded.

All through this corner of Wyoming there are various other side roads, vistas, and campsites. On the whole, Crook County makes for a sort of Indian-enchanted island of refreshment, surrounded by an ocean of barren plains, ranges, and badlands.

The stump-like Devils Tower, Paul Bunyonesque in its enormity, as the setting sun colors its face. (opposite) Two climbers seem dwarfed by Devils Tower's massive columns.

Moorcroft was named by the English Miller brothers, owners of a big horse ranch nearby, after their ancestral estate at home, Moorcroft Acres. The town became a stock-loading center after the first railroad came along. From Moorcroft on, you are quite definitely out on the plains of what is generally rather broadly designated as the Powder River Basin; though at this point the river itself is a good 50 miles (80 km) to the west. The direct route is Interstate 90 to Gillette.

If you want to linger awhile in the Black Hills, however, then head east on old U.S. Route 14 to the junction of Wyoming State Highway 116, under Interstate 90, just west of Sundance. This road passes west of Inyan Kara and near the area of Custer's Floral Valley. Handsome, open, rolling country, with forested hills, lies all about. Eventually comes **Upton**, almost on the plains, but not quite. It's built on a long, lone, low, pine-crested ridge, the last gasp of the Black Hills and of such woodland greenery for a hundred miles south and west. Upton greets the traveler with the surprising sight of a town golf course, and then a sign proclaiming that it's the best little ol' town in the world (more or less). It isn't; though nice enough.

From Upton, U.S. Route 16 goes northwest diagonally back up to Moorcroft and Interstate 90, passing through a section of the **Thunder Basin Grasslands**, which covers a large part of the plains to the south.

Dinner around the chuckwagon at a Warren Livestock Co. roundup. (Courtesy, American Heritage Center, University of Wyoming)

THUNDER BASIN

WHEN YOU LEAVE MOORCROFT, YOU CROSS THE BORDER into Campbell County and onto the Great Plains. The drive from Cheyenne to Newcastle might give any traveler a sufficiently good taste of such plains; but on that route they are continuously broken up by buttes and rivers, valleys, farmlands, towns, and views of distant mountains. This section of Wyoming, on the other hand, presents an unadulterated sweep of almost total emptiness.

From the Appalachians to the Wind Rivers, the North Pole to the Laramies, there's nothing to stop the wind. This slice of Wyoming remains pretty much the same as the trappers, Indians, soldiers, immigrants, and still-resident cowboys and sheepherders saw and see it (though oddly enough, it hasn't the special historical color of the eastern border). The only things really different from the past are the actual road you drive on, the few, usually distant traces of oil and coal you come upon, and a secretive coal railroad (Burlington), which you don't see until you get to Bill. Most tourists don't tour this part of Wyoming, for obvious reasons, but it's an essential part of the state's atmosphere. After all, the name "Wyoming" means "bright and shining plains."

For the some 150 miles (250 km) down from the Montana border to the Platte River, there's nothing, except Gillette. For another sweep of 100 miles (170 km) west, from Casper (on the Platte) to Shoshoni, you get more such plains, but these are always in sight of some sizable mountains, however distant, and there are quite a few little settlements along the way. In the vast area from Douglas north to Gillette, and way beyond, however, it's just space all the way.

To give an idea of the vastness of Wyoming's plains, imagine a straight, diagonal line of flight from Gillette to Rock Springs. It would pass over virtually nothing at all but uninhabited terrain and some mines and oil wells. It would cross only three main highways—Interstate 25, and U.S. routes 26 and 287. The Sweetwater would be your biggest stream, the Antelope Hills or Green Mountains your only serious bumps. You would cross the continental divide twice on the line of flight over the Great Divide Basin. At last, you would strike Interstate 80, thick with its trucks and travelers, and the comparative metropolis of Rock Springs.

There's a question of just how much of this space can be profitably absorbed by the average traveler. It depends first of all on conditions. Steady rains or completely cloudy weather are most unfavorable. Terrific heat or cold are most unpleasant. But varied

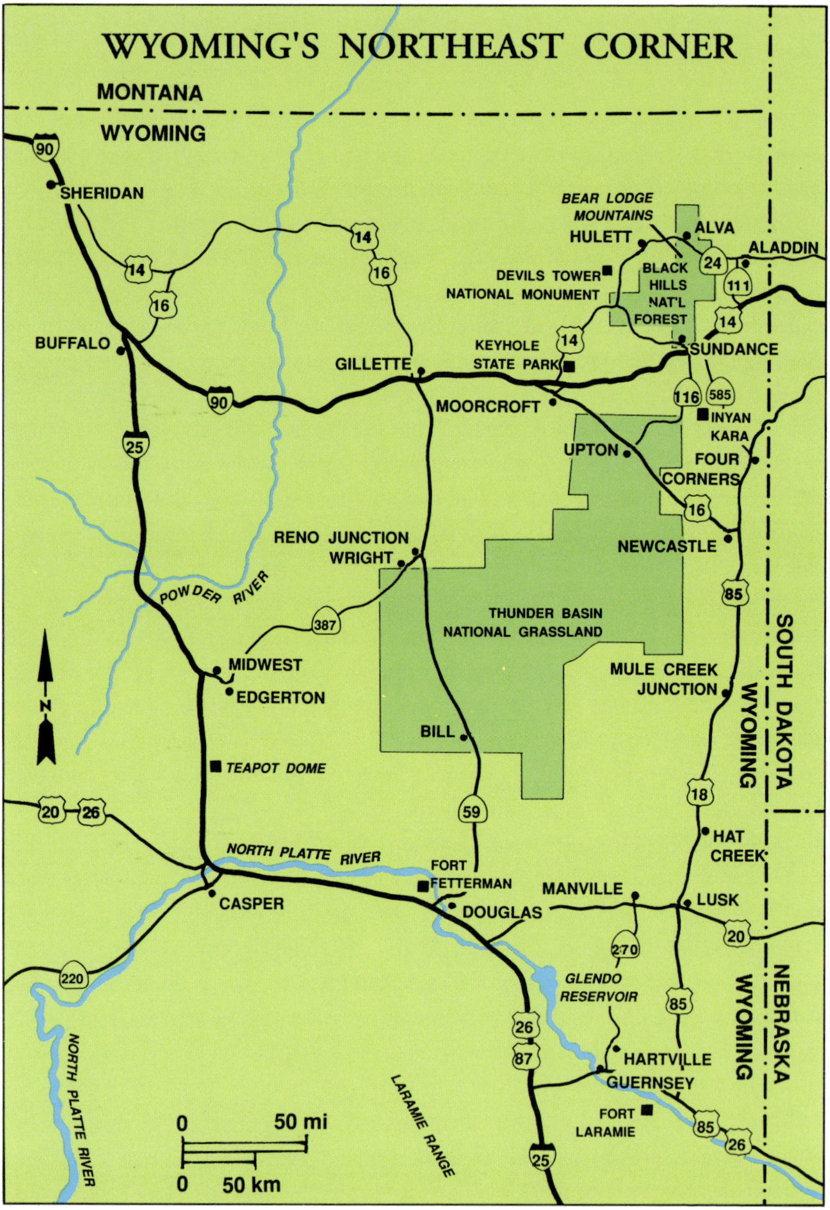
WYOMING'S NORTHEAST CORNER
MONTANA
WYOMING
SHERIDAN
BUFFALO
BEAR LODGE MOUNTAINS
HULETT
ALVA
ALADDIN
DEVILS TOWER NATIONAL MONUMENT
BLACK HILLS NAT'L FOREST
KEYHOLE STATE PARK
SUNDANCE
GILLETTE
MOORCROFT
INYAN KARA
UPTON
FOUR CORNERS
RENO JUNCTION
WRIGHT
NEWCASTLE
POWDER RIVER
THUNDER BASIN NATIONAL GRASSLAND
MIDWEST
EDGERTON
MULE CREEK JUNCTION
SOUTH DAKOTA
WYOMING
BILL
TEAPOT DOME
HAT CREEK
NORTH PLATTE RIVER
FORT FETTERMAN
MANVILLE
LUSK
CASPER
DOUGLAS
GLENDO RESERVOIR
HARTVILLE
GUERNSEY
NEBRASKA
WYOMING
FORT LARAMIE
LARAMIE RANGE
NORTH PLATTE RIVER
0 50 mi
0 50 km
N
90 14 16 25 20 26 387 59 24 111 116 585 85 18 220 270 87

skies, especially earlier and later in the day, can be particularly glorious. These empty, enormous stretches have an oceanic quality of purity and variety under proper conditions. In the broad, hot glare of noon, the landscape flattens out and loses all its color. By later afternoon a miracle of transformation takes place, and by evening light, what seemed total desolation becomes a symphony of blues and browns and greens and magical distances; and toward the edges, remote peaks and pinnacles.

This aspect of the state presents what the Chamber of Commerce must recognize as a touristic problem of considerable dimensions. To get from one group of pretty parts in the southeast and northeast, to another in the northwest, you have to traverse this barren diagonal somewhere. You can avoid most of it, notably by a dash from the Black Hills to Buffalo via Interstate 90; but then you will certainly miss a big slice of native Wyoming, austere, but in its own way beautiful.

■ GILLETTE

Gillette is fairly austere also. It has only one basic reason for economic existence: coal. It's the center for strip mining of low sulphur coal, still useful for power plants. The area roundabout is full of huge gouges where the coal comes from. As far back as the early 1800s, trappers and explorers were puzzled and terrified, as were the Indians before them, by the pall of smoke that sometimes hung over the area from fires in subterranean coal seams. These, ignited by lightning, sometimes burned for years, opening sudden smoldering rifts into which unwary horsemen might ride to their deaths. No trees or natural greenery surround Gillette. It's too far from either the Black Hills or the Bighorns for mountain views. There's not even a sizable river.

Yet Gillette itself is a hive of activity and source of wealth. Until recently, it was a boom town of oil *and* coal. Now it's still supported, but well supported, by that old standby, coal. Roundabout there is still a great stock-raising area. As a result of this prosperity, the school system is the envy of the state. It has its own planetarium, and culture is encouraged through symphonic concerts, theater, and art exhibits.

There are, however, two Gillettes: the old town on the north side, along the railroad tracks, and the new town along Interstate 90, southward. Old Gillette is a compact, rather snug city. You still see brown prairies at the end of most streets. The business section is neatly impressive, with big, modern bank buildings and planted trees, which are such a pleasing new touch in Wyoming cities. There are good stores and restaurants, and a general air of solid establishment. The residential section is one of close-packed small houses, thickly shaded by trees and bushes, as though to protect them against blizzards. There is a beautiful green cemetery next to a town park on the heights, southward, and on the high points of town a few elegant houses with far glimpses of the rangelands beyond. The inevitable gridiron is distinguished by its named streets patriotically commemorating not presidents, but Wyoming's founding fathers, such as Carey, Kendrick, and Warren (whose memorial plaques adorn the capitol rotunda in Cheyenne). You still hear train whistles from the long coal trains rumbling through town, down below.

New Gillette, the obvious result of the late boom, is a horrific phantasmagoria of modern synthetic culture—every syndicated fast-food joint in the United States, from McDonald's to Pizza Hut; big, bare shopping malls; massive, luxurious, impersonal motels, and packed traffic going south toward Interstate 90. This is perhaps the most flagrant contrast between an urban Old West of a stable, indigenous sort, and a New West of national standardization with nothing Wyoming about it whatsoever. There is also a "new part of town," with snappy, modern houses huddled together up on bare buttes; what might be called suburbia. For that the tourist travels 10,000 miles?

■ Routes Through the Plains

There are several different routes south from Gillette to the Platte River. Wyoming State Highway 59, discussed in the next section, takes you through the ultimate in Wyoming's wide-open spaces.

An alternate route for those particularly interested in oil history and development swings southwest from Highway 59 onto Wyoming State Highway 387, past the brand-new mining town of Wright, and through the oil fields of Edgerton and Midwest. From there, Wyoming State Highway 259 heads southwest past Teapot Dome to Interstate 25, and then to Casper. (This route will be discussed later in this chapter.)

The unadventurous route is just to bypass Gillette, taking Interstate 90 from Moorcroft to Buffalo, and then Interstate 25 down to Casper. The scenery along that route is gorgeous—the Big Horn Mountains, badlands, great rangelands, and the Laramies as you approach Casper—but of course you won't see "life."

A variant route leading north from Gillette on old U.S. routes 14 and 16 also takes you through beautiful country, a spectacular crossing of the Powder River in its canyon, and then either to Buffalo (Route 16) or Sheridan (Route 14) by increasingly picturesque landscapes.

All these different routes have their beauties and interests; but the emphasis here is on the more offbeat Wyoming State Highway 59 as being more characteristic, less traveled, and a real exposure to these absolute plains.

■ Thunder Basin

Highway 59 cuts down from Interstate 90, just south of Gillette. You pass Reno Junction after 38 miles (63 km). After another 40 miles (67 km), you pass Bill. In 35 more miles (58 km), you're in Douglas. That's it. This route is pretty much a test case of how the traveler feels about wide-open spaces. If you feel expanded and released and inclined to yell "Whoopee!" and "Don't fence me in!" this is certainly your place. If not, it's not.

What you see is something called the **Thunder Basin National Grassland** (a distant cousin of the national parks and forests). This enormous stretch of more than two million acres has been set aside by the government as a soil preservation and conservation experiment. During the thirties, when dust bowls became a national menace, it became obvious that the well-meaning and open-hearted homestead program, instead of making for happy rural prosperity, was creating a wasteland. Soil that should not have been plowed, was. The idea behind these grasslands was to try to restore nature's status quo. National grasslands are scattered about the plains states, notably Nebraska and eastern Colorado, but Thunder Basin is by far the largest and longest established. The Bureau of Land Management not only controls Thunder Basin grazing, but also oil exploratory roads, and even archaeological digs and access—anything that might permanently damage the rich, but fragile, ground cover. Many dust bowls, past and present, might have been prevented if this policy had been inaugurated sooner and in more places.

Coming down from Gillette, the country is first all grass—grass not only on flat places, but covering the buttes and ridges. Little oil pumps bob up and down; but the most striking single sight along the road is the big buffalo ranch some dozen miles (20 km) below town. There the green, hilly range near the roadside is populated with dozens of the great, black beasts of both sexes and all ages. Though they are really domestic stock, just like sheep or cattle, the setting here is so like a Catlin scene that you expect any moment to see naked Indians on ponies roaring and yelping in pursuit from around the grassy bumps. Antelope also hang about, and of course, cattle and horses.

The only town on Highway 59 is brand-new **Wright**. It's off to the west at Reno Junction, a sort of model company town attached to new coal excavations. You don't see these from Highway 59, but only the town itself, which looks very new and spic-and-span. It's sort of a shock, sitting bare out in the middle of the enormous space and silence.

After Wright, the country flattens, grows less fertile and much emptier—sagebrush, rather than just grass. Far to the east is the dim, grim tall castle of a coal mine establishment. Otherwise, all is earth and sky... and sheep. Eventually you cross one of the usually dry forks of the Cheyenne River, with its inevitable cottonwoods. Here a new Wyoming rest area provides a pleasant, much-needed stopping place. Then you come to Bill.

Except for Reno Junction and Wright, **Bill** is the only dot on the map before Douglas. It's been on the map for years, but unfortunately Bill's future is uncertain. Bill is a small store and post office operated for years by an old-timer, sure enough named Bill. But Bill, the postmaster, eventually died, and Bill, the town, was put up for sale. Patronized by local ranchers, passersby, and railroad men from the Burlington (which has been sneaking down parallel from Gillette, and now appears alongside the road), Bill must serve a purpose vital enough to preserve it. After all, there's nothing closer than Wright or Douglas. It should still have some future.

By this time, the countryside has begun to degenerate visually. Like some interminable German symphony, things begin to dawdle scenically (just before a finale with all the trumpets blasting): few or no hills, the railroad close by to destroy the sense of isolation and freedom, not even much in the way of far vistas. And then the road crosses the tracks and turns away west. Suddenly, first a blue glimpse of Laramie Peak over the undulating rangelands, then (about 10 miles north of Douglas) one of the apocalyptic visions which highlight travel in Wyoming: from a rising sweep of the road, the whole panorama of the Laramies strung out before you, southeast to northwest. After the long preparation of the grasslands, it's dramatic and exciting beyond expression.

■ DOUGLAS

Douglas, with a population of about 6,000, is no longer on the plains, but in the Platte River valley. Here, that great immigrant trail comes around the foot of the Laramie Mountains, following the water and trees, and bringing green cultivation.

(previous pages) Some of the loveliest ranching country in Wyoming lies near the tiny Powder River Basin settlement of Recluse.

The foothills crowd out the grand view of peaks, but are themselves imposing. All sorts of scenic excursions are possible back into the mountains from all the nearby riverside towns—a very different world from Wright or Gillette.

You're now back in "civilization." Douglas is a relaxed, pleasant town with nice, comfortable residential areas, big houses shaded by big trees, and an old-fashioned business section somewhat disorganized by railroad sidings. Down along the river are the fairgrounds, where the famous annual Wyoming State Fair is held in August. After the bare immensity of the plains, Douglas seems a very welcome refreshment.

Douglas is also famous (perhaps better, infamous) for its **jackalope**, the largest in the state. Jackalopes are supposed to be the miscegenation of the antelope and the jackrabbit, both denizens of the plains to the north. In the old days, dudes were fooled into thinking they were real animals. Dudes these days are too sophisticated for this old joke, but it's sort of quaint.

A more genuine spectacle is **Ayre's Natural Bridge**, a handsome rock arch in the mountains to the south. Roads to it off Interstate 25 are marked. There is a wealth

Pioneer Museum, Douglas

The people of Douglas point with pride to their spacious local museum, located just inside the fairgrounds. Here you will find the rifle of Nate Champion, a suspected rustler murdered in the Johnson County Wars; an army trumpet and bullets from the Custer massacre site, and saddles that once belonged to outlaw Tom Horn and to Governor Joseph Carey. Check out the special "running irons" used by rustlers to alter cattle brands, and the bison-fur mittens worn by Portugee Phillips on his famous ride from Fort Kearny.

On a kinder, gentler note, take a look at the large doll collection and the unusual collection of women's fans, along with a description of "fan language." Back rooms house a gorgeous, old Wurlitzer jukebox, various fossils, and several wagons and carriages, including an army escort wagon from the 1880s. The extraordinary collection of Indian artifacts includes a Sioux wooden flute, beaded moccasins, an Indian bow from the Wagon Box fight, hundreds of arrowheads and other implements from the Spanish Diggings site southwest of Lusk, and even a stone war club from the Black Hills. Before you exit this fine museum, drop a penny in the slot to check your weight on the old-fashioned scales.

—Don Pitcher

(top) Driver Ray Martin is dwarfed by the 240-ton truck used to haul coal at Black Thunder Coal Mine near Wright. (bottom) An explosive charge loosens the deep seam of coal at Black Thunder. (opposite) Welders Tim Boyd and Mike Radcliff, in front of a dragline used to strip overburden at Black Thunder.

of natural beauty and possible excursions up in the Laramies, but it would be well to check out road conditions and directions locally. Hiking and riding trails abound.

You could now board Interstate 25 and divorce yourself from reality; but not to be missed is **Fort Fetterman**, named in honor of one of the more unfortunate military victims of the Powder River Indian wars (see "Historical Interlude"). The fort, in operation from 1867 to 1882, can be reached from just west of town on a good minor road, Wyoming State Highway 93. It's hard to explain the odd impact of the fort. Unlike Fort Laramie, there is really nothing left that's original. One restored old building houses a nice, small museum which explains the fort's history with exhibits and a 15-minute video show. However, the site itself conjures up history.

At the time Fort Fetterman was activated, it was the only military post in the vast region west of Fort Laramie and directly south of the Powder River forts, which were closed in 1867. The high, bare promontory on which the fort sits—with mountains behind, the big, green course of the Platte winding below, and the great tan plains endlessly north—is somehow the perfect setting for the epic of those days. Soldiers, Indians, immigrants, and cowboys inevitably people the scene in imagination. It's as evocative as Fort Laramie, but the setting is more scenically beautiful.

Wyoming State Highway 93 continues across the river and northwest through the rangelands, with mountain views emerging behind. Joining State Highway 95, it returns to the river at Glenrock. From there on you're in OIL. Casper is 30 miles (50 km) west. You can keep on Wyoming State Highway 20 (and 26) from Glenrock to see a mixture of pleasant river valley of ranches and refineries, or more efficiently, go up Interstate 25, which zips along through surprisingly bare rangeland. In any case, when you get to Casper you had better get onto the interstate to avoid needless traffic on the outskirts.

■ The Oil Road to Casper

A better preparation for the *oil*-town character of Casper might be the alternative route (Wyoming State Highway 387 at Reno Junction) from Gillette that goes right through Midwest and the Salt Creek oil fields, where Casper's first oil spouted a hundred years ago. The scenery around **Midwest** is dramatic—sharp buttes thrusting up towers over gulches and badlands. One of these buttes south of Midwest is the notorious **Teapot Dome** (if you could possibly recognize it).

Midwest itself is a striking example of the impact of industrialism. Coming out of the empty range, you suddenly enter a valley of rumpled pink and white badlands, completely covered in every direction by oil pumps and electric lines and century-old evidence of use and abuse. It's quite a shock. Just as shocking is the by-now antique and terribly shabby shack-town of Midwest, huddled slightly to the north of the fields in struggling greenery, with many of its bungalows boarded up, but still game to celebrate its centennial. It's a fascinating place, but certainly not pretty. The whole history of Casper is intimately involved with the goings-on here.

Casper, an extraordinary oil boomtown during the early 1980s, has seen hard times more recently, and its business district shows the effects. Casper did not lie along the original railroad route that brought to life so many Wyoming towns, instead cutting its teeth first on travelers along the Oregon Trail, and then on refining oil from the vast Salt Creek field 40 miles north near the twin towns of Midwest and Edgerton. More than 600 million barrels of oil and 700 million cubic feet of natural gas have been recovered here since an oil gusher in 1908 created Wyoming's first big oil boom. When the second oil boom hit in the late 1970s and early 1980s, Casper (along with Rock Springs, Evanston, and Green River) turned into a madhouse of pickup trucks, heavily muscled oil workers, honky-tonk bars, striptease joints, fast food outlets, and trailer courts. Wyoming still holds top honors as the state with the highest percentage of mobile homes. Although the oil boomtimes have faded (they could easily return if oil prices rise again), coal mining continues to increase in Wyoming, especially around Gillette, Wright, and Rock Springs. Trains of a hundred black coal cars pulled by four diesel engines rumble through the towns constantly, on their way to distant power plants. Wyoming is now the nation's largest coal producer, more the 160 million tons per year of low sulfur coal, primarily from monstrous strip mines in the Powder River Basin. With perhaps a trillion tons of coal still below the surface, Wyoming is truly one of the largest energy storehouses anywhere on the planet.

—Don Pitcher, *Wyoming Handbook*, 1991

(top) Ranchers Tooter and Jo Rogers in front of the entire town of Spotted Horse—consisting of a combination cafe, gas station, and bar. (bottom) Dick Pickerel cuts Dale Moore's hair at Douglas Corner Barber Shop. (opposite) "Fat Ed" Rogina hams it up at his Douglas eatery.

FAT EDS
DINNING
TO PUBLIC
FULL MENU
DAILY
COOKED
ROLLS
FAT ED

OREGON TRAIL ROUTE

CASPER IS THE OFF-AND-ON BIGGEST CITY OF WYOMING. Sometime in the 1990s, it is supposed to shrink again to second place, trailing Cheyenne. Casper's fortunes are based on oil, and oil isn't what it was, as Texans well know. The rest of the state regards it with mixed emotions—envy and some pride, especially when the oil is gushing, or distrust and some scorn on the part of those who prefer Wyoming as a wilderness or stock range. These latter consider Casper to be a suburb of Houston, and refer to the often non-natives active there as "boomers." By now, at the end of Wyoming's first century, older towns like Laramie and Cheyenne have developed a sort of staid, settled, tree-shaded character that's almost mellow. Nobody ever thought that of Casper. Casper is Up-to-Date.

It does, however, have history (of which one significant remnant remains); and it's a sufficiently active and bloody Wyoming sort of history. The very name of the town commemorates slaughter, though in a peculiarly confused fashion. It is named after rash, young Lieutenant Caspar W. Collins, who died in an attempt to rescue an army wagon train from Indians in 1865.

From the 1840s on, immigrants on the Oregon Trail took the route west through the future site of the city, coming along the North Platte and going up the Sweetwater to South Pass. The site of Casper, where many crossed the river, was crawling with immigrants for two decades. A Mormon ferry crossed the North Platte as early as 1847, and in 1859 troops were stationed there to protect travelers. That same year, a rickety bridge that succeeded the ferry was replaced by a fancy new one costing $60,000. Finally, a military post was established at the bridgehead in 1863.

On July 26, 1865, 3,000 Indians on the warpath after the Sand Creek Massacre in Colorado (see "Historical Interlude") assembled in the hills above the river. Sergeant Amos T. Custard, heading a party of army wagons coming from the Sweetwater toward the Platte, was ambushed by Indians 17 miles (28 km) upriver at Willow Springs. Twenty-one-year-old Lieut. Collins, who had just reported to the post at the bridge the night before, was ordered to lead a party of 25 men to rescue Custard.

Collins crossed the new bridge and followed a road northwest, where he was attacked by a force of some 600 charging Cheyennes and 1,800 Sioux. He was, shall we say, outnumbered. The fighting, however, was hard. In attempting to rescue a fallen soldier, Collins tried to lift the wounded man to his saddle, and his horse ran away straight into Indian forces. Caspar's body was found the next day, mutilated almost beyond recognition. All of Custard's party was killed, but only four of Collins's. The following autumn, Maj. General Pope declared the army post at the Platte River bridge to be "hereafter known as Fort Caspar"—*not*, incidentally, Fort Collins, as might be expected. That name had already been given to the fort (now city) in Colorado, in honor of Caspar's father. The name in Wyoming is still Fort Caspar, but unfortunately for Caspar's memory, the names of the town and the mountain behind it are, for some obscure reason, spelled *Casper* not *Caspar*. No one knows why. One explanation is that some ignorant mail clerk made the mistake on all the mailings. In any case, Caspar is the fort, and Casper the city.

Fort Caspar is nicely reconstructed, with a big and especially prestigious **historical museum**. It's on the far southwest side of town, on a bend of the Platte, and is easily reached by the wonderful Wyoming State Highway 258, which encircles the whole city. (This road, incidentally, is really worth the drive all by itself, since you get a panoramic view of the city, looking north, and a splendid view of Casper Mountain, looking south.) The restoration and museum are well worth the detour, but the park in which they stand is a disappointment. Instead of a nice, big, cottonwood city park in this bend of the river, it's a skimpy area surrounded by commerce on all sides, and unworthy of both the fort and the city. Too bad. This should by rights be Casper's big pleasure ground.

■ Founding Fathers

The first ranch house in the vicinity was built in 1876 on the CY Ranch of Judge Joseph M. Carey, founder of one of the state's most famous families, who trailed his 12,000 head of cattle up from Austin. (Carey later became a U.S. senator, and governor of Wyoming.) The nearby Goose Egg Ranch was founded by the Searight brothers, who arrived from Texas with 27,000 head of cattle. They built a large stone ranch house in 1877 that was used by Owen Wister in *The Virginian* as the scene for that Saturday night dance where all the babies were deliberately mixed up by prankish cowboys. (The babies had been lined up on the floor during the course of the dance. When the parents got home, miles away, the resulting mix-up took awhile to straighten out.) All this less than two decades after Lt. Caspar Collins lost his life.

The usual rough stuff went on during Casper's founding. It started as a cattle ship-

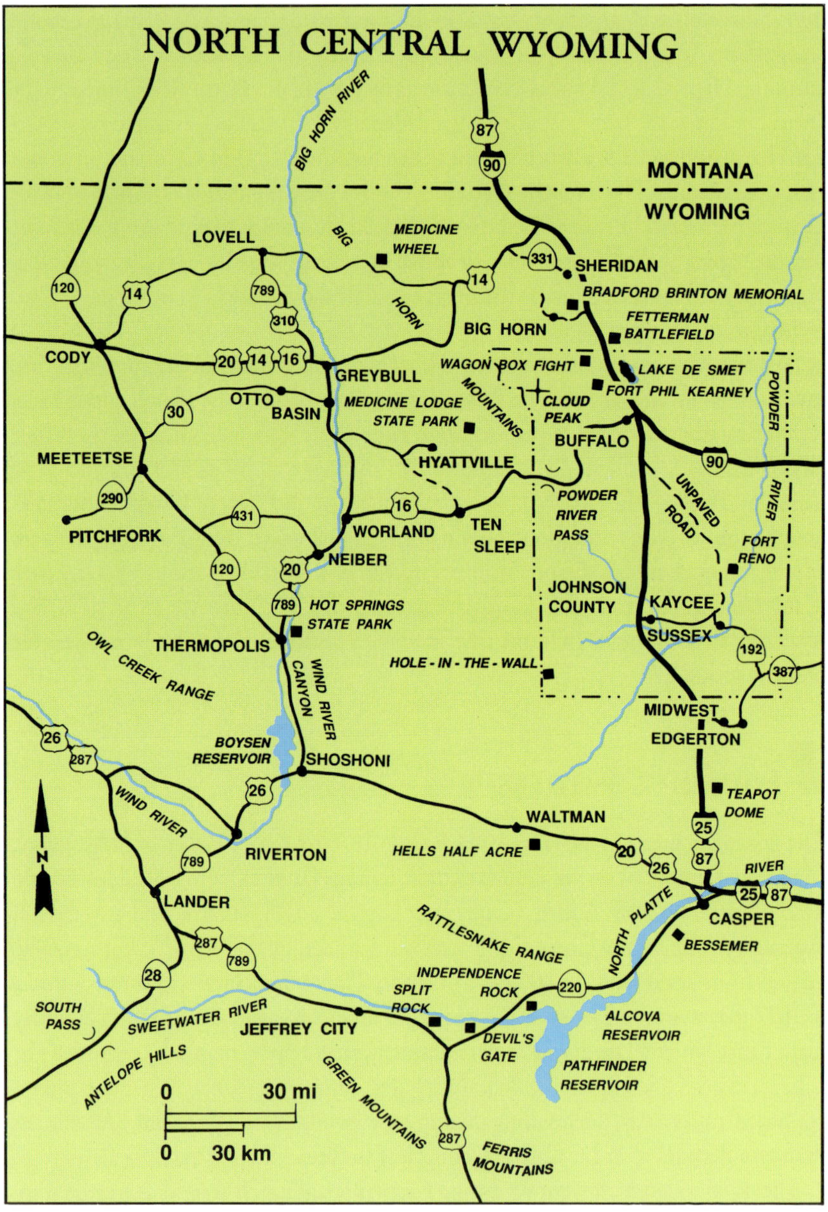
NORTH CENTRAL WYOMING
MONTANA
WYOMING
BIG HORN RIVER
BIG HORN
MEDICINE WHEEL
LOVELL
SHERIDAN
BRADFORD BRINTON MEMORIAL
FETTERMAN BATTLEFIELD
BIG HORN
CODY
GREYBULL
WAGON BOX FIGHT
LAKE DE SMET
FORT PHIL KEARNEY
OTTO
BASIN
MEDICINE LODGE STATE PARK
MOUNTAINS
CLOUD PEAK
BUFFALO
POWDER RIVER
MEETEETSE
HYATTVILLE
UNPAVED ROAD
PITCHFORK
POWDER RIVER PASS
WORLAND
TEN SLEEP
NEIBER
FORT RENO
HOT SPRINGS STATE PARK
JOHNSON COUNTY
KAYCEE
SUSSEX
THERMOPOLIS
OWL CREEK RANGE
HOLE-IN-THE-WALL
WIND RIVER CANYON
MIDWEST
EDGERTON
BOYSEN RESERVOIR
SHOSHONI
TEAPOT DOME
WIND RIVER
WALTMAN
RIVERTON
HELLS HALF ACRE
RIVER
LANDER
CASPER
RATTLESNAKE RANGE
NORTH PLATTE
BESSEMER
INDEPENDENCE ROCK
SPLIT ROCK
SOUTH PASS
SWEETWATER RIVER
JEFFREY CITY
ALCOVA RESERVOIR
DEVIL'S GATE
PATHFINDER RESERVOIR
ANTELOPE HILLS
GREEN MOUNTAINS
FERRIS MOUNTAINS
0 30 mi
0 30 km
N
87
90
14
331
120
789
310
20
16
30
290
431
26
287
28
25
192
387
220

ping center (Chicago & Northern) when, in 1885, Judge Carey of the CY designated part of his ranch as a possible site for a new town and railroad station. By the time the first passenger coach pulled in on June 15, nearly 100 people already lived there. The town was platted, lots were sold for about $250 each, lumber for construction was carted down from the forests on Casper Mountain, and the city was ready to go.

By 1889, there were eight saloons along Main Street, and the town was incorporated. Although there was a town ordinance prohibiting the discharge of firearms on the streets, within a year the mayor himself had beaten his man to the draw in a duel on Main Street while passersby ducked for cover. It was also unlawful for any woman to "use any vile, profane, or indecent language, or to act in a boisterous or lewd manner, or to smoke any cigar, cigarette, or pipe on Casper's streets, or to frequent the barroom of any saloon between 7 a.m. and 10 p.m." This, of course, didn't interfere with business at all. Ten p.m. to 7 a.m. was the real shank of the evening. As usual, the public school and the Congregational church were starting up at this same time. Virtue and vice grew side by side.

Natrona County was authorized in 1886, but "owing to financial inability" didn't function till 1890. There was a fight with the neighboring settlement of Bessemer, which intended to surpass Casper quickly and snatch away the honor of county seat. Casper won. Bessemer just faded away.

■ Oil

Casper won that fight just in time, for in that same year of 1890, when Natrona County began to function, the first oil gushed in the Salt Creek field to the north. The Pennsylvania Oil and Gas Company, composed of refugees from the dying fields back east, erected the first refinery in Wyoming in Casper as of 1895. Crude oil was hauled by wagon from the fields, 20 miles (33 km) away, which inhibited prosperity until pipelines were finally built in 1916.

By that time the boom created by World War I was in full blast, and Casper's destiny was determined. All the familiar antics of Wyoming's many booms were repeated once again. Everyone contracted speculative fever. Doctors and lawyers left their offices to buy and sell oil stocks. Most of the trading took place in the lobby of the Midwest Hotel (then the Hemming), and new oil companies were organized daily. Out in the field, land grabbers and claim jumpers forced the legitimate companies to hire line-riders to protect their leases. The Midwest Oil Company grew in ten years from a tiny local corporation to a $50-million outfit before it was swallowed by the even-more-giant Standard Oil.

The town population jetted up to 30,000 in 1925, with 2,000 more outside the city limits. The value of lots and land skyrocketed. Luxurious hotels and office buildings sprang up. A million dollars was spent on a new high school. Casper aimed to supplant both Denver as the metropolis of the Far West, and Cheyenne as the capital of Wyoming. But in the later 1920s the boom collapsed, and the depression of the 1930s completed the debacle. In that decade, the population halved to about 16,000. The same phenomenon took place in the 1980s.

It was under the Harding administration of the post-World War I era that Casper made headlines, along with Standard Oil and the Teapot Dome. The dome was an old stagecoach landmark that may once have actually resembled some sort of teapot. (Erosion, however, has been at work.) By 1910, it was in the center of Casper's oil fields. President Taft closed the area around the dome to private exploitation, and made it a naval oil reserve. Early in his administration, Harding transferred it from the Navy to the Department of the Interior, where his great and good friend, Albert B. Fall, was secretary. Fall leased it secretly, without competitive bids, to *his* great and good friend, Harry Sinclair, whose local operation was the Mammoth Crude Oil Company. One of the first Sinclair wells drilled there proved to be the largest gusher in state history, producing some 25,000 barrels a day. Between 1922 and 1927, Mammoth drilled 87 wells there. Oil gushed, but scandal leaked out. In early 1929, the Supreme Court invalidated the lease and restored control to the Navy. Sinclair was imprisoned for three months and fined all of

Harry F. Sinclair served time in prison for his role in the Teapot Dome scandal of the 1920s. (Courtesy, American Heritage Center, University of Wyoming)

$500, laughing all the way to jail. He went right back to pumping oil. Fall, however, got a three-year sentence and was fined $300,000. He was the first United States cabinet officer to land in jail. It was one of the major scandals of that disgraceful administration, and the name "Teapot Dome" was known all over the country to people who didn't have any idea where or what it was.

■ Modern Casper

Casper itself nowadays has no interest in being Old Western. It's the Chicago, let's say, of Wyoming, and just wants to Get Ahead. It's brisk, clean, busy, full of fine new buildings, has nice new residential sections up the slopes south of town, and is altogether a place of many advantages. There are all sorts of driving, hiking, riding, and camping options up in the mountains, as well as plenty of wide-open rangeland to the north. Water recreation and wildlife areas are also found not far away to the west on the beautiful Alcova, Pathfinder, and Seminoe reservoirs.

But to those from bigger, more "progressive" cities, Casper really doesn't have much different to say, despite its advantages. Certainly nothing aboriginally Wyoming. There are the **Nicolaysen Art Museum**, the fine Casper College up on the hills, good shops and restaurants downtown, and grandiose motels all about near the Interstate. The central streets in town have been most imaginatively landscaped and beautified with trees and flowers, and there are some startlingly impressive examples of new architecture, notably a bank that looks like a marble mosque with an electric-sign minaret. Altogether, as a *modern* city recovering with spunk from a bad slump, Casper is quite a model (except of course for the horrors of its approaches). But it's impossible to reconstruct the former mayor's duel in the middle of Main Street, or those laws governing ladies' conduct. In cities like Cheyenne and Sheridan, there is still ample architectural evidence of old times in the downtown area, and one can easily summon up the atmosphere of the bad old days. Not in Casper.

■ Central Plains

When you finally leave Casper and its rather extensive fringe of development, you're back in the Wild West with a vengeance. Through Natrona County and into the east-

Summer thunderstorms frequent the skies of central Wyoming.

ern part of Fremont County lies another great swath of plains stretching horizontally, so to speak: east to west, unlike the north-south-running plains between Gillette and Douglas. There is a distinct physical difference between these two areas. Whereas the eastern plains were uninterrupted prairie, the terrain west of Casper is broken and surrounded by all sorts of mountains, buttes, ridges, and badlands, and carved by river valleys, notably that of the Sweetwater. It's hard not to be in sight of mountains most of the time as you pass through. Right in the middle is the rugged, but bare and forbidding, and no doubt aptly named, **Rattlesnake Range**. Along the southern edge are the curious short ranges of the central belt. To the north, the Owl Creeks and the very end of the Big Horn Mountains cut off these plains from the Big Horn Basin.

So, this second, westering installment of the plains has a good deal more to offer visually than the plains farther east. Furthermore, the trip west from Casper along the Platte and Sweetwater rivers is not only beautiful, but chock-full of historic interest. This route follows the immigrant Oregon Trail until it branches west toward South Pass, almost on the still-existent traces of wagon wheels. History follows you all the way.

Shortly after leaving Casper, following the North Platte River west on Wyoming

(opposite) Floor hand James Lock works an oil drilling rig in central Wyoming.

State Highway 220, you pass the site of **Bessemer**, which once challenged Casper for supremacy. One might expect to find ruins of some great steel mill there, but such things never existed. The historical marker that once pointed the place out seems to have vanished. The town was founded in 1888 as a grandiose real estate development, planned to be the "Queen City of the West"— 49 city blocks were platted for a future capital of Wyoming; but by 1891 it was abandoned. Casper was never seriously threatened.

Thirty miles (50 km) beyond Casper, you come to an area of spectacular dams on the Platte, creating **Alcova, Pathfinder**, and **Seminoe reservoirs**. Though miles of beautiful riverside wilderness were submerged and destroyed, the lakes created are also very beautiful, and provide campsites, a game refuge, and recreation areas. A road detours southward from State Highway 220 to small Alcova, west to large Pathfinder, then back to the main highway. It gives you a wonderful series of views of bare, but fascinating, subtly colored, vast, open spaces, and oddly shaped mountain masses. This whole area, in fact, especially from Casper to Muddy Gap, is the quintessence and ideal of Wyoming's characteristic plains-and-mountain scenery. Grim under the glare of noon or leaden skies, it blossoms miraculously under other more gracious lighting effects and times of day. If you find the landscape dour, barren, forbidding, or boring (which indeed it is in places), hurry on north. If you can respond to the constant enticement of the varied distant ranges, the enormous open spaces, a meandering river valley, moving patterns of shade and sun, subtle color variations, the buildup of storm clouds, and the effects of early-morning and late-afternoon light, then you're properly initiated into the special beauties of Wyoming.

■ Independence Rock

Thirteen miles (22 km) beyond Alcova lies **Independence Rock**, the most striking and famous milestone on the Oregon Trail. Having crossed Poison Spider Creek and bypassed the Rattlesnake Range on their way west, the immigrants stopped with relief on the wide, watered meadows that surround the rock. Rounded, pink, and isolated, it juts out of the flat valley like a miniature Australian Ayers Rock. The naked hump has been described by geologists as "one of the most significant erosion remnants in the West." However, what makes it more significant is its long history as a beacon and campsite along the trail.

It may have been seen and even named by the returning Astorian, Robert Stuart, on Independence Day in 1812. It is mentioned as Independence Rock in a diary of 1837. Father Pierre Jean De Smet in 1840 referred to it as the "famous Rock Independence, register of the desert." Lieutenant John C. Frémont, in 1842, described the rock's inscriptions: "Everywhere within six or eight feet of the ground and in some places 60 to 80 feet above, the rock was inscribed with the names of travelers. I engraved on this rock of the far west a large cross covered with black rubber . . . to resist wind and rain." But this particular souvenir was destroyed, in any case, by a gunpowder blast during Fourth of July celebrations in 1847. The fact that Frémont left this "Catholic symbol" on the rock was used against him in his unsuccessful presidential campaign

Cattle Kate

Wyoming, despite its rather overpowering atmosphere of aggressive masculinity, has also been pretty aggressively feminist. The Equality State commissioned the country's first female justice of the peace, Esther Hobart Morris, and elected the first female state governor, Nellie Tayloe Ross. These worthy ladies have been balanced by some others perhaps not as worthy, but who are still prime examples of independent women, among them Calamity Jane and Cattle Kate.

Calamity Jane's Indian fighting, and her love affair with Wild Bill Hickok during the Black Hills gold rush, play a prominent part in Western legend. Unfortunately, in the harsh light of modern revisionism, it seems that none of her self-made story is backed by stern fact. She seems to have made the whole thing up, including her famous affair with Hickok.

Cattle Kate is less famous, more unsavory, and perhaps more authentic. Her real name was Ella Watson. She and her supposed husband Jim Averill were involved in a store and saloon business in the now vanished "town" of Bothwell, 10 miles (16 km) east of Independence Rock. Averill accepted cash from thirsty cowboys in his bar. Kate, who had a homestead nearby, accepted donations of stray calves onto which she put her brand. Soon, her brand was on a sizable bunch of the neighbors' cattle, and in their irritation these neighbors suggested that the Averills leave the country. When they refused, the neighbors strung both of them up to a tree. Needless to say, nothing was done about this except to cut the pair down and bury them near the former saloon. Cattle Kate thus has the distinction of being among Wyoming's female Firsts—the first woman lynched in the state.

in 1856, when he ran as the first Republican candidate. (One thing that has not changed is politics.) Brigham Young passed in 1847. A bronze plaque honors Narcissa Prentiss Whitman, wife of the missionary Marcus, and her companion Eliza Hart Spalding, the first white women to cross the continent. Another tablet commemorates Wyoming's first Masonic meeting, held on top of the rock (agile Masons) on July 4, 1862. Almost all of the some 50,000 names once inscribed on the rock are now obliterated, thus rather spoiling the historical impact. Alongside, there are still dim traces of the wagon tracks, and if you walk along the bottom of the rock through nettles and flowers southward from the plaque area, you can discover on your own a few faint old inscriptions; but Register Cliff near Guernsey is far better preserved, if generally less impressive.

All along this reach of highway, the road plays hide and seek with the Sweetwater River, which so succored and guided the travelers on their way toward South Pass. Odd protrusions of the central belt mountains, a series of disjunct and curiously contrasting elevations, also accompany the road, to the south. East to west, they are the **Shirley Mountains, Seminoes, Ferris Mountains, Green Mountains**, and the **Antelope Hills.** To the north emerges a separate range—the **Stoneys**, or **Granites**—very appropriately named since it looks like immense piles of gray stones (not unlike the Vedauwoo).

■ Devil's Gate

About five miles (eight km) from Independence Rock you pass by **Devil's Gate**, an odd, short canyon cut through the short fag end of the Stoneys. It seems to have no visible geological reason for existence. The Sweetwater runs through it, but any ordinary river wouldn't have taken the trouble. (There are indeed deep, mysterious geological reasons for it.) Despite its sinister name, it really doesn't amount to much. But it *is* queer. An 18-year-old, Caroline Todd, fell into the chasm traveling west with her immigrant family, who buried her under a tombstone inscribed:

> "Here lies the body of Caroline Todd
> whose soul has lately gone to God
> Ere redemption was too late
> she was redeemed at Devil's Gate."

Which is one way of looking at it. Far more horrendous was the fate of Captain Howard Martin's company of 576 English immigrants a short distance west at Martin's

(opposite) A few names remain from the 350,000 Oregon Trail emigrants who camped at Independence Rock.

MAY 28

Cove, in 1856. These were part of a group of a thousand Mormon converts leaving England for Utah, who found when they arrived in America that the Mormons could not afford to provide wagons and oxen to transport them from the end of the railroad in Iowa. They were forced to push *handcarts* with their belongings for the remaining thousand miles. They started across the continent in two groups, soon losing the few stock they had to marauding Indians, but managed to get to the Sweetwater, where they made two separate camps a few weeks apart, in October and November, 1855. They were both marooned there by blizzards. The group that camped at Martin's Cove suffered most. At least a hundred people died and were buried in a single trench. The survivors were eventually rescued by fellow Mormons from Salt Lake.

■ Beyond Muddy Gap

Muddy Gap Pass marks the end of Wyoming State Highway 220 and the junction with U.S. Route 287, which comes from the south through the desolate eastern edge of the Great Divide Basin. At this point, the Oregon Trail turned north and west to follow the Sweetwater. Historical markers at turnouts tell about the trail, its events and curiosities. To the south, the belt mountains, in their curious shapes and sizes, continue. The Ferris Mountains are tall, steep, sharply serrated, and only moderately timbered. The Green Mountains are softly rounded and heavily green with timber, as their name indicates. Still farther west are the bare, brown, castellated Antelope Hills; then the south end of the huge Wind Rivers.

West of Muddy Gap, **Split Rock** is an oddly shaped, bare, pink butte, conspicuously split into two sections. Like Independence Rock, it was very visible to the Oregon Trailers.

The scenery becomes less and less compelling, however, as you head northwest on Route 287. The Green Mountains subside, the Stoneys peel away northward, the landscape becomes sagebrush flat, and though the Sweetwater runs alongside, it, too, distances itself from the road. There is only one bit of habitation along this part of the Sweetwater Valley: **Jeffrey City**, a modern uranium camp that once boomed with a population of some 2,000. Now it's derelict, and, on the whole, deserted. The paved roads, once lined with white trailers, are now lined with weeds. A big store along the highway reads JEFFREY CITY GROCERY; somebody has painted a big "?" afterward. It's shut tight. However, on a bluff farther along is a bit of suburbia on a circular drive, so something must still go on there. Surely not many would live there out of pure choice.

Once more, just as in the approach to Douglas, things begin to seem pretty desolate. Then, once again, about ten miles (16 km) beyond semi-deserted Jeffrey City, the road rises and the Wind Rivers emerge. From now on, they grow closer and closer, more and more majestic. Tantalizingly, they appear beyond the final crossing of the Sweetwater, where the river and the Oregon Trail veer off toward South Pass; but the real apocalypse occurs ten miles (16 km) beyond the Sweetwater crossing. At the top of a long descent into the enormous valley of negligible Beaver Creek, there's a big truck pull-off. It's marked by the conventional sign warning of a steep downgrade, but there's no indication whatsoever of the fact that this is one of the most magnificent viewpoints in the whole state of Wyoming. Stopping here, you look across the deep, wide, rough valley, and behold the entire epic panorama of the white-capped Wind Rivers. It's unfortunately typical of the Highway Department that though they'll attack you every few miles with often rather trivial historical turn-offs, this epochal view point is placed here just for the convenience of tired trucks.

■ Wind River Basin

As you approach Lander, the land gradually becomes greener and the mountains closer, while the peaks become hidden by foothills. You are entering the south fringes of the Wind River Basin. To complete this tour of the central plains, you should turn north at Lander on State Highway 789 toward Riverton, Shoshoni, and the Big Horn Basin. (Lander and the Wind River Indian Reservation are discussed in the "Indian Country" chapter.)

The 46-mile (77 km) drive from Lander to Shoshoni on State Highway 789, unfortunately, is pretty homely. When you drive it in the opposite direction, you face the Wind Rivers in their majesty all along; going north, you don't. At first there's rural scenery with oil in it, then the total debauch of hideous, crowded commercialism on the Strip outside of Riverton, then rather bland farmlands and bare buttes to Shoshoni. From Boysen Reservoir and Shoshoni itself, things improve.

Riverton aims to be stylish, but its upsurge has been interrupted by the collapse of the uranium boom in the Gas Hills to the east, and the general decline of oil prices. Once a farming center, with big grain elevators around, Riverton has begun to think of itself as a little Casper. There are fancy new residential areas and shops, but the changeover is far from complete. The big event of the year remains the annual fair.

As for Riverton's Strip itself—it may be bleak, but it does contain motels: a great, very grim Holiday Inn and the nice, old-fashioned HI-LO Motel. There's a huge, handsome Golden Corral cafeteria next to the HI-LO. There's also a stylish Brokers Restaurant on Riverton's main street in the center of town.

■ Shoshoni Shortcut

An alternate route from Casper to Shoshoni, more direct but much less interesting, is U.S. Route 20/26. One of the state's more desolate highways, it follows the Bridger Trail, marked out by Jim Bridger in hopes of redirecting traffic from the fatal Bozeman Trail through the Powder River Basin, farther east. Unfortunately, it didn't work. The route passes through 100 miles (167 km) of semidesert—rough, dry buttes and gullies, and enormous, wide-open distances. The Bridger Trail then turned north into the Big Horn Basin, through the mountains, and so to Virginia City, Montana.

The modern highway goes straight to Shoshoni through quite a few tiny dots on the map. You see glimpses of mountains along the whole route; far and faint, but there. Side roads lead off to energy sites, notably the defunct Gas Hills uranium development. Some 45 miles (75 km) from Casper, near a dot on the map called Waltman, is a curious little wonder called **Hell's Half Acre.** It's a smallish, Grand-Canyon type of hole-in-the-desert, full of fantastic, eroded pink pinnacles. It should be called Hell's Half Mile for it's a lot more than half an acre. It's entered by way of a rather shabby area of private development, a big restaurant, and a run-down motel; but the view itself is spectacular and well worth the stop. It's the only such "sight" on the highway.

BIG HORN BASIN

THE HISTORICAL APPROACH TO THE BIG HORNS—the way most pioneers, fur trappers, and settlers approached them—was from the east, either from the Yellowstone River in Montana, direct from the Black Hills, or up from the North Platte. This is also the normal approach for contemporary tourists from the east, but it is not really the preferred route. It's quick to zip along Interstate 90, west, or Interstate 25, north; but it's a comparatively dull, superficial way to go.

A better way is the back door from the south through the Wind River Canyon to Thermopolis, which you might otherwise miss. The suggested route then takes you twice across the beautiful plateau of the Big Horn Mountains, first eastward, then westward.

Entering the Big Horn Basin from this back door, the traveler enters the area of Wyoming's most massive scenic splendor. This northwestern part of Wyoming—roughly two-fifths of the state—is where most of what tourists want to see flourishes: mountains, forests, lakes, canyons, game and fish, and curiosities like geysers. Indians and cowboys tend to flourish on the great plains rather than in the mountains. Such towns as do exist in this northwest corner, however, are liable to be more specifically "Western" than ones farther south and east. As mountains, the Laramies, Snowies, and Black Hills are all very well, but they don't begin to compare with the Big Horns, Absarokas, Wind Rivers, and Tetons. There are some little lakes and sizable reservoirs back in eastern Wyoming, but nothing like Yellowstone Lake or the lakes of Jackson Hole. A few peaks of the Medicine Bows and Sierra Madre are over 11,000 feet (3,400 m), but nothing like the barrier of 12,000- to 13,000-footers (3,700-3,900 m) you'll see in the Wind Rivers.

■ BIG HORN BASIN OVERVIEW

A basin is a "hole" in Western parlance; that is, a valley more or less completely surrounded by hills (mountains, in another Western parlance). The particular hills in this case are the Owl Creeks to the south of the Big Horn Basin; the Big Horn Mountains, east; vague ranges like the Pryors, north; and the Absarokas, west.

The Big Horn Basin is a great, *big* hole, with a good deal of varied topography and character inside it, and so spacious that in the middle of it the mountains are more or less invisible. It slopes down towards the north end into a desert depression well below 4,000 feet (1,200 m). This is pretty low for Wyoming. Quite a bit of the basin is badlands, but some is irrigated farmland. To the south and west, below Cody, it's big, open cattle country. It contains lots of towns, especially for Wyoming: Thermopolis, Worland, Ten Sleep, Basin, Greybull, Lovell, Powell, Cody, and Meeteetse. Yet, it is still full of empty spaces. Some of the basin is interesting and good to look at, some isn't. Much of it is a pleasure ground for paleontologists, chock-full of bones and fossils. It's oil rich, too.

The Big Horn Basin was the bastion and home grounds for the Crow Indians after the Sioux drove them out of the Powder River area. The Crow and Sioux were hereditary enemies. Lots of horse stealing and fighting and counting of coups went on over the decades before the white men came. But there is much evidence here, too, of those mysterious tribes of prehistoric times. (Who were they? What happened to them? Were they direct ancestors of the plains tribes or not?) Later on, trappers explored the basin, and cattlemen came to stay. There were no significant Indian-white conflicts, unlike the Powder River; but later on, the cattle-sheep war culminated here.

The Big Horn Basin, however, presents a special problem to travelers. There's really no logical or sensible way to view it. Neither a trip up the middle, nor a circle round the circumference makes sense, touristically, so in this case a rather peculiar zigzag back and forth, up and down, is suggested, which in the end will give a taste of the varied beauties and curiosities of the basin without subjecting the visitor to the less pleasant parts. For, to tell the truth, the center of the valley from Thermopolis, at the very south, up to Lovell in the north, is deadly dreary. There are some attractions en route, but not many. The terrain alongside and above the Big Horn River valley is semidesert of a peculiarly drab sort—somewhere between sheeped-off range and just plain, gray-brown dirt—with not much mountain scenery in the distance till you get far north and closer to the Big Horns. It's also the main route for trucks going north. Altogether, a steady south-to-north trip palls. So from Thermopolis, a varied diet is recommended.

■ Wind River Canyon

Nothing, however, could exceed the grand introduction presented by the **Wind River Canyon**. It's one of the great sights of the West. The preparation for it begins right beyond Shoshoni with the Owl Creeks, which seem inconspicuous when seen from a

(opposite) The 2,500-foot (760-m) cliffs of Wind River Canyon leave only a narrow swath of sky overhead.

distance. Suddenly, they begin to loom in a grim, broken, desert-brown grandeur. Meanwhile, alongside is the blinding-blue (on a bright day) **Boysen Reservoir**, totally artificial in this badland setting, but in wonderful contrast. Just as you come to the mountains, some great, pointed, dark red rock-thrusts shoot up at the edge. Marinas and a bare, new picnic ground are situated alongside the lake. Then comes the dam and you are in the canyon.

Thousand-foot-high cliffs and pinnacles and castles close in. The Wind River rushes green to the left, with a little railroad running on the other side of it. Geological information signs point to the rocks, which you daren't look at if you're driving; and the whole is such a violent contrast to anything you'd have seen anywhere else in southeast Wyoming that you might think you're in the deserts of Utah.

This awe-inspiring traverse is only 32 miles (53 km) long, from Shoshoni to Thermopolis, but worth the trip. When you emerge at the north end, the by-now big river alongside is definitely and specifically the Big Horn, *not* the Wind River, and you come almost immediately to Thermopolis and its hot springs. The town is rather new, even by Wyoming standards, but the springs have been known and used for ages. The Indian legend is that the strong, continuous wind that blows down the canyon wafted a feather, which led the first Indians to the springs, hence the name Wind River. For decades, the waters were considered to confer perpetual youth and assist courtship. Great Chief Washakie of the Shoshones had his private bathhouse there, and the springs were once part of the Wind River Reservation.

The rather unconvincing explanation of how one river has two names is that, without consulting one another, the white settlers up above named it *Big Horn*, and the Indians and settlers down below called it *Wind River*. So the two names stuck in the two regions, and now it's too late to change the situation.

■ THERMOPOLIS

With a population of about 3,800, **Thermopolis** is unique among Wyoming towns in having a classical name. The West doesn't go in much for such names (unlike New York State with its Syracuse, Utica and Ithaca), and this particular name is part of the confused history of the place. There was originally a rough, tough, little cow town to the north called Andersonville, founded in 1890. There, outlaws from the Hole-in-the-Wall gang to the southeast used to drop in, and on one occasion tried to take over the town during an election. A gun battle cleared them out. Later, in 1894, a first version of Thermopolis was founded in anticipation of the hoped-for opening of the hot springs, then part of the Wind River reservation, to white settlers. This opening occurred in 1897, when a treaty with the Indians removed this corner from their jurisdiction. Andersonville and Thermopolis packed up and moved together to the new site, where they remain to this day.

Dr. Julius A. Schuelke is credited with naming the town—"city of hot springs" in Greek (*thermos* means "hot"; *polis* means "city"). It immediately became the spa it is now. It also became the county seat when Hot Springs County was created in 1911.

However, town and springs are now quite separate. The town is a rather pleasant, ramshackle, and random place whose gridiron has spread it all up and down surrounding hills in an accidentally picturesque fashion. It boasts of having 300 sunny days a year, and bright town gardens seem to prove it. A grand boulevard main street was first laid out with a grass median like New York's Park Avenue, but the grass plots are now parking lots, and most of the older stone buildings along it are in a state of disarray. U.S. Route 20 passes through, south to north, with a continual growling of trucks. But on either side, there are rewards: on the west, a big, typical, two-story town museum full of everything local; and on the east, an excellent restaurant, the Pumpernick. But there are no actual springs in the City of Thermos.

The springs, and **Hot Springs State Park**, are just north of town and across the river, eastward. The park is indeed an impressive place, a combination German spa and large county fairground. The springs themselves are pretty impressive too—and peculiar.

Hot Springs Historical Museum, Thermopolis

The Thermopolis museum calls itself "one of the best small museums in the country." It lives up to this billing with an impressive collection of old photos, wagons, Indian artifacts, and displays of frontier life, such as a newspaper shop, a dentist's office (take a look at those frightening tools!), a blacksmith shop, and a general store. The cherrywood bar from the Hole-in-the-Wall Saloon is particularly popular; here members of the famous outlaw gang tipped their glasses with sympathetic locals. Look for their photos on the wall. Downstairs you will find an elk hide painted by Chief Washakie of the Shoshones, and across the street an old schoolhouse, petroleum building, and a caboose.

A single hot, bubbling green pool of water emerges from the very foot of a towering, roof-topped, deep-red mesa, and spreads out and over in large terraces toward the river. These by-now tepid waters slip over a long, high, gray cliff made of mineral deposits, and drip directly into the Big Horn River. Around the southern edge of the thermal springs—the largest of their kind in America and perhaps the world, spewing out four million gallons of hot water a day—is a line of bathing establishments in which you can soak or swim. There's a capacious outdoor pool, and a water slide for kids alongside the red cliffs, to the east. In the middle of the complex is a perpetual fountain under a cupola, and surrounded by watered lawns—a nice place to cool off. There are flower beds, full of roses in season, and it is indeed very German, as though in memoriam to Dr. Schuelke. Farther back in the pleasant park are various buildings, including a Holiday Inn. During the summer, all of Wyoming is at the springs, splashing and sun bathing, and the dream of the good Herr Doctor seems thoroughly realized.

After you leave the town and springs, you enter the Big Horn Basin itself, either by driving west from Main Street onto beautiful, lonely Wyoming State Highway 120 to Cody, or north on the less beautiful and much less lonely U.S. Route 20.

Topography around Thermopolis is a mixture of farms and badlands.

■ Thermopolis to Worland

Route 20 between Thermopolis and Worland gives you a taste of the long river valley that bisects the basin. The road goes along bare benches just west of the greenery below, where lie little villages like Lucerne and Kirby. There was an oil boom westward in the Grass Creek Field in 1917-18, and there's still plenty of oil out there.

The first permanent settlements in the basin—mostly cattle ranches—were in this southern area. As early as 1871, J.D. Woodruff built the first house in the valley. The nearby Embar (M—) Ranch ran 50,000 head, and there still are plenty of cattle here. Down along the river, alfalfa grows in Lucerne, and there was once coal at Gebo and Kirby. Across the river, farther along, is **Tie-Down Hill**, where once lived Tie-Down Brown, so named for his skill in tying down and branding other people's calves. But in 1880, his partner killed him with an axe, and for a good many years his ghost rode up and down the hill looking for revenge. On another hill north of Neiber is the site of an old Shoshone burial yard. All this, however, is skirted nowadays by the big, not very pleasant, truck-laden route north to Worland.

Worland, with a population of about 6,000, is situated in the midst of irrigated farmlands. It's the county seat of Washakie, another memorial to the great chief, yet a twentieth-century town of lawns and trees in its residential area. Like Torrington, Worland grew up with the sugar beet refinery and the railroad from 1906 onward. Rangeland—so often denuded in the Big Horn Basin as to be really badlands—lies beyond the reach of irrigation. The Big Horns rise to the east, Owl Creeks to the south, and Absarokas very dim and far to the west.

■ Meeteetse Detour

The direct way east to Buffalo over the mountains would be to proceed from Worland to Ten Sleep on U.S. Route 16. This, however, would prevent you from seeing anything else of interest in the lower Big Horn Basin itself. So instead, turn west at Neiber, nine miles (15 km) below Worland, onto Wyoming State Highway 431. This empty road begins tamely, heading up a flat, open creek bed, with low, drab ridges north and south, framing scanty green ranch pastures. As you glide smoothly over this excellent highway, gradually the scenery grows more grand. The ridges alongside push up into crags. The blue Absarokas ahead loom larger. Halfway along, due north, is a gulf of superb **badlands**—pink, white, red, buff, blue, gray—in all sorts of jumbled towers, palaces, temples, and ruins. These badlands accompany you off and on almost until you swing back into Hot Springs County, where you soon run into State Highway 120 swerving up from Thermopolis. From here on, the scenery becomes still more exalted, with high, mountainous, cedar-spotted ridges, and near-glimpses of the great Absarokas. The road crosses into Park County, with an immediate increase in scenic beauty, and descends into the Greybull Valley to Meeteetse (maTEETsee). The elevation here is 5,795 feet (1,766 m), whereas Worland is only 4,061 feet (1,238 m)—which accounts for some of the exhilaration of this trip.

Meeteetse, with about 500 people, is a cow town, and still has an Old West atmosphere, despite the automobile. Its old buildings are scattered about a crossroads (State Highway 290 leads west to Pitchfork). There are two historical points of interest—the **Meeteetse Archives**, in an old, pink stone bank building on the west side, and the **Meeteetse Museum** in the town center.

Pitchfork was and is the site of the Pitchfork Ranch of Charlie Belden, famous photographer of cowboy life in the 1920s and 1930s. Its previous owner was Otto Franc, whose real full name was Count Otto Franc von Lichtenstein. He settled the site in 1878, and was one of the great cattle ranchers of the area, as well as a notable big-game hunter. One of the most odd incidents of his career was his involvement with famous outlaw Butch Cassidy. Cassidy, then called George Cassidy (his real name was George Leroy Parker), was arrested for the possession of horses stolen from Franc. After a dubious series of mistrials, he was found guilty and served a jail sentence from 1894 to 1896. The prosecutor who convicted him was Bill Simpson, progenitor of a notable Wyoming family, including a governor (Milward) and a senator (Alan). Butch never forgave Franc, and claimed he took seriously to a life of crime after his jail term. The rights and wrongs of the case are as confused as most Wyoming incidents, but there was no doubt about Cassidy's success in his newly chosen profession.

Franc lived in high style on the Pitchfork, but the style became higher when the Belden-Phelps regime took over in 1901—the next and permanent owners. In 1918, a great, gabled frame and stone ranch house was built, which is still headquarters for Belden descendants. Charlie Belden's pictures of cow life and the world around him have never been surpassed in beauty and authenticity. Specimens of his work are in the museum at Cody, and indeed all over the state.

From Meeteetse, State Highway 120 proceeds north for 31 beautiful miles (52 km) to Cody, with increasingly spectacular views of the Absarokas; but our route takes off back east on Wyoming State Highway 30, some six miles (10 km) beyond Meeteetse, and down the rich, green Greybull River valley. This is some of the most typical of Western sceneries: a lush valley of huge cottonwoods and vivid pastures, flanked on both sides by the grim, bare cliffs of often fantastically carved, red badlands. As long as you're in Park County, for about 20 miles (30 km), all is well. But in Big Horn County, eastward, the river valley gradually widens, and you've lost sight of the Absarokas and the cliffs alongside. The delta of the Greybull assumes the scruffy look characteristic of the central Big Horn Basin. However, the little town of **Otto** reminds one of the romantic past; that is, it's named after Otto Franc von Lichtenstein. Sadly, there is nothing noble or romantic about the place.

The town of **Basin** is at the junction with U.S. Route 20, coming up from Worland. Basin won the honor of being county seat of Big Horn County by a close vote in 1896: Basin, 481 votes, Otto 420, and far off Cody trailing with only 243. Basin was also the scene of the famous sheep-and-cattle war court trials of a slightly later era. It still possesses its fine courthouse, but unfortunately little else. By now commerce has been sucked away to bigger, newer Greybull, eight miles (13 km) north.

■ Sheep vs. Cattle

This area is famous, or infamous, in Wyoming as the country where the long, bitter sheep and cattle wars came to a climax at the turn of the century. This was one of those unnecessary confrontations that could have been solved by some common sense. It resulted from the greedy, unregulated American enterprise of that post-Civil War period. Sheep owners simply ignored the prior claims of cattlemen to the ranges. They penetrated the Powder River Basin and then moved into the Big Horn Basin. In the process, they ruined the range for cattle and so threatened to ruin the cattle ranchers. Instead of trying to settle the matter by persuasion, arbitration, and law, cattlemen in typically high-handed fashion just slaughtered the sheep. They shot them, poisoned them, drove them over rimrock precipices, and still failed to stop the inexorable advance. This war reached a violent climax near the Big Horn Basin town of Ten Sleep.

In 1903 some herders were shot by masked men, and their sheep slaughtered. During the next six years, the violence continued, and 11 bands of sheep valued at $100,000 were dynamited, rimrocked, and attacked by dogs. The sheep persisted, however. The sheep men didn't retaliate against the violence; they just went on obstinately overgrazing. In the fall of 1908, a lamb shipment valued at $2 million was shipped from the Big Horn Basin.

Cattle rancher and Washakie County State Rep. John Rankine.

In the spring of 1909, Joe Allemand and a partner brought five thousand sheep into the Big Horn. On April 3, 20 masked men killed them and a herder on Spring Creek, and cremated the bodies in their own wagons. This brought the feud to a head. The National Woolgrowers Association offered a bounty of $20,000 for the arrest and prosecution of the Ten Sleep raiders. A grand jury investigation was launched, while jurors, sheriffs, and witnesses were threatened. One witness committed suicide. Finally, seven men were arrested in May. When conviction became certain, influential friends of the cattlemen intervened. A deal was arranged so that the accused could plead guilty to lesser crimes than murder, and receive lesser jail sentences of three to six years. Justice perhaps was not exactly done; but the result was efficacious. Everyone calmed down. Deadlines were now determined by law, limits were fixed beyond which sheep could not graze. Entire counties, like Teton, were thus set off-limits, and though sheep men and cattlemen could never be friends, at least no one got shot. Why didn't anyone think of that 20 years sooner?

Nowadays, most ranges are fenced or under government control to prevent overgrazing. Big owners run both sheep and cattle. But cattlemen and cow hands still despise woollies and think sheep herders are morose "furriners," many of them mysterious Basques who go crazy listening to that bleating and can't ride a horse worth a damn.

(opposite) Sheepherder John Abyta prepares for a day among his 1,600 sheep in the Big Horn Mountains.

■ Medicine Lodge State Park

Our route through the Big Horn Basin turns south to Manderson, a tiny post office in a grove of big trees, where Wyoming State Highway 31 takes off for Hyattville. This is the site of the **Medicine Lodge State Park**, an absolutely obligatory detour.

The scenery becomes progressively more striking as you go up Nowood Creek (which supports plenty of cottonwoods) and turn east into the foothills of the great, hulking Big Horns. The state park lies, rather inconspicuously, up Paintrock Creek (aptly named for the intensely red cliffs that wedge into the intensely green ranch val-

We had noticed with a great deal of anxiety that the wrinkles had commenced to accumulate on our cattle's horns, as a new wrinkle grows each year after an animal is two years old, and we had been advised by several cattlemen who had been in the habit of taking their cattle by rail to market in place of driving them, to procure files and rasps and remove these wrinkles before we got to Omaha. So we secured a lot of rasps and files at Cheyenne and had Jackdo carry them for us, and when we caught up with the train we went to work to take off the sign of old age which had come on our stock since shipping them, as the Nebraska corn-raisers only want young stock to feed. When we first loaded our cattle we were informed that they were a little bit too fat for the killers, but, of course, the next day, they was about four pounds too thin for the killers, but too fat for the feeders. However, by this time they were nothing but petrified skeletons, and Dillbery Ike wanted to leave the wrinkles on their horns and sell the entire outfit for antiques. But the more we discussed it, the more we made up our minds that as this railroad done a large business hauling stock, the antique cattle market must be overstocked. So we finally concluded to take off the wrinkles that had grown since we started and sell the cattle on their merits. We arranged to run two day shifts and one night shift of six hours each and to commence up the engine and work back. So getting in the first car we climbed astride the critters' necks and commenced to file. Day after day, night after night, we kept at this wearisome task, and when our files and rasps became worn we sent Jackdo (who wouldn't work, but who didn't mind tramping) to the nearest town to get fresh files and rasps. Sometimes we became discouraged when we saw the wrinkles starting again that we had removed to commence with, and our eyes filled with bitter tears when we thought how much better it would have been to have trailed our cattle through, or even sold them to some Nebraska sucker and taken his draft on a commission house.

—Frank Benton, *Cowboy Life on the Sidetrack,* 1903

ley), and then up Medicine Lodge Creek, and beyond through a small gate leading to a shady campground. Across the creek is one of the wonders of Wyoming—a wide, smooth, pink cliff, covered with yards of petroglyphs (incised designs) and some pictographs (painted designs). Prehistoric tribes camped along this same cliff and stream. At least 60 cultural levels have been excavated, covering some 10,000 years of occupation. Solar heat from the cliff in winter, summer shade, and nearby water and quartzite for arrowheads all made this a permanently attractive place. It still is. A stone canopy along the cliff top has helped preserve the images, which are mostly circular designs with decorations inside and protuberances outside. Some are recognizably animal, some human. This is the most beautiful, easily seen, and imaginatively compelling cliff decoration in the state. The setting alone makes it worth a visit—a lushly treed private ranch, with the beautiful, clear creek running through it. So far the prehistoric designs seem to have escaped the insane vandalism that so often destroys monuments such as Register Cliff—the real beastliness of modern tourists—though a pair of cowboys more than 70 years ago did their best. With black paint, "Jinks Burgess" and "Speed Martin" immortalized (or damned) themselves for posterity on "8/10/16"—almost prehistoric by Wyoming standards.

At this point, it's best to return to the junction of the marked road up Nowood Creek to Ten Sleep. Turning south, you drive through wild, craggy, turreted rangeland, once a battleground of the sheep-cattle wars, where both sheep and cattle now range in peace. After some 20 miles (33 km) you reach Ten Sleep.

■ Ten Sleep

With about 400 people, **Ten Sleep** gets its queer name from the Indians. It was ten sleeps (overnight camps) away from somewhere for the Crows, but no one seems absolutely sure from where. The Crows are now settled on their reservation in Montana.

The Crows occupied the Big Horn Basin before the first whites penetrated. John Colter, one of the first mountain men to pass through, had escaped brushes with other tribes, notably the Blackfeet; but the Crows welcomed him. Ed Rose and other trappers followed Colter. The basin was officially explored in 1859-1860 by the Raynolds-Maynadier expedition, accompanied by the famous scientist, Ferdinand V. Hayden, later the true begetter of Yellowstone National Park. The Raynolds-Maynadier expedition had difficulties getting through the Wind River canyon, and even lost its wagons, but the group made the first scientific report on the region.

When John Bozeman proposed a trail up through the Powder River Basin to gain access to gold in Montana, trapper-guide Jim Bridger warned him of the Indian troubles his route would (and did) start. Bridger instead suggested breaking a trail through the Big Horn Basin, passing by the more amiable Crows. Bridger and Bozeman had a sort of race to determine which route was quicker. Unfortunately, Bozeman reached Virginia City first. From then on it was bloodshed all the way on the Powder River; but not on the Bridger Trail through the Big Horn Basin.

The original cattle coming into the basin were trailed in from Oregon, of all places, in 1879. By 1883, the entire basin was stocked by largely English, Scottish, and German (Otto Franc) big owners. Then came sheep, irrigation, homesteads, oil and coal, railroads, and sugar beets, with Mexican, Russian, and Japanese field hands. All the general influx of modern times; but somehow, except for the Ten Sleep murders, with less conflict and tension than on the plains.

■ The Big Horn Mountains

U.S. Route 16 takes you away from Ten Sleep and into the mountains through spectacular **Ten Sleep Canyon**, rather like the Wind River Canyon in its towering yellow castles, but more open and smiling. High over the canyon on a pinnacle to the south is the **Leigh Monument**. This marks a point where an English gentleman, Gilbert Leigh, who had settled near Ten Sleep and liked to wander about the mountains hunting game, fell to his death in 1884 from a 600-foot-high (200-m) precipice. Buzzards led searchers to his body.

The road goes from bare, brown rangelands along Nowood Creek up into the green forests and pastures of the Big Horn National Forest, which surrounds Cloud Peak—at 13,165 feet (4,011 m), the tallest in the Big Horns. Wide views begin to emerge as the road wriggles over the Powder River pass (9,666 feet/2,945 m) and across the wide, forested plateau. The eastern descent is particularly engaging, with great grass-and-flower open meadows, and views north of snow-capped peaks. All the way along the route are campsites. There are also two pleasant guest ranches beside the road—South Park Inn, by a rushing stream, and the Pines Lodge. Both have guest cabins and meals.

The trees begin to thin out as you make the long descent to Buffalo. Some time before you actually get to Buffalo itself, you know you are very definitely back on the plains.

(opposite) Wyoming experiences a riot of colors as the seasons progress. Indian paintbrush (lower left) is the official state flower.

HISTORICAL INTERLUDE: THE POWDER RIVER MYSTIQUE

AT THIS POINT, IN ORDER TO GIVE TRAVELERS A REAL understanding of what they're seeing, especially east of the Big Horns and in the Powder River Basin, it's necessary to take a fairly extensive historical detour. What you should see is not so much the empty, barren landscape eastward from the mountains, but the essence of Wyoming's most dramatic past. This is what makes this particular section of Wyoming the crucible in which the spirit of the state was distilled, the anvil on which it was hammered out.

Unlike the Big Horn Basin, where there were few immigrant trains or Indian troubles, Powder River Basin had its fill of both. The history of the area from the Civil War and beyond was one of constant action. It was Wyoming's ultimate Indian-soldier-cowboy country, and its blood-soaked and epic history, full of heroics and horror, gives it a special glamour that no other part of the state, and few places in the Union, can match.

As a result, Powder River has become a symbol and a battle cry. Quite literally, for soldiers from Wyoming in World War I would cry "Powder River, let 'er buck!" when charging into battle. If there is one section of the state that has inspired that bucking horse on the license plate, it is the Powder River watershed.

■ INDIANS

As rivers go, the Powder is pretty minimal. Few people live on its banks. That it's "an inch deep, a mile wide, and runs uphill all the way" is not quite true, but it *is* mean, sour, full of quicksand, and thoroughly unproductive. That word "ornery," so close to the heart of Wyoming, certainly does apply here.

When the Sioux arrived from the east and drove the Crows into the Big Horn Basin, they lorded over the area from the Big Horns east to the Black Hills. The Black Hills in general remained a sacred place for the Sioux, while the plains between the two ranges, centered on the Powder River, were their chief hunting and camping grounds.

The essential difficulty between the plains Indians and Americans of European descent was a basic misunderstanding of property rights. To all Europeans, property was something sacred, bounded by borders or walls that belonged to somebody as his most

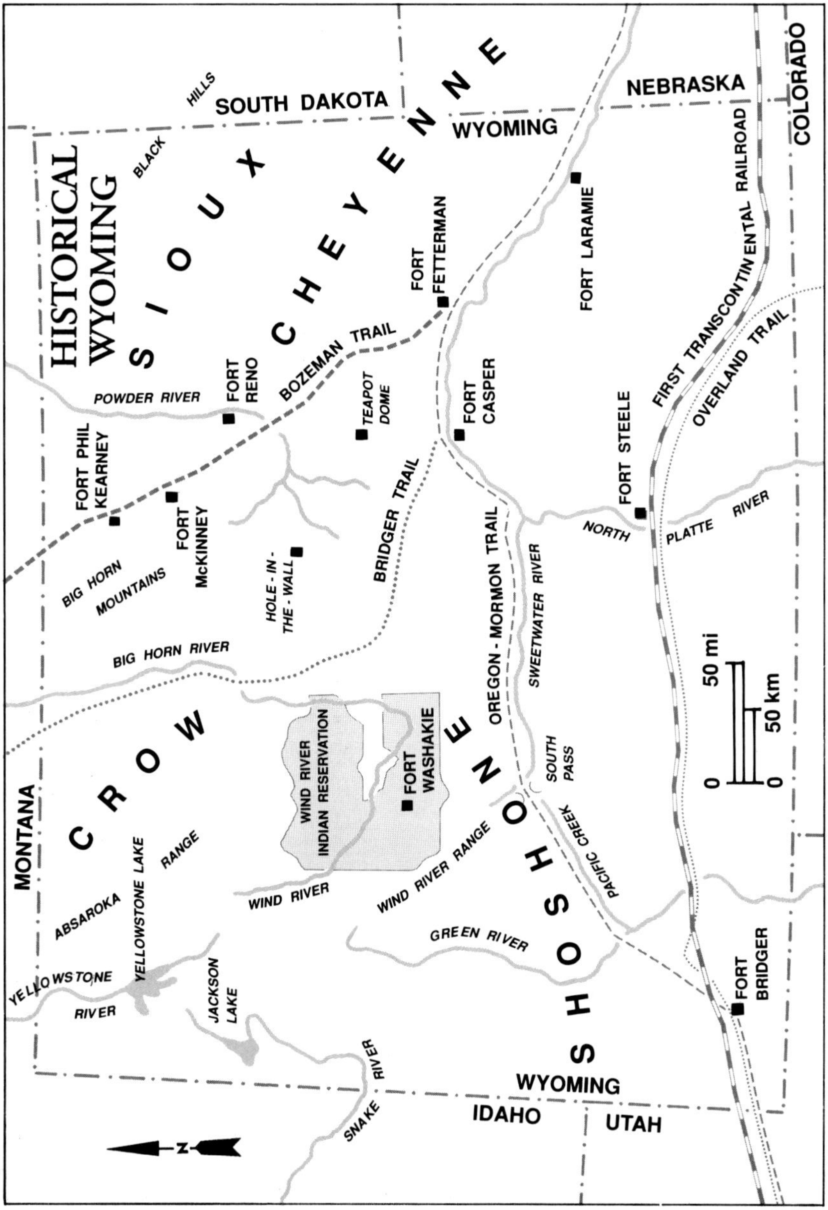
HISTORICAL WYOMING
SIOUX
CHEYENNE
CROW
SHOSHONE
SOUTH DAKOTA
NEBRASKA
COLORADO
WYOMING
MONTANA
IDAHO
UTAH
BLACK HILLS
FORT LARAMIE
FORT FETTERMAN
FORT RENO
FORT PHIL KEARNEY
FORT McKINNEY
FORT CASPER
FORT STEELE
FORT WASHAKIE
FORT BRIDGER
FIRST TRANSCONTINENTAL RAILROAD
OVERLAND TRAIL
BOZEMAN TRAIL
BRIDGER TRAIL
OREGON - MORMON TRAIL
POWDER RIVER
TEAPOT DOME
HOLE - IN - THE - WALL
BIG HORN MOUNTAINS
BIG HORN RIVER
NORTH PLATTE RIVER
SWEETWATER RIVER
SOUTH PASS
PACIFIC CREEK
WIND RIVER INDIAN RESERVATION
WIND RIVER
WIND RIVER RANGE
GREEN RIVER
ABSAROKA RANGE
YELLOWSTONE LAKE
YELLOWSTONE RIVER
JACKSON LAKE
SNAKE RIVER
50 mi
50 km
0
N

precious possession. It could be inherited by descendants, and was fought for, tooth and nail. Agriculture, not nomadic hunting, was the essential basis of possession.

To the Indian, this idea of *possession* was totally alien. Land didn't *belong* to any person. The right of the tribe to hunt and camp through a huge, comfortable area "belonged" to the tribe strong and numerous and brave enough to hold it against other tribes. The Sioux thought of themselves as the bravest tribe around, and so they had the "right" to drive the Crows out of the Powder River. The Sioux were unable to comprehend that people "owned" ranches or that the United States government "possessed" all their hunting grounds.

On the other hand, the United States couldn't shake off the European idea that the Sioux were either "rebellious subjects" or "national enemies." The only possible way the Indians and the white men could ever live together was for the whites to adopt the Indian way of life, as the trappers often did; or for the Indians to be converted into property owners, as the reservation system has tried to do; or just to turn the whole of the American northwest over to the tribes, and not settle there. Well-meaning whites tried to covert them to "civilization." Ill-meaning ones tried to exterminate them. Neither policy worked. The government vacillated between the two extremes.

It was a while before this inevitable conflict of customs and ideas really became a problem along the Powder. The fur traders had little effect; as often as not, they were converted to the Indian way of life. The trading posts, however, though few and far between, and the army posts that followed them, like Fort Laramie on the North Platte, *did* affect Indian culture. Indians brought furs to the posts and bartered for trinkets, tools, guns, and most fatally, whiskey. The encounter was usually disastrous. The so-called "ration Indians" who hung about the forts waiting for handouts were a sad lot.

Trappers did not really affect the Sioux; they worked in the mountains farther west. The early immigrants went through on the Platte, farther south. The hordes of travelers going by stage from Cheyenne to Deadwood, South Dakota, through the sacred Black Hills, or to Virginia City, Montana, through Sioux hunting grounds on the Powder River are what brought about the final war.

■ The Bozeman Trail

This stage of the Powder River Indian troubles began with the Bozeman Trail. John Bozeman, a trapper contemporary of Bridger, determined in 1863 to lay out a trail along the eastern foothills of the Big Horns. It was to be an easy, if roundabout, way to western Montana and its gold strikes. The trail, which followed somewhat along the present route of Interstates 25 and 90, would cut right through the hitherto secluded Sioux heartland. The Sioux resented this. Jim Bridger, the savvy trapper who knew what would happen, tried to persuade Bozeman to put the route up through the Big Horn Basin and the grounds of the more amenable Crows. Bozeman and his partner, John Jacobs, wouldn't listen. The Sioux, as expected, reacted belligerently. They were already on the warpath, and the road was just the last straw of provocation. The Sand Creek Massacre had been enough.

Fortunately for the reputation of Wyoming, the Sand Creek Massacre of 1864 belongs entirely to Colorado, but its effects were widespread. Probably the most thoroughly unpleasant character in Western history was the Reverend John M. Chivington, colonel of the Colorado volunteer cavalry. In private life, he'd been a Methodist minister before serving active duty in the Civil War. Some renegade Cheyenne and Arapaho bands had been making trouble in northern Colorado, and Chivington was sent with his regiment to chastise them. He took his mission seriously. He exhorted his troops, before starting out, to kill and scalp all Indians, big and little, especially all children (since "nits make lice"). He permitted his men to use torture to obtain confessions.

Unfortunately for everyone concerned, he had false information. He mistook a camp on Sand Creek of (at least temporarily) peaceful Cheyennes and Arapahos for the camp of his "malefactors," and attacked. The Indians were asleep in their teepees. Chivington set on them without warning and killed every man, woman, and child he could find—over a hundred in all. However, a number of Indians did survive and escape, alerting the whole Indian population, and picking up recruits on the way to stir up their allies, the Sioux. They marched from Colorado to the Black Hills, and then around to the winter quarters of the Sioux on the Powder River; 400 miles in December and January with women, children, old folks, and all their stock. Their progress stirred the tribes to the north into a frenzy of revenge. En route, the moving cavalcade killed more whites than Chivington had killed Indians. When they reached the lodges of the Powder River Sioux, the whole Indian confederacy was on the warpath: Sioux, Cheyennes, Arapahos, Oglalas, Brulés—most of them previously friendly Indians. They devastated the whole area of the Oregon Trail through Wyoming, burned stage stations and wagon trains, scalped and massacred anyone they found along their way. (This was part of the force that killed Lieutenant Caspar Collins.) The telegraph lines were cut, and the stage route closed for a hundred miles. For a time, the mail to California had to be sent via Nicaragua by way of the old route. The military, totally surprised, just holed up in their lonely forts.

This was the beginning of the final years of the Indian wars that lasted intermittently from 1864 to 1877. The provocations of Sand Creek and the Bozeman Trail destroyed any possibility of peace. As the Indians were outraged by Sand Creek, so the United States Army was outraged by the slaughter of whites along the Oregon Trail that followed as a direct consequence. General P.S. Connor, a veteran of earlier Indian troubles, was sent in the spring of 1865 to build a strong fort and make a demonstration of army presence on the Powder, in the heart of Sioux country. He was then supposed to move up along the Big Horns and meet up with two other units coming from the north and west. The combined forces were supposed to be five thousand strong, and the Sioux were to be "taught a lesson." However, no one seemed to know exactly what lesson they were to be taught. The war, in fact, just sort of evolved on its own. In Washington, politicians were besieged by voters pressing from two sides. Some voters, mostly Western, were all for exterminating the Indians. Others, mostly Easterners, were for placating, cherishing, and above all converting them to Christianity. Congress spent the years backing and filling, switching from side to side.

In this case, the vacillation took the form of bungling the Connor expedition. Connor got off from Fort Laramie much too late, in midsummer, with only a third of the troops he was supposed to have with him. He got to the Powder and built his fort, as ordered, and then marched farther north to meet the other two forces led by Colonels Cole and Walker. The three never met, Cole and Walker having gotten lost in the Powder River badlands. Connor continued to march up along the Big Horns, attacking a camp of Cheyennes and Arapahoes under Old David and Black Bear on the Tongue River. They captured 1,000 horses and killed 65 Indians, with the loss of eight soldiers, but the main force of the Sioux wasn't touched, and the whole point of Connor's expedition was frustrated. The Sioux learned no lessons, except perhaps the army's incompetence.

Connor was recalled in disgrace. His fort was later moved closer to the river and renamed Fort Reno. Altogether, the first episode of the war was a fiasco. Except for Connor's Tongue River skirmish, no real fighting occurred.

Up to 1865, not one white man had been killed along the Powder. Things certainly changed.

■ 1865

Connor's fort was built, and his skirmish occurred on the Tongue River. A month later, Indians attacked an expedition led by Colonel James Sawyer, and besieged his troops for 13 days in a camp six miles west of Connor's Tongue River assault. Still, there were few casualties, and Sawyer's men were rescued by Connor's cavalry.

■ 1866

After Connor left and his fort was moved, Colonel Carrington relieved Connor's unseasoned volunteer troops at the fort with 700 seasoned regulars, and moved north to build two more forts: Fort Kearny, 40 miles (66 km) north of Fort Reno, and Fort C.F. Smith, in Montana. Fort Kearny was in particular an affront to the Sioux. It was built specifically to protect the hated Bozeman Trail, and was located in country the Sioux regarded as the center of their home grounds. Of all the Wyoming forts, it had the most sanguinary history. Finished on October 31, 1866, Kearny was a strong, well-built affair on a poor site—a low bench in an unprotected valley, not close enough to water, and far from wood. Already ten men had been killed during construction. During the first six months of the fort's existence, 154 more were killed. The Sioux could put up, reluctantly, with troops situated only as far north as Fort Reno, but Fort Kearny was definitely going too far. Particularly ironic was the fact that by this time, travel on the Bozeman Trail was practically nonexistent.

In December of 1866, just after Fort Kearny was finished, and just north of it, occurred the Fetterman Massacre. Three officers and 76 privates under Colonel W.J. Fetterman were killed by Sioux under Red Cloud, the leader of the war against these invaders of Sioux country. Much like Lieutenant Grattan down on the North Platte 20 years before, Fetterman was an eager hothead, chafing for action. He'd been distinguished for his bravery in the Civil War and wanted more of the same kind of glory.

A train carrying wood to the fort started from the Big Horns on the morning of December 21. A cavalry scout alerted the fort that the party had been attacked. A company of 76 men under sensible Captain James Powell was assigned to relieve the wood cutters, but the rash Fetterman pleaded to go instead. Carrington injudiciously gave in, choosing the wrong man. Fetterman was given strict orders not to pursue the Indians for any distance. Fetterman disobeyed that order. Having dispersed the marauders attacking the wagons, he allowed himself to be lured into an ambush. There were some two thousand Indians hidden in wait for the soldiers, and though few had guns, the entire Fetterman party was massacred by hatchets, clubs, arrows, and spears. The only signs of Indian casualties were ten dead Indian ponies and some 50 pools of blood on the ground. Indians always liked to take their dead off the battlefield. The Sioux at the time claimed only ten killed; but later the Cheyennes admitted that 50 or 60 had died. Fetterman and one of his officers shot one another rather than face torture and mutilation. Red Cloud had directed the ambush. His outstanding warrior, Crazy Horse, had done most of the damage.

The fort itself was saved from attack by a blizzard. That night of the 21st, the temperature dropped to 30° F below zero, and the snow drifted so high that Carrington's men shoveled all night so the Indians wouldn't be able to sneak over the high drifts into the fort, which, in fact, they had no intention of trying. Indians preferred fighting in good weather. Carrington called for volunteers to ride down to Fort Laramie for help—some 230 miles (380 km) southeast. A man called John Portugee Phillips volunteered. He was a civilian scout. No one thought it would be possible to get through. In one of the most extraordinary feats in the history of Wyoming, Portugee Phillips, taking Colonel Carrington's own Arabian thoroughbred with a sack of oats and some hardtack biscuits, traveled through the blizzard for three days and two nights till he reached Horseshoe Creek, near the present town of Glendo. He telegraphed Fort Laramie, then rode on. The telegraph message was never delivered. Phillips's hands, knees, and feet were frostbitten. He reached the fort on Christmas Eve. The younger officers were giving a party in their quarters, "Old Bedlam." Phillips staggered into the merriment, told his story, and collapsed. His horse was dying outside. Kearny was relieved and saved. Phillips was rewarded by a purse of $300; but the Sioux, one year later, attacked his ranch, killed his cattle, and ruined him. (Carrington married the widow of one of the three officers killed in the massacre, but like Connor he, too, was relieved in disgrace and sent to Fort Caspar.)

■ 1867-1868

Next summer, Captain Powell, whom Fetterman had replaced before the massacre, had his revenge at the Wagon Box Fight. Fort Kearny was by now better prepared for attack, but Red Cloud renewed his harassment in the spring. Once again there was

(opposite) A Nez Percé encampment along the Yellowstone River. (Photo by William H. Jackson. Courtesy, Horace Albright Museum, Yellowstone National Park)

trouble with a wood detail. This time it was Captain Powell and his men who were chopping wood in the Big Horn foothills, some five miles from the fort. Twelve men under a sergeant's command cut wood, 13 others and a sergeant stood guard. Captain Powell had taken no chances. He made a rough temporary fort by dismounting the boxes from his wood wagons to form a corral, then piling sacks of grain on top. Across openings between the boxes he dragged the wagon carriages. He had plenty of provisions and ammunition. On August 2, Red Cloud, Crazy Horse, and at least 1,500 Sioux warriors struck. They first stampeded the wood party's horses, and chased the woodchoppers out of the timber. Four woodchoppers were killed outright; the rest made it to the makeshift fort. Thirty-two men were inside the fort, including two civilian scouts. The Sioux came roaring down on horseback. Powell held his fire until the Indians were almost at the fort. The soldiers were fighting for the first time with new Springfield-Allin breech-loading rifles, with their deadly continuous fire, and the Indians were forced to retreat. They tried again, this time creeping up through tall grass. Again they were turned back. None of the defenders had even been wounded. The next charge was on foot, in such close-packed ranks that they almost overwhelmed the fort; but again the

charge was broken, and after a last desperate horseback attack, they were finally routed. As they removed their dead and wounded from the field in the dusk, the relief from Fort Kearny arrived. In the end, seven of the defenders died, including the four woodchoppers, and three were wounded. It was a devastating defeat for the Sioux. A force of 1,500 of their best warriors had been routed. Another battle up in Montana—the so-called Hay Field Fight, near Fort Smith on the day before the Wagon Box—had been equally disastrous for the Sioux. Red Cloud's reputation as a warrior was permanently tarnished.

The Sioux retired, licking their wounds—some 180 warriors killed at Wagon Box, and total humiliation. Things quieted down. And then to celebrate this great victory, the government totally changed its mind. The whole Powder River Basin was given back to the Sioux, along with the Black Hills. A deadline was established beyond which no white man was to use the Bozeman Trail, and soldiers were now to be stationed only to enforce the deadline. In a way, Red Cloud had lost the battle but won the war.

In August of 1868, the garrison evacuated Fort Phil Kearny. Red Cloud and his warriors watched them go, then charged down to the fort. The soldiers could see a huge column of black smoke going up when they looked back.

■ Aftermath

This was only the first chapter of the war with the Sioux. Between 1868 and 1874, instead of fighting the Sioux, the government supported them. Red Cloud toured the East Coast as a Chautauqua lecturer. In 1870, he addressed a great multitude at the Cooper Union in New York, making a splendid impression. He was dignified, sincere, and full of common sense. Red Cloud never led his people to war again. He ended up on the Pine Ridge reservation in South Dakota, an unhappy man.

Then, in 1874, Custer was sent with his magnificent expedition to evaluate the Black Hills. There was gold in those hills, and the land suddenly became very valuable indeed. Gold seekers were pouring in willy-nilly, and it was hopeless to keep it sacred to the Sioux. The government had already given the Sioux $6 million between 1868 and 1874 for support. The Sioux were now offered $6 million more by the government for repossession of the Black Hills. Refusing the offer, the Sioux instead demanded six *hundred* million and support for seven generations. Government officials lost their patience; a peace conference at White River, Nebraska, broke up; and the war resumed. The Sioux "wild" bands—those not already on reservations—were peremptorily ordered to surrender and relocate on reservations by January 1, 1876—or else.

None of them paid the slightest attention. On March 1, the army under General Crook (after whom the northeast county of Wyoming is named) marched from the new Fort Fetterman on the North Platte with 1,000 men to enforce the law. Once more, the Sioux were to be taught a lesson. The expedition was not a success. There was a skirmish with Crazy Horse, now leader of the Sioux on Tongue River, where Connor had his small victory in 1865. Then Crook, with his soldiers freezing and his supplies low, marched back to Fort Fetterman.

Sitting Bull—Tatanka Yotanka—succeeded Red Cloud as leader of the Sioux forces. But the center of action by 1876 had moved up to Montana, and it was there that the disastrous final Indian victory at Little Bighorn took place about 40 miles (60 km) north of the Wyoming border.

The ironies were compounded. The army victory at Wagon Box was followed by the total capitulation of the government to the Sioux. The Indian victory at Little Bighorn was followed by a determined war of attrition that permanently defeated the Sioux, and drove them forever off their hunting grounds to the reservations in the Dakotas. However, this last phase of the war was not really a part of Powder River history.

The military sites of the Powder River Basin Indian wars are now preserved as historical monuments. **Fort Kearny** is 17 miles (28 km) north of Buffalo, and has a visitor center and museum. The Fetterman massacre site is marked by a monument a few miles up on the other side of the highway. Twenty-two miles (37 km) above Buffalo, near the small town of Story and old Wyoming State Highway 196, is the site of the Wagon Box Fight. The battlefield where Connor surprised the Cheyenne and Arapaho camp on the Tongue River is 11 miles (18 km) north of Sheridan on U.S. Route 14, where it starts west over the Big Horns.

■ CATTLE

As soon as the curtain fell on the drama of the Indian wars, it rose on that of the cattle boom and later, the Johnson County War.

Without government prohibition and Indian attack, the grasslands of the great basin between the Black Hills, Big Horns, Montana state line, and the North Platte became wide-open for cattlemen. This vacuum was quickly filled, beginning in the 1870s, by cattle driven up from Texas along Wyoming's eastern border. Once they had come up only for summer pasture, but now they came to stay, and in the decade from 1877 to 1887 occurred Wyoming's most spectacular and colorful boom-and-bust extravaganza. All through the area, but particularly along the strip at the base of the Big Horns, from south of Buffalo to north of Sheridan, a feudal cattle barony suddenly came into being, almost overnight, that in its swagger, arrogance, extravagance, and initially wild financial success set a permanent seal on the state in general and the area in particular. This golden age of cattle and the cowboy only lasted a decade, but its effect on the psychology of Wyoming has lasted a century. That bucking horse on the license plate remains a symbol a hundred years later.

The swagger and pride of the horseman is an ancient tradition in European culture, reaching its climax with the knights of the Middle Ages. The mystique was transferred to America by the Spanish conquistadors, blossomed in Texas after the Civil War, and struck Wyoming in full force in the late 1870s. The fact that the Plains Indians had also been the most dashing of horsemen fortified the mystique. The U.S. cavalry that had fought them had its panache too, with its exploits from the Civil War, and the Southern cavalier tradition before that. So, when the cattle culture and the cowboy struck the Powder River, the country was prepared.

Unlike, say, coal mining, where bosses and owners are not likely to work underground, owners of cattle ranches were usually working horsemen themselves. Many of them were old cowhands or soldiers. Others were Britishers with country fox-hunting background, or German hussars.

The semi-feudal setup of the ranch in the firm hierarchy of owner, foremen, and hired hands was democratized by this common bond of the horse and the universal admiration for good horsemanship. This feudal system in itself was anything but rigid.

Rounding up cattle near Cheyenne. (Courtesy, American Heritage Center, University of Wyoming)

Any good hand could become a foreman, or even an owner. Many owners had once been foremen and cowhands. This in any case was the ideal. In real life, of course, many owners were absentee money grubbers, foremen were hard-nosed and dishonest, hands were worthless and lazy. But that's not the legend as it endures right to the present. Like the very different, older mystique of the woodsman-trapper, the cowman-horseman was, and remains, a central symbol of far Western glamour. In this place and this time—Powder River of the 1870s and 1880s—the legend crystallized. Wyoming citizens will never be made to believe the validity of claims from other far Western states. The cowboy was really born on the Powder River, and that is that.

Today, most of Wyoming's economy isn't based on cattle. Except for this one brief period, it probably never really has been. Sheep raising, farming, mining (especially coal), oil, and now tourism have, especially during the twentieth century, competed with cattle for land, political power, and money. But one of the few things you can do with those wide-open spaces is run stock on them. Cattle can't be run without cowhands, and cowhands can't operate without horses. So the cow, the cow horse, and the cowboy still remain central to the economy of the state, if by no means dominant. Those involved in the business have a prestige to which no other group in the state can really aspire.

The towns of Buffalo and Sheridan owe their origins to cattle. In their vicinity cattle ranches sprang up, some of them pretty grandiose in the first, flush days. Even before the Indian wars were over, cattle began arriving from Texas. By 1871, over 40,000 longhorns had invaded the state, and this was just the beginning. The southeast and central areas along the North Platte and the Sweetwater got cattle first. The north, of course, was closed. It belonged officially to the Sioux by the treaty of 1868. Even up in the Big Horn Basin, cattle were being run before the boom began on the Powder.

A special quality of the cattle boom throughout the West, but particularly along the Big Horns, was Anglo-Scottish ownership. Of the 20 big Wyoming cattle companies operating by 1884, half were controlled by Scottish or English owners, with a combined capitalization of over $20 million returning dividends of 10 to 20 percent. In the British Isles, this constituted an investment bonanza, like that of the eighteenth-century South Sea Bubble.

The secret of this bonanza, while it lasted, was the open range. You didn't have to own your feeding grounds. They stretched about the ranch for miles and miles, all tax free. Though some ranches were enormous, ten or twenty thousand acres, the surrounding seas of unowned grass seemed unlimited.

A rather extreme example of this large scale and its seemingly unlimited possibilities was the Powder River Cattle Company of the English Frewen brothers, Moreton and Richard. Their brand was 76. By 1885, they ran 66,000 cattle on the Powder as far north as Conner's Tongue River and as far south as Fall's Teapot Dome. Their operations extended west into the Hole-in-the-Wall, with line camps all along the Middle and South forks of the Powder River. Log-cabin ranch houses resembled royal hunting lodges; one, in fact, was nicknamed Castle Frewen. The brothers threw hunting parties in the fall and house parties in the summer, for which private stages brought the guests in relays up from the nearest railroad station, 250 miles (417 km) to the south. They used the same stages to import hothouse flowers from Denver, so that lady guests could wear corsages for dinner. Only a few years earlier, Indians had camped on the site where the ranch houses were. Not so long before, Portugee Phillips had made his winter ride across the Powder River to Fort Laramie. And the cousins Moncrieffe and Wallop of Sheridan were younger sons of English titles, whose families have survived into modern times in Wyoming.

Most of the great spreads, however, including that of the Frewens, suddenly collapsed in the great blizzard of 1887-88. By then, however, things were already beginning to go wrong. The boom, like all booms, brought overexpansion; the ranges, even the seemingly unbounded ones of the Powder River, began to be overcrowded and overgrazed. Owners tended to be overconfident, lax, and increasingly absentee. They spent perhaps too much time in Cheyenne at the Cheyenne Club drinking "rare wines," playing Boston, and contemplating the famous bullet-ridden copy of Paul Potter's picture of a bull, instead of riding the ranges. (This copy of a famous Dutch painting hung in the Cheyenne Club, where a drunken member had plugged it full of holes.) Foremen got greedy and dishonest, and padded the inventory figures, while surreptitiously subtracting items for themselves.

Then came the terrible winter of 1887-88. The summer of '87 had been abnormally dry, and feed was scarce. Cattle were already thin. The snow began falling heavily in October, and never melted. December was a month of blizzards. In January came a fatal chinook, a warm wind that melted the top layer of snow, which then froze when the temperature dropped again. Cattle could make it through snow, but not a coating of ice. The temperature plummeted to 40-50° F below zero. Cattle drifted into the beleaguered towns to die in the snow-clogged streets. Herds of thousands were reduced to hundreds. By spring, many cattle barons on the Powder were ruined, and the days of the unlimited open range and corsages from Denver were done.

■ JOHNSON COUNTY WAR

The bonanza was over, and the open range increasingly restricted by private or government ownership and control, but cattle was still king along the Powder. However, the last lurid phase of trouble around the Big Horns still centered about cows; a battle between the remaining big cattlemen and a new generation of small cattlemen. This also involved a new breed of bad men, gunmen, and outlaws who became involved in the cattlemen's quarrel. Then there was the intrusion of homesteading farmers (called "grangers") onto the cattle range, and the slow advance of sheep. All these kept things bloodily busy for the next two decades into the twentieth century.

Since the big owners couldn't continue to control the range, especially after so many of them had gone bankrupt, a new breed of cattlemen, usually former cowboys who had amassed small herds of their own (not always beyond suspicion of having borrowed calves from the big herds), began to compete on the market and on the range. Accusations of rustling by the big owners and of coercion by the small owners finally became so pointed that the situation evolved into a real (if somewhat comic-opera) battle usually called the Johnson County, or the TA, War.

In back of the big owners was the absolutist Wyoming Stock Growers' Association (WSGA), based in Cheyenne—and the Cheyenne Club. They precipitated the conflict by a series of high-handed actions, the most suspicious and drastic of which were the unsolved murders of various small ranchers—dry-gulched (i.e., murdered in canyons), shot in ambushes, besieged in their cabins. No one knew who the murderers were. Everyone claimed innocence. But everyone knew it was the big ranchers and their hired gunmen trying to terrorize the small ranchers.

The issue that actually started the war was legalistic. The all-powerful Wyoming Stock Growers' Association had always told the cattlemen of the state when to hold their roundups, and when to drive their cattle to shipping points. This was all a salutary way of preventing confusion, disorder, and unbridled, competitive, cutthroat tactics. The Johnson County cattlemen, however, considered it dictatorship, and founded their own Northern Wyoming Farmers and Stock Growers' Association. They defied the big men and the WSGA, and said they'd hold their roundups whenever they damn well pleased. The state association then instructed shipping inspectors to seize and sell all "blacklisted" stock, and to turn the money over to the association. This had always been a way to control rustlers and those ranchers who let rustlers use them as a respectable facade for selling stolen goods. In this case, the Wyoming association claimed

Enforcer Tom Horn awaits his execution in the Laramie County jail. (Courtesy, American Heritage Center, University of Wyoming)

that the Johnson County ranchers were rustlers or false fronts for rustlers, and some of them probably were. But in the spring of 1892, the small ranchers were going to hold their blacklisted roundup no matter what.

On April 6, a train arrived in the Cheyenne rail yards two days after the annual meeting of the Wyoming Stock Growers' Association. That night, the train pulled out, the blinds of the coach cars were drawn, and all telegraph lines north of Douglas were cut. Hidden on the train was a score of expert Texas gunmen with their horses, saddles, and ammunition, as well as a complete camp outfit and three wagons on freight cars behind. At Cheyenne, an equal number of Wyoming men had joined the group on the train, most of them foremen or owners of big Powder River outfits, including the TA ranch. The total holdings of the ranchers represented was estimated as some 100,000 head of cattle, 5,000 horses, and 86,000 acres of land. The object of this expedition was obviously to break up by force the "illegal" northern association's roundup.

Two young strangers joined the expedition for the fun of it: an Englishman, Henry Wallace, and a Philadelphian, Dr. Charles Penrose. The latter offered to act as surgeon for the party.

The group got off the train at Casper and headed for Buffalo. They never got there. There was supposed to be a list of "rustlers" to be executed en route. Some of these in actual fact *were* rustlers and bad men, notably Nate Champion and his partner, Nick Ray. They had become involved with Johnson County rebels, were looked upon as heroes, and had made themselves thoroughly unpopular with the other side. "The Invaders," as the mysterious group got to be called, first visited a run-down cabin on a ranch named the KC (now memorialized by the town off Interstate 25 named Kaycee). The Invaders laid siege to the cabin, hoping to flush out Champion and Ray. Two innocent trappers were also in the cabin, having just dropped in for the night. They were captured and held prisoner when they went outdoors to wash in the creek.

The two outlaws, Ray and Champion, however, were besieged. Ray, obviously not quite aware of what was going on, went out to fetch water from the well and was wounded. He managed to get back to the cabin, though dying. From dawn to dusk Champion fought a single-handed battle, and most remarkably, kept a diary while doing so. It was found in the cabin afterward. Eventually the Invaders fired the cabin, forced Champion out, and shot him. On his chest they pinned a note saying "Cattle Thieves Beware." This, of course, made Champion not so much a hero as a patron saint and martyr. His death was celebrated in a ballad, the words edited from the entries in the diary, but made to rhyme. The introductory words went as follows:

It was a little blood-stained book which a bullet had torn in twain.
It told the fate of Nick and Nate, which is known to all of you.
He had the nerve to write it down while bullets fell like rain.
At your request I'll do my best to read these lines again.

. . . and at the end:

The light is out, the curtains drawn, the last sad act is played.
You know the fate that met poor Nate and of the run he made.
But now across the Big Divide and at the Home Ranch door
I know he'll meet and warmly greet the boys that went before.

This bit of strong arm justice en route cost the Invaders the success of the entire enterprise. A neighboring rancher had seen the siege from a bluff and rode to Buffalo in a hurry to alert the town. By nightfall, 200 armed Johnson County men were riding down-country to stop the invasion. A bloodbath was in the making.

The Invaders had gotten separated from their supply wagons on the way to the KC. Then they heard the Johnson vigilantes were coming, and galloped to the friendly TA Ranch, 30 miles (50 km) north. They managed to get there in time to fortify it. They were now the besieged ones, instead of Nate.

Meanwhile, the news reached Cheyenne. On orders from the capital, down from Fort McKinney (a new fort several miles west of Buffalo) rode three U.S. cavalry troops, who arrived just as the Buffalo besiegers were about to plant dynamite bombs and end the siege by blowing up the TA. In the end, casualties were light. Besides Nate and Nick, one Texan was killed by the accidental discharge of his own gun, and three others were wounded, two by Nate at the KC. This was the exciting, if almost ludicrous, end to what might have been a very serious affair.

The Invaders surrendered with relief to the soldiers and were taken for trial to Cheyenne—where, naturally, they were very popular. Waiting to be tried, they were housed in jail at night and were free to roam the streets by day. When they were released on bail, the Texans were told to be sure and report back to Wyoming for the trial. They promptly went home and were never heard of again. The case was dismissed in January, with the excuse that Johnson County had refused to pay the cost of prosecution. Wyoming justice, as always, had been served without too much quibbling about rights and wrongs, legality and illegality. The main thing was: nobody was shooting anybody anymore.

As for poor, young Dr. Penrose, he escaped and took refuge in Douglas, a center of rabid small-cattle sentiment. He was about to be lynched as an Invader when the new governor, Amos W. Barber, also a doctor and fellow graduate of the University of Pennsylvania Medical School, sent a marshal to arrest (and rescue) Penrose. Barber sat Penrose on the cowcatcher of a train headed eastward and told him not to get off till he crossed the Nebraska line. Penrose didn't dare come back to Wyoming for twenty years.

■ Bad Men

One of the exasperating complications of this desperate (but also a bit humorous) Johnson County War was that the bad guys were heavily involved on the front lines of both sides. On the Buffalo side were those martyrs Nate and Nick. Not much is known about them, but they were rumored to have been part of the so-called Red Sash Gang in Texas, whose members wore red sashes to dances. Champion was supposed to have been run out of Colorado for rustling, Ray to have killed two men in Texas. Heroes they may have been, but also, no doubt, gunmen and thieves.

Another hero in Buffalo was the unsavory Arapaho Brown. He became a leader in the vigilante attack on the TA, and for awhile, a local idol. He was a huge, bearded, gangling Tennessee hillbilly who settled on a Powder River ranch, where he was rumored to have murdered his partner and the partner's family, and then appropriated the ranch. Eventually, he was murdered by two inexpert young robbers in an extremely bloody fashion. Despite his popularity, he was generally considered a dangerous character.

Things were no better on the big cattlemen's side. Tom Horn was neither bearded nor gangling, and nobody's hero. He was the epitome of the calm, suave, deadly marksman who killed for hire, a successful businessman. Nobody could ever catch him or trace his crimes. He was officially a stock inspector, had served as a scout in the army, and was a champion rodeo roper. He was hired to terrify opponents of the Wyoming Stock Growers' Association. No one ever knew for sure if he had committed the crimes. The secrets went with him to his grave. He was finally caught in such a stupidly awkward fashion that everyone felt there must have been some mistake. He shot a fourteen-year-old boy going out to the ranch corral in place of his father. How could such an old master as Tom be so careless? He made a confession, and his hanging in Cheyenne in 1903 was the sensation of the year. Speculation was, and still is, rife. How could such a canny fellow be caught red-handed doing such a foolish thing? Was his confession genuine? Was he framed by the association because he knew too much? Had he been promised that he'd be rescued at the last minute if he confessed? Perhaps he really was rescued and a dummy was used in his place? Whatever the truth is, Tom Horn remains a dark, legendary figure, half-admired still as he was when alive. He probably did make that one fatal mistake and was really hanged. But his character and looks—cool, collected, canny, mustached, darkly handsome—and even his somewhat sinister name, all remain parts of a memorable legend.

Another of Wyoming's favorite bad men was Butch Cassidy. Butch was everything that Arapaho Brown and Tom Horn weren't: charming, humorous, sort of handsome, too, but in a cocky, easygoing, devil-may-care, Irish way. Like Horn and most such professionals, he practiced his trade all over the West (there's hardly a town in Wyoming that doesn't boast of a visit by Butch), but he was particularly identified with the Powder River and the Black Hills. He had a prosaic real name—George Leroy Parker. Though involved with some tough characters, such as notorious gang leader Harve Logan, Cassidy himself emerged with a Robin Hood reputation.

He was particularly associated with the famous Hole-in-the-Wall gang—or "Wild Bunch," as they liked to call themselves. The **Hole-in-the-Wall** was (and is), as its name indicates, a "hole"— a valley enclosed by hills, like Jackson Hole. This particular one is located southwest of Kaycee in a far corner of Johnson County. Its reputation as a hideout has given people the impression that it must be some deeply secluded canyon, surrounded by cliffs and entered through a secret passage. It is, in fact, entered by a gorge lined by red cliffs. But inside it is a wide, open range, bordered with fairly low hills, except for a long, red cliff to the east. Anything but a mysterious, secret hiding place. The Frewens had a line camp there, and it was they who named it Hole-in-the-Wall, supposedly after a famous old tavern in London. Its reputation as a gang hideout may have been exaggerated, but the gang that adopted its name was certainly famous enough.

Leader Harvey Logan and partner Cassidy emerged into local Wyoming reputation with the Belle Fourche robbery in the Black Hills, in 1897. In addition to Cassidy were Logan's other lieutenants, such as Big Nose George Curry (see pages 178-179), Harry Longabaugh (also known as the Sundance Kid), and numerous others. They operated all over the West and forged liaisons with other famous gangs. They had other hideouts, too, such as one southwest of Baggs on the Colorado border. Some of these men, like

The Wild Bunch: Harry Longabaugh (Sundance Kid), Bill Carver, Ben Kilpatrick, Harvey Logan (Kid Curry), and George Parker (Butch Cassidy). (Courtesy, Buffalo Bill Historical Center, Cody, Wyoming)

Logan, were deadly. Logan is presumed to have killed at least nine men. He was, like Tom Horn, the calm, polite sort.

Butch Cassidy, on the other hand, was genial and generous. Incredibly, he was never known to have killed or even injured anyone on purpose. He was a crack shot, however. He wore his sombrero cocked over his red hair, his blue eyes sparked with mischief and humor. The Robin Hood legend suited him personally, but was earned also by the gang in general. They stole from the rich (banks and trains) and not from the poor (small ranchers), and so they became local idols. Banks and railroads got what they deserved. He was, however, finally caught. He stood trial in Wyoming, but was released on the condition that he would never again operate in the state. Wyoming's gain was Montana's loss. He went right across the border and robbed a bank there to pay for his Wyoming trial, but he was as good as his word, and never practiced in Wyoming again.

The legend is that he and the Sundance Kid were killed in South America, but that legend is contradicted by another theory that he returned to the States and became a respectable burgher in Tacoma on the Pacific Coast. Everyone hoped it was true. All sorts of people claimed they saw him later, alive. They missed Butch. He was fond of practical jokes: once he shot the legs out from under a sleeping (no doubt drunk) man's chair, rung by rung, until at last the chair collapsed (a sound sleeper!). Tom Horn remains a delightfully sinister myth, Cassidy a delightfully amiable one. The presence of these gentlemen in Powder River country made people uncomfortable, but today the state is pretty proud of them.

■ INTRUDERS

Much more disruptive of the cattle kingdom than mere outlaws at the turn of the century was the intrusion on the range of homesteaders ("grangers") and sheep men. The sheep oozed slowly west despite violent, sometimes murderous, opposition by cattlemen, which climaxed in the Big Horn Basin. The grangers were a different problem. Cattlemen claimed that the sheep poisoned the range for cattle and overgrazed it, but at least the range remained range, however contaminated or denuded. Homesteading farmers plowed it up and destroyed it for good. They preempted water, and introduced a whole way of life entirely opposed to that of the "horsemen of the plains" (a bit like the earlier conflict of nomadic Indians and white settlers). In some respects, the presence of the grangers was very salutary. They brought a spirit of neighborly communal life to a countryside where it had not really existed before. Green fields, snug ranches, churches, and schools flourished in places where farming was appropriate and successful. But unfortunately, all the homesteaders on the plains, particularly dry farmers, didn't settle where they should have, such as in potentially rich river valleys. Some settled on dry, high places and broke soil fit only for grazing, which the wind blew away in dust storms. Deserted ruins of farmhouses all over the eastern counties testified to this disaster, particularly by the 1930s. (This was what national grasslands were intended to cure and prevent.)

A certain amount of zoning and control has now made things less disruptive. It is significant that their association was the Northern Wyoming *Farmers* and Stock Growers' Association. New dams and reservoirs, which provide irrigation for farmers somewhere downstream, also mean less rangeland for cattle and sheep; and all those dams have changed the character of Wyoming. This intrusion of the Midwest into the Far West, as represented by eastern border towns like Torrington, does not please those who prefer the latter to the former.

POWDER RIVER BASIN

TWO COUNTY SEATS—BUFFALO (JOHNSON COUNTY) to the south, and Sheridan (Sheridan County) to the north—are the civic centers of the Powder River Basin, the area east of the Big Horn Mountains, including the actual watershed basin of the Powder River. Historically, these two towns represented the two factions of the TA War. The Northern Wyoming Farmers and Stock Growers' Association was based in Buffalo, while Sheridan was dominated by big cattle owners.

■ BUFFALO STORIES

Buffalo is the smaller (about 3,800 people) of the two, and more distinctly a cow town, as it has been from its beginnings in 1879. Though right at the foot of the Big Horns, it's more a plains than a mountain town. From Buffalo south to Casper, the plains dominate all the way, with cattle as far down as Kaycee. This open and desolate stretch is full of stories of grim events, not only the killing of Nate Champion at Kaycee, but earlier tales as well.

Two prospectors stumbled into Fort Reno, southeast of Buffalo, in 1865, claiming that they and their companions had found a fabulously rich gold lode on the south fork of Crazy Woman Creek. They had built a cabin there, extracting seven thousand dollars worth of gold in a week, before Indians attacked and killed all but these two survivors. A new party was thrown together and started back to the site... and were never heard from again. The cabin and mine disappeared for good. Another version of the story has one survivor leading the second party back to the mine when he went crazy. The Lost Cabin story survives in many versions and variations. No one else has ever found gold on Crazy Woman Creek.

In 1861, four misguided missionaries built a log mission near Kaycee, hoping to convert the Crows. They didn't. In the first place, the Crows were no longer there, having been chased up into the Big Horn Basin by the Sioux. One of the missionaries deserted and one was killed. The two survivors gave up and headed east, and the Sioux, thoroughly unconverted, burnt the mission. No traces remain.

Buffalo was the nearest drinking place for the Hole-in-the-Wall gang, and entertained such folk heroes as Butch Cassidy, "Flat-nose" George, and the Sundance Kid.

CONTEMPORARY BUFFALO

Buffalo nowadays remains one of the most distinctive Wyoming towns. It has the immense good fortune of a crooked main street, derived from a crooked ford across a crooked creek in midtown. This was early built up with stalwart brick and stone buildings, many of them hotels, so that the street couldn't be widened and straightened without total disaster. The result is a town center that looks like a town center instead of a collection of wayside tourist traps on a superhighway. It's a town where you can wander up and down the business street with amusement and pleasure, and rest on a memorial platform-bridge with seats that straddles the creek which tumbles through the middle of the city. A Historic Buffalo movement is making an effort to save the town and its picturesqueness.

Buffalo's focal point is a splendid Victorian brick courthouse on a hill right in the center of where the two main streets meet. In back of it is the **Jim Gatchell Historical Society and Museum**, comprising the main brick building with permanent installations, and an old Carnegie Library building with temporary exhibits. Recently, the library displayed wonderful photos of the great cattle roundup on the Powder River of 1884, at the height of the boom, and of the Frewen castle. (Wyoming is almost plastered with such striking old photographs, always characteristic and evocative. Evidently a dull snapshot was impossible until modern times.) The Frewen castle in the photo, however, looks rather seedy. One finds it hard to imagine those corsages; but the castle did have two stories and a shingled roof, astoundingly palatial for the place and times. (Incidentally, a Frewen brother married a sister of Jennie Jerome, Winston Churchill's mother. It's a small world, and some of it centered briefly on the Powder River.)

Strangely enough the name "Buffalo" does not derive, as it should, from the once-local beast, but from faraway Buffalo, New York. Too bad.

All the old hotels are closed, though the buildings and the signs on their facades remain. Motels abound on the outskirts, of course. One of the nicest in the state is the Z Bar, a few blocks west on U.S. Route 16, which has small log cabins and a big green lawn with spruces and a few apple trees, scarce in Wyoming. The local restaurant is Steve's, a big place done up rather Art Deco, very good and elegant. Another splendid motel on the Strip is the Super 8, distinguished by a carousel imported from Ocean City, New Jersey, with bucking horses added by a local sculptor. It revolves to the accompaniment of many turn-of-the-century tunes and present-day squealing kids, and is altogether a rare delight, especially out here. The variety store next door is an enjoyable place to browse.

■ Johnson County Circle Tour

If you want to understand Buffalo in its proper setting as the one and only civic center of Johnson County, and to realize what Johnson County is really like, this mildly adventurous circle tour is strongly advised.

Take Wyoming State Highway 196 south from town on the main street, and almost immediately you are on the range. One of those fine, paved Wyoming highways with nobody else on them, it passes through grasslands and by the gates of big cattle spreads. The Big Horns run right alongside, to the west. Slowly, the country gets wilder and sparser. After 45 miles (75 km), you reach **Kaycee** (KC), famous in song and story, where Nate met his dramatic end. There's not much there now, but it's on a stream that soon becomes the Powder River itself. Even more adventurous trips west to Hole-in-the-Wall country can start from here.

Next, Wyoming State Highway 192 takes off along the Powder River, due east. After about 20 miles (33 km) through more and more naked, rugged country, with the pleasantly cottonwood-dotted Powder to the right, the highway makes a sharp turn south to cross the river. At this point (marked Sussex on the map, though there's not the slightest trace of Sussex), a smaller road turns off to the north. This isn't marked until you get right up to it. It leads, supposedly, in the direction of the site of Fort Reno. Even if you could find the fort site, there is, in fact, nothing there. Beyond, the unnamed road soars north along the course of the Powder, but high above it. After a short distance, another road plainly labeled "Bozeman Trail" turns away inland and to the left; but the road to take proceeds north, to open up an incomparable vista of the rough and rugged Powder River country: precipitous benches over which the road wanders; deep, craggy draws; the river meandering far below, and steep ridges and far-stretching range to the east, across the river. If ever the mystique of Powder River can be made visible, it's along this perfectly feasible but seemingly reckless route. Eventually the road curves westward toward the mountains, and you have yet another of those wonderful plains-and-mountain Wyoming encounters. Suddenly, for no observable reason (perhaps someone bribed the highway department), the road becomes paved. More ranches are visible, horses and cows more frequent. The Big Horns loom larger, and as an anticlimax you run perforce into Interstate 25 and traffic and road signs and Modern Times. But the surrounding landscape remains empty as ever.

■ North of Buffalo

Heading north to Sheridan on Interstate 90, you pass **Lake De Smet**, a big, blue gem set in a frame of treeless, brownish-pink buttes. You can exit from the Interstate and drive up to a Father De Smet memorial, but it's not really worth it. However, the lake is beautiful in its way, and one of the few historically peaceful mementoes in this whole region. Here, the first Catholic missionary in this part of the Rockies, Father Pierre Jean De Smet, discovered the lake, and no doubt preached to the Indians. The lake is a curiosity, and local lore includes various silly stories of water monsters and Indian maidens (always "maidens," never just "girls"); but it is most curious that there should be a natural lake there at all. There's not another for hundreds of miles east and south.

Soon, there's an exit deceptively labeled Piney Creek, and, as an afterthought, **Fort Phil Kearny**. A back road, Highway 193, takes you through pastoral country to a cut-off that leads left to the splendidly scenic site of the fort. It's a small plateau that would certainly seem ideal for a fort, but unfortunately it is ringed by bare heights in most directions behind which Indians could creep up unobserved. No original buildings

Dirt roads reach miles to ranches in the Barnum area.

(opposite) Many roads in the Powder River Basin are built from crushed clinker, a red rock created when coal is burned underground.

stand (the Indians took care of that when the fort was abandoned), only a small, yet informative, historical museum with photos of all those army folk—Fetterman, Carrington, Powell—and their ladies, notably the Mmes. Carrington I and II. All of this gives you vivid impressions of the fort and its inmates.

An even more bushy and wandering country road, also well-marked, leads by ranch gates and through groves to the site of the **Wagon Box Fight.** One is indeed astonished at how far the soldiers had to go to get their wood, and how far from the forested foothills the Wagon Box site itself is. There's a big monument to the three soldiers who died in that great victory, but nothing at all in honor of Powell, to whom all the credit

Johnson County Jim Gatchell Memorial Museum, Buffalo

The country around Buffalo absolutely overflows with history. The "Bloody Bozeman" trail ran nearby, creating countless conflicts between Indians and the invading settlers and soldiers. The infamous Johnson County War was also fought not far away, and the Powder River drainage was a favorite haunt of Butch Cassidy's Hole-in-the-Wall gang.

During the first half of this century, Theodore James Gatchell, a friend of local Indians as well as whites, collected or was given thousands of historic items. Originally displayed in his drug store, they are now the core of a collection that includes more than 10,000 artifacts, making Buffalo's county museum a real treat. It houses dioramas and displays of items found at the Wagon Box Fight, the TA Ranch siege (Johnson County War), and the Fetterman Massacre. You'll find guns, bayonets, bones, old clay pipes, and even jasper arrowpoints taken from a soldier killed by Indians at Fort Fetterman. Most touching is the flattened horn of Bugler Adolph Metzger. His body was the only one the Indians did not mutilate after the massacre; instead they covered him in a buffalo robe out of respect for his valor.

Scattered around one room are some other surprises: a pair of Cheyenne medicine rattles used in the Dance of Victory after Custer's defeat at Little Bighorn, an arrowhead that belonged to Red Cloud, a cartridge belt made by famed mountain man Jim Bridger, and the outlaw Tom Horn's spurs and a bridle, braided while he was awaiting execution in Laramie. Ask the folks at the museum to point out a rifle probably used by the cavalry at Little Bighorn and a shell that was fired from Custer's handgun.

—Don Pitcher

should be given. The famous failures—Caspar Collins, Fetterman, Crook, Custer—are amply honored by things named after them. Not Powell, the only sensible, victorious one of the whole lot! Such are the rewards of virtue.

Another bushy road leads on north to tree-hidden Story, and meets Wyoming State Highway 193 again at Banner. This in turn debauches onto U.S. Route 87, where you turn south to get to the **Fetterman Monument**, which lies east of the road on a high hill, looking down over the scene of the battle. There's not much else. Again, a long way by horseback from Fort Kearny. Turning north again towards Sheridan, you willl soon come to Wyoming State Highway 335, which goes west toward the mountains and the town of **Big Horn.**

Big Horn looks more like an Old West cow town than anything else you're liable to see: two false-front, flourishing bars and a few other assorted old buildings. Along the road to it are beautiful, tucked-away ranches and houses. One extraordinary yet typical specimen of local ranch glory is the nearby **Bradford Brinton Memorial**. The estate looks as though it were flown in from Manchester, Vermont, and dropped intact on Little Goose Creek. It lies in a beautiful, shady grove, but instead of giant elms there

Farmers in Big Horn Basin irrigated cropland in 1920. (Courtesy, Powell Museum)

(right) Sugar beets remain an important crop in the Big Horn Basin; Eddie Abraham and Shawn Schwope work for Abraham Farms near Byron.

(below) Sugar beet farmers in Big Horn Basin, circa 1920. (Courtesy, Powell Museum)

Cowboys on the PK Ranch west of Sheridan move cattle to fresh pasture, a century-old tradition.

are giant cottonwoods, and the stone walls are made of round, river cobblestones. Established by the Moncrieffe family in 1892 during the Johnson County War, the original ranch was bought and enlarged by Brinton in 1923. Its ranch brand is Quarter Circle A. The house is a white, clapboard, neo-colonial mansion, like so many in New England, filled with handsome East Coast furniture, but also many Western touches—pictures, statues, books, and Indian objects. Brinton himself was from neither East nor West, but was a gentleman of means from Chicago. He devoted his life to cattle and collecting. What isn't in the beautiful house overflows into a spacious gallery behind the parking lot, where permanent collections and rotating exhibits of western art are housed. Especially if you've just come from the rough, tough banks of the Powder River and the blood-soaked grounds of Fort Kearny, it's all hard to believe.

Not far from the Quarter Circle A is the ranch of the Wallops, kin of the Moncrieffes, where Queen Elizabeth stayed when she visited. The Moncrieffe and Wallop clans were established here by younger sons of British titled families. One of them, after the death of his elder brothers, found himself heir to the title. He returned back to England to sit in the House of Lords, but refused to give up his Wyoming citizenship until forced to do so by law.

Off Wyoming State Highway 335, west of the Brinton Memorial, is the well-marked Spahn Bed-and-Breakfast Lodge, a stylish log cabin built by the owner. It has spectacular views of the plains below, and a host whose knowledge of the country, both plains and mountains, is encyclopedic.

Up the Red Grade Road west of the Brinton Memorial and Spahn's, you head into the mountains, climbing abruptly from the bare plains to the forested heights of the Big Horn plateau. The road is poorly graded, but you can make it with caution, in low gear. At the top, you emerge onto a broad, smooth forest service road that wanders about the lush mountain scenery of the Big Horns, through open meadows thick with wildflowers and deep woods of fir and pine, past small blue lakes, with striking views southwest to the Big Horns' highest mountains, Cloud Peak and Black Tooth Mountain. With luck, you might also catch sight of moose, elk, and deer. All it takes is grit getting up there.

■ SHERIDAN

When you finally get there, Sheridan seems overwhelmingly urban. In fact, along with Cheyenne, Laramie, and Casper, it's one of the few places that seems a real city in the whole state. Even the larger Rock Springs and Green River don't have the same sense of cosmopolitanism. The entire length of Main Street is lined and occupied by mostly turn-of-the-century, two and three-story buildings, stone or brick, occupied by businesses, and thoroughly "city center." It resembles Cheyenne in this respect, but is more extensive and well-preserved. Though the usual commercial strip extends out towards Interstate 90, eastward, no one can doubt where life goes on—such a totally different effect from Gillette, where all the action takes place out in Pizza Hut land, near the Interstate.

Though the cattle business still dominates the town in fact and in spirit—weekly local ranch rodeos in the summer and annual public cattle drives in early July are part of the area's activities—other industries add to the economy. Coal has long been important here. There used to be mines to the south along the mountains, and some mines still exist to the east; but no one has ever thought of Sheridan as a coal town like Gillette. Coal brought an Old World mining population to town, and ethnic celebrations have become customary. Descendants of miners with Polish or Middle European names have become leading citizens. Oil is a presence, too. That, however, doesn't determine Sheridan's character in the way that its old cattle history does.

Oil derricks crowd the slopes of Wells Spring Valley in 1903. (Courtesy, Thermopolis Museum)

As Buffalo represents post-boom cattle, Sheridan represents boom-time cattle. It still retains some of the aroma of the great days before the blizzard. The low altitude (3,725 feet, or 1,135 meters), and water from the mountains permit flowers and fruit trees that would perish farther south to flourish here. The first polo field in the nation remained for years as a legacy of the Scottish-English influx. The preserved Brinton and Kendrick mansions are other mementos of Sheridan's traditional high life. The Burlington railroad built a spur up to Sheridan, where, in the spirit of the Adirondacks, it owned and managed the grand old Sheridan Inn, with gambrel roof, dormer windows, and a big summer piazza. Dozens of famous people stayed there, from Colonel Cody on, but there have been difficulties with the present management. Down in Buffalo, all this kind of thing is considered pretty effete and dudish.

It is appropriate that the dude ranch, that curious blend of the extremely Western and extremely Eastern, had its origins here in Sheridan, with Eaton's and the Horton's HF Bar still flourishing as the two oldest and most famous of their kind. There are dude ranches now all over the West, but Wyoming is still the center of proper dude ranches at their best and most indigenous.

Sheridan itself is the creation of one enterprising man, J.D. Loucks. The first settlement was a log house on Little Goose Creek, with a big corral in back reputed to be the hideout of "Big-Nose" George Curry, later reputedly killed and skinned in Rawlins (some say this occurred in Castle Gate, Utah). Bad men surely did get about the country. A trapper, Jim Mason, built the first house of record in 1878, which was converted into a store and post office named Mandel by a later owner. It was bought by Loucks in 1882. He laid out a town plat on brown wrapping paper and sent this informal plan to Cheyenne with a three-dollar registration fee. On May 10 of the same year, the town was staked on a 40-acre plot and named after Loucks's commander in the Civil War, General Philip H. Sheridan.

Lots sold for $2.50, which compares unfavorably to the $250 and more paid for lots in railroad boom towns. The town was incorporated in 1883, and Loucks, the only begetter, was, of course, mayor. He recorded only one person arrested there in the first two years of the town's existence. Nobody shot? What a contrast to centers farther south! By the end of 1883, there were 50 buildings, and soon, two rival newspapers, the *Sheridan Post* and the *Enterprise.*

Even before Sheridan began, however, it had its famous characters. Martha Canary, better known as Calamity Jane, got her nickname on Goose Creek before Sheridan was conceived. She was already a well-known scout by then, and as such was out with

The historic Sheridan Inn, the "House of 69 Gables," was completed in 1893.

troops sent to quell an Indian uprising in the region. Her commanding officer, a Captain Egan, was shot. Calamity (still just Martha) rescued him, and when they got back to the fort he recovered and said to her, "I name you Calamity Jane, the heroine of the plains." That's the account found in her memoirs, at any rate. She didn't settle in Sheridan, but went on to become one of the West's more picturesque figures, particularly in Deadwood during the gold rush, but her first reputation was made in Wyoming.

The *real* history of Sheridan began with that flamboyant cattle boom of the 1880s. The influx and influence of the early cattle barons put a permanent stamp of high-living on the town. Along with the Bradford Brinton Memorial, the other principal sight in the area is the Kendrick house, **Trail End**, which is also on public display. Unlike the Brinton ranch, Trail End is definitely a town house, located up the hill on Clarendon Street, west of Main, in the center of the city. John B. Kendrick, immortalized by a plaque in the Cheyenne capitol, retired here after he had made his pile in cattle. He drove cattle up from Texas in the late 1870s, and became not only one of the state's great cattlemen, but a governor and U.S. senator. Trail End was finished in 1913, and is very different architecturally from the Quarter Circle A. It has borrowed not from Vermont, but Tuxedo Park, New York—dark woodwork, heavily handsome turn-of-the-century furniture and decor in a baronial style. The Flemish exterior is surrounded by a green garden area in which is preserved the first cabin built on the site of Sheridan in 1878.

Once the **Mandel Post Office**, the cabin was reconstructed in 1976 by the Colonial Dames of Wyoming, active in Sheridan, and preserves what's left of materials bought for $50 by Founder Loucks in 1882. It was moved in 1883 to the corner of Main and Loucks streets, and incorporated in a large building which became the city's first bank in 1885. The old cabin was shoved to the back of the lot and covered with clapboards and plaster—and so got preserved. The swift changes from, say, 1880 to 1910, a mere 30 years, are admirably illustrated by these two neighboring buildings, a cabin and a mansion.

On the way down from the hill, Lewis and Dow streets curve around Goose Creek (concrete-lined to protect the city from floods) and pass by a **monument to General George Crook**, after whom Wyoming's northeastern county is named. Crook tried to substitute mules for horses here in Sheridan before starting north for his ill-fated encounter with Crazy Horse and Sitting Bull on the Rosebud in Montana. The mules were unbroken, and the cavalrymen riding them were expected to break their own mounts on the spot. The result was a riot of bucking mules that is still remembered in local history with pleasure. The monument says nothing about this, of course.

BIG NOSE GEORGE CURRY

Big Nose George

Wyoming's most famous badman may have been George Leroy Parker, better known as Butch Cassidy, leader of the Hole-in-the-Wall gang. But the most notorious and most elusive outlaw in his time was Big Nose George Curry. Historians disagree about Big Nose's career, how he met his Maker, and what happened to him after he died.

Even his name is slippery. Some say Big Nose George Curry, Flat Nose George Parrott, and Long Nose George Manuse were one and the same nose, er, outlaw.

Carl Sifakis writes in his *Encyclopedia of Crime* that Curry lived from 1841 to 1882. A prolific stagecoach and train robber, Big Nose also was the biggest cattle rustler of the 1870s in Wyoming's Powder River region. By all accounts, Curry was a braggart, drunkard, womanizer, and friend-betrayer. A ballad penned by Jean Osborne describes him thus: "This George, he robbed the UP train / And doubled-crossed his pals / Then freely spent his stolen loot /A-boozin' with the gals."

Depending on whom you consult, Curry was either hanged, hanged twice, shot, or some combination thereof. Sifakis writes that the outlaw was apprehended for the 1880 holdup of a Union Pacific train and murder of two deputy sheriffs, and sentenced to hang on April 3, 1882, in Rawlins. He broke out of jail but was immediately captured by a mob that resolved to hang him on the spot. Big Nose was "ordered to climb a ladder set against a lamp post, put a rope around his own neck and jump," writes Sifakis. "Big Nose did, but the rope broke. While some of the mob said another rope should be secured, others felt it wasn't worth the effort and shot Big Nose to death as he lay on the ground." An account of Big Nose's demise, given by Jay Robert Nash in *Bloodletters and Badmen*, is quite different. "After participating in several bank and train robberies in the Southwest following the turn of the century, George Curry rode back to the Hole-in-the-Wall and began

pen-and-ink drawing by Harold S. Robins

rustling cattle. He was caught red-handed while changing a brand by the sheriff of Vernal, Utah." Curry leaped on his horse and galloped off. The sheriff gave chase for 10 miles, shots were exchanged, until finally "a lucky shot hit Curry in the skull and he dropped from the saddle—dead."

Casper Star-Tribune reporter Bill Bragg, though, believes Big Nose botched a train job near Medicine Bow, after which he and his gang were trailed by a couple of lawmen near Elk Mountain.

"Both lawmen were killed and Big Nose fled to Montana," Bragg writes. "One of the members of the gang was caught and a mad mob took him from the law at Carbon and lynched him. . . . Later Big Nose was captured, and when he passed through Carbon, the same gang waylaid Carbon County Sheriff Rankin, and tried to lynch Big Nose too. But, even though they used the same telegraph pole, they didn't get the job done, and relented. So, Big Nose got to go to Rawlins where he was jailed." A mob seized Big Nose from the jail and tried to lynch him, but they too failed. Finally, they succeeded on March 22, 1881. One eyewitness allegedly reported "how [Curry's] boots made such an eerie sound at night scraping the bridge as he swung in the wind."

Dead at last, Big Nose's "life" took a bizarre turn. Dr. John E. Osborne (who would later serve as governor and senator of Wyoming) performed the autopsy. For reasons best known to himself, the good doctor sawed off the top half of Curry's skull and presented it to his assistant, Dr. Lillian Heath, who used it for many years as a doorstop. He then stripped the hide from Curry's chest, tanned it, and stitched either a pair of slippers and a tobacco pouch, or a covering for his favorite pair of shoes, and his medicine bag. He pickled the rest in a whiskey barrel.

Both Curry's death mask and a Union Pacific photo of him reveal that his nose was larger than average. Writes Bennett R. Pearce, in *The West*, "The *Cheyenne Daily Leader* reported that the body was buried in a pauper's grave. One local wit related the tale many years later in his old age. He reported that Curry's nose was so large that the undertaker had some difficulty in nailing the coffin lid down."

To the south lies Alger Street and the **Public Library**, surely one of the most beautiful modern buildings in the state, designed by Adrian Malone. The library contains a striking collection of paintings by Gollings, Wyoming's most important artist, who ended his rather wandering career as a permanent resident of Sheridan. Along with the Heritage Center in Laramie, Sheridan is the best place to see his work.

On Main Street itself, **King's Saddle and Rope Emporium** should not be missed. It's the greatest traditional center for cowboy gear in Wyoming. Not only does it sell saddles, clothes, sombreros, hackamores, and other Western paraphernalia, but behind the store, across the alley and through a black door, an annex houses a fine selection of ropes and riatas, as well as a famous collection of saddles. For anybody interested in Western lore, it's at once enticing and nostalgic. In this archetypical all-cowboy emporium, there's a big, framed photo of Queen Elizabeth, commemorating her presence in Sheridan. She rested in the happy aroma of horses out in Big Horn, and of course she visited King's.

Nearby, at 151 Main Street, is the famous **Mint Bar**, a hangout for local citizenry, with cattle brands and Charlie Belden photographs on the walls. In contrast is a handsome red building at 122 Main, formerly the Bank of Commerce, but now occupied by **The Book Shop**, center of the town's literary life, featuring lectures and poetry readings. Next door is the Spotted Horse Restaurant, run by the daughter of the local architect, Adrian Malone, and a center for sophisticated cooking. Altogether, Main Street is a parade of such old business buildings adapted to modern usage—antique by Wyoming standards and described and dated minutely in a pamphlet, *Sheridan Main Street District Walking Tour*, available at The Book Shop. This whole exhibit of so-called plains-style architecture, still well-preserved above the first-floor modern shop windows, has been enrolled in toto on the Register of Historic Places, as of 1982—one of the few streets so favored.

This only scratches the surface of Sheridan's odd blend of cows and culture, Old West and new sophistication. The town's startlingly un-bloody history is rare for Wyoming.

■ Return Routes over the Big Horns

Our circuitous tour of the Big Horn Mountains, which first crossed west to east over Powder River Pass, now turns west again, this time over the north end of the mountains.

From Sheridan, Interstate 90 takes you briskly for some 15 miles (25 km) to Ranchester and U.S. Route 14. It is possible to detour around this bit by finding and taking Wyoming State Highway 331 west out of Sheridan, then curving around by gravel roads north and west past the entrance to Wolf, the private post office of the Eaton Ranch. It's a beautiful trip across the golden, open foothills, but the chances of going astray are significant.

There's no problem finding your way to **Ranchester** on the Interstate, however. Ranchester is an old ranching center, another example of the Anglo-Western mixture of the area. Even its name combines *ranch* with *chester*, the latter a common ending for many town names all over the British Isles, and derived from the Latin word *castra*, meaning *camp*.

From Ranchester, U.S. Route 14 heads west through **Dayton**, an unspoiled ranching town, before beginning the breathtaking ascent up that abrupt eastern flank of the Big Horn Mountains. The road up to the plateau is broad but constantly curving, climbing some 20 miles (32 km) through forest and meadow, past lakes and streams, campsites and fishing spots, to **Burgess Junction**, in the middle of wide, open, mountain meadows.

Here you have a choice of routes west to the Big Horn Basin and Cody. It's a difficult choice: **Alternate Route 14** takes off almost directly west through increasingly high, open country along the edge of timberline. Just before the highway begins its vertiginous descent, a small, marked road leads north to the **Medicine Wheel**, one of Wyoming's most excitingly mysterious archaeological sites. **Regular Route14**, on the other hand, turns almost due south through Granite Pass (8,950 feet, or 2,730 m), and west through Shell Canyon with its dramatic falls and gorge.

Which way to Cody? Alternate 14 is uplifting as long as it stays high on the plateau. The great zigzag descent straight down into the Big Horn Basin, with all the valley spread out below, can only be described as an awesome automotive experience; but once you're down, the road becomes a chore. It goes through a tiresome, urbanized stretch for 47 miles (78 km), via Lovell and Powell. **Powell** is the center of famous paleontological digs, home of many remarkable fossils. **Lovell** has been recently rocked by a nationally publicized scandal involving the town's favorite doctor. However, this alone does not make the towns fun to drive through.

Regular Route 14, on the other hand, once it emerges from the curious wonders of Shell Canyon, heads due west to Cody, interrupted only by pleasant Greybull. The central stretch of this road, especially from Greybull west, also is nothing to write home

about, but at least it's a fine, absolutely straight road that gets you there. This route would be the obvious choice, except for one crucial fact: nobody who's this close should fail to visit the Medicine Wheel.

The best solution, if time and energy permit, is simply to drive up beautiful Alternate Route 14 to the Medicine Wheel, and then drive back to Burgess Junction, about an hour's detour all told, and certainly worth it. No use trying if there's still snow on the ground in June or September, or even early July. You see snowbanks not far above on the hillside even in August.

The Medicine Wheel

The Medicine Wheel is a prehistoric construction dating back 1,000 to 10,000 years—part of the same horseless culture that produced the petroglyphs of Medicine Lodge. From the rock-pile hub in the center of a big circle formed by stones, 28 spokes radiate outward to the circumference, like the spokes of a wagon wheel. The hub and spokes were apparently used to calculate astronomical phenomena, such as the sunrise of the summer solstice and various star-paths. Its significance was religious (astrological), rather on the order of the English Stonehenge. Though this is the most famous and accessible of such constructions, it is by no means unique. Other wheels are scattered about the West, always on such bare heights. But the knowledge of who built them, and exactly what purpose they served, has been lost in time.

Strips of cloth left in Indian ceremonies add to the mystique of the Medicine Wheel archaeological site.

The Medicine Wheel is surrounded by an odd, outwardly flanged, wire fence, on which Indians have tied "flags" or fetishes. Though the Wheel has no connection with the Plains Indians of his-

(opposite) Devil Canyon in Bighorn Canyon National Recreation Area is a popular spot for local boaters.

toric times, they have adopted this as a sacred place—with good reason, for it does indeed have that aura. A thoroughly inaccurate and cursory forest service sign tells you nothing essential about the Wheel. What's really needed is an observation platform from which you can look down on the construction to see its convolutions, with some pertinent descriptions of the design. Meanwhile, the whole setting and remarkable survival of this prehistoric site, like the descent to the valley below, is awesome.

■ West to Cody

Back east, from Burgess Junction, the descent from the Big Horn plateau via U.S. Route 14 is at first rather tame—nice forest, meadow, and mountain scenery. But suddenly, the whole aspect changes. Everything becomes semidesert, bare yellow and red crags tower overhead, and the previously mild Shell Creek suddenly crashes down in a splendid waterfall through frighteningly narrow, deep, rocky **Shell Canyon.** A fine, new visitor center alongside the road lets you see all these things and tells you more than you probably want to know about the geology, flora, and fauna of the place. (Restrooms, but no food.)

From here on the road descends precipitously from the top to the bottom of the canyon, so you now look *up*, not *down*, at the brightly colored cliff walls. At last, the road emerges into the Big Horn Basin, with red monuments roundabout, notably a striking, deep, scarlet plinth to the south that looks like a cathedral tower. The tiny town of **Shell** is a pleasant place with cabins and gardens.

As you go westward, things gradually get drearier. That mangy, barren, gray-dirt, central basin rangeland obtrudes, and soon you cross the mighty Big Horn River itself and into neat **Greybull**, an up-and-coming city of about 2,000 people, with oil refineries, brisk stores, neat gardens around the houses, and a nice, small museum full of fossils—ammonites—whorled ancestors, huge or tiny, of the modern squid. Across the street is a nice K Bar Motel, and a block east, toward the new bridge over the Big Horn, is Lisa's, a stylish, even exotic, new restaurant.

After winding through town, the highway heads straight west for 54 miles (90 km) to Cody. For the first 20 miles, it's flat, irrigated farmland with no mountain views. Speed ahead and hope not to be arrested. (Wyoming persists in the 55-mph speed limit, though the highway department seems determined to make you exceed it.) After a non-place called Emblem, the farmland suddenly stops. Now it's perfectly flat sagebrush range. But very gradually hills begin to close about, and the Absarokas loom more and more majestically. You cross the border into Park County, and sure enough everything becomes beautiful. Once again there's that characteristic Wyoming experience of vast plains heading for vast mountains. The oddly characteristic ram's horn peak of Heart Mountain is silhouetted to the northwest, and before you know it you're in Cody.

The dogs dug down through five inches of new snow until they reached dirt and lay in their cone-beds with their backs to the wind. McKay brought the horses in and saddled one of them. He had decided to open the pasture gates to let in the cattle, who cannot paw through snow to eat, drift in. "Open gates, cut wire, do whatever you have to during a blizzard or the cattle will walk into a draw and suffocate there," his father had always warned him.

As he rode, Heart Mountain disappeared from sight. The cloud that took it did so quickly, like a hunger, McKay thought. Now the peak broke the skin of the cloud. Nothing about it resembled a heart. It was, instead, a broken horn or a Cubist breast, as McKay's mother had once remarked. Behind it the Beartooth Mountains veered north. Forty million years ago Heart Mountain broke off from the Rockies and skidded twenty-five miles on a detachment fault to its present site. There was no other limestone in the area like it and at its base was one of the most fertile hayfields on the ranch.

As McKay rode under the limestone tusk he looked up. A half moon hooked its side. So that's how love works, he thought and chuckled out loud. He reduced his mother's geology lesson to a list of words: detachment, skidding, breast, horn, heart. As he said the words a bank of snow clouds took over every mountain west of the ranch and McKay kicked his horse into a lope. When he reached the first gate, the cattle were already waiting.

—Gretel Ehrlich, *Wyoming Stories*, 1986

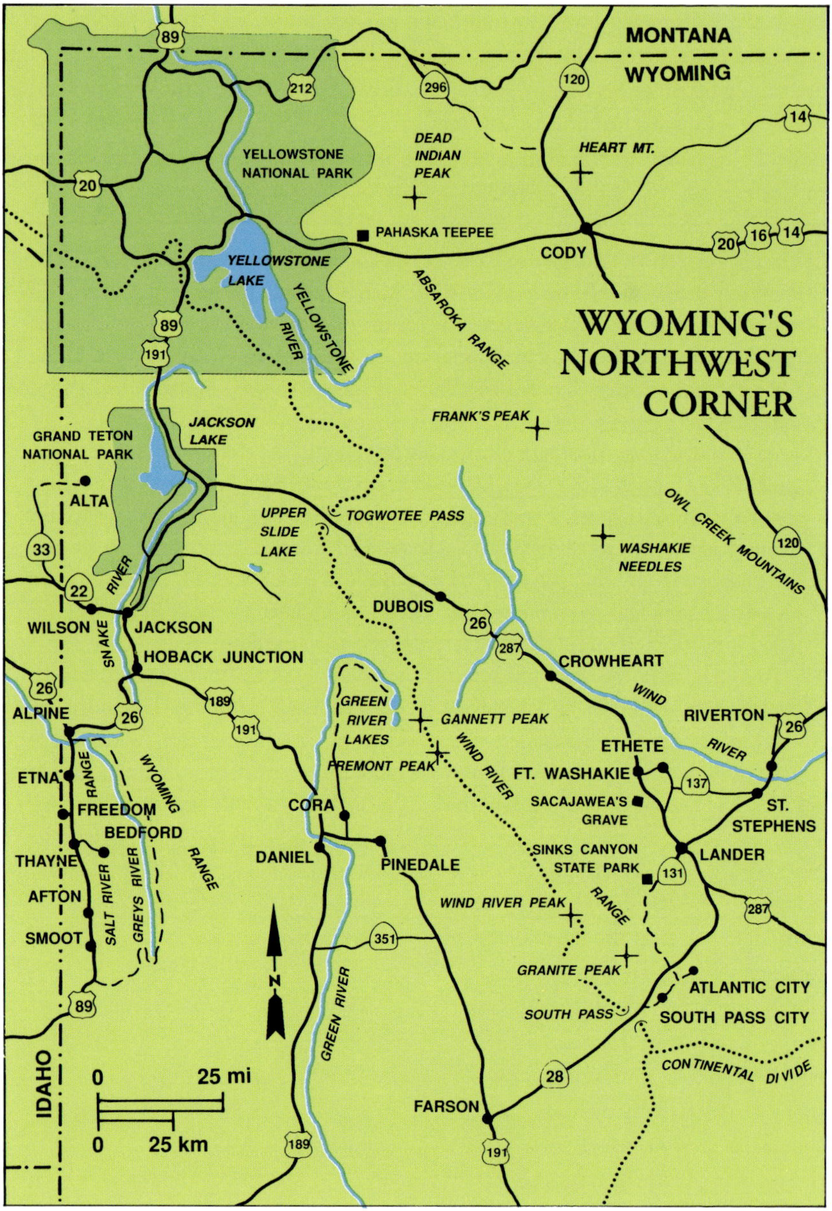
WYOMING'S NORTHWEST CORNER
MONTANA
WYOMING
IDAHO
YELLOWSTONE NATIONAL PARK
YELLOWSTONE LAKE
YELLOWSTONE RIVER
DEAD INDIAN PEAK
HEART MT.
PAHASKA TEEPEE
CODY
ABSAROKA RANGE
FRANK'S PEAK
JACKSON LAKE
GRAND TETON NATIONAL PARK
ALTA
UPPER SLIDE LAKE
TOGWOTEE PASS
OWL CREEK MOUNTAINS
WASHAKIE NEEDLES
SNAKE RIVER
WILSON
JACKSON
DUBOIS
HOBACK JUNCTION
CROWHEART
WIND RIVER
ALPINE
GREEN RIVER LAKES
GANNETT PEAK
WIND RIVER
RIVERTON
ETHETE
FREMONT PEAK
FT. WASHAKIE
ETNA
RANGE
WYOMING
FREEDOM
BEDFORD
RANGE
CORA
SACAJAWEA'S GRAVE
ST. STEPHENS
THAYNE
DANIEL
PINEDALE
SINKS CANYON STATE PARK
LANDER
AFTON
SALT RIVER
GREYS RIVER
WIND RIVER PEAK
RANGE
SMOOT
N
GRANITE PEAK
ATLANTIC CITY
SOUTH PASS
SOUTH PASS CITY
GREEN RIVER
CONTINENTAL DIVIDE
0
25 mi
0
25 km
FARSON
89
212
296
120
14
20
16
14
20
89
191
33
22
26
287
26
189
191
26
137
131
287
351
89
28
189
191

A B S A R O K A S

ONCE YOU CROSS INTO PARK COUNTY, you are in the part of Wyoming that's the true goal of all the state's tourists, as it has been almost since the state was created a century ago. This northwest corner, including Park County and the Absaroka Range, Yellowstone park, and Jackson Hole, attracts far more visitors than any other part of Wyoming, and for many it is the only reason for coming to Wyoming at all. The cheap, smart-aleck crack "Wyoming is just Yellowstone and Grand Teton and Rock Springs in the rearview mirror" sums up the more ignorant touristic attitudes. Yet this region is at the same time generally the most removed and wildest section of the state. Though the competition is pretty severe, perhaps no other Far Western state has such a solid concentration of world-famous spectacles.

From the Montana line down to the south tip of the Wind Rivers at South Pass, from the northwest corner of Yellowstone down through Jackson Hole and Swan Valley, this slice of the state is so different from Wyoming as a whole that it seems a separate province, of which most is totally uninhabited. Cody, Lander, Riverton, and fast-growing Jackson are the only towns of even modest size or significance. Central to the complex is Yellowstone Park, which alone would make the region famous. There's nothing in the whole world quite like Yellowstone; and all around lies some of the most beautiful mountain wilderness in America.

■ THE ABSAROKAS

With a population of about 6,700, Cody is the largest and oldest of Yellowstone's gateway towns. East of Cody sprawls the Big Horn Basin, with the Big Horn Mountains looming distant on the horizon. West of Cody stretches one of the country's most formidable mountain barriers, the **Absaroka Range**. It's not a single, serrated wall, like the Tetons or the Wind Rivers, but rather a mixed-up mass of wilderness, all part of the Shoshone and Bridger-Teton national forests, occupied principally by bear, moose, elk, deer, and a few mountain sheep. This barrier of almost random peaks can be explored and seen only by horse or on foot in summer, and in winter on skis or snowshoes (and in some places, snowmobile—though that's as much a violation of true wilderness as a bicycle or motorcycle would be).

The Absarokas contain an incredible variety of scenery and many hidden summits over 11,000 feet. Toward the north are Pilot Peak (11,708 feet/3,569 m), Black Mountain (11,562 feet/3,524 m), Dead Indian (12,213 feet/3,723 m), Trout (12,294 feet/3,747 m) peaks, and Sunlight Peak (11,922 feet/3,634 m), which overhangs beautiful, hidden Sunlight Basin and its choice dude ranches. To the south are Ptarmigan (12,250/3,734 m), Fortress (12,075/3,681 m), Pinnacle (11,485/3,501 m) and Needle (12,130/3,697 m) mountains, the Red Tops (12,202/3,719 m), Wiggins Peak (12,160/3,706 m), and highest of all, Frank's Peak (13,140/4,005 m), named after Otto Franc of the Pitchfork, but misspelled. Dominating the Wind River Basin are the Washakie Needles (12,495/3,809 m), north of Washakie's own Wind River Indian Reservation. There are many, many more, some of which can be seen from roads; most can't. They form a random, rugged, and wide barricade for a hundred miles (160 km) from Montana down to the Wind River—beyond which rise the even more spectacular Wind River Mountains. Some of this great mountain area is protected by national parks and wilderness areas. The rest of it is at once protected, and nowadays only too often (according to environmentalists) exploited, by the forest service. All of it is beautiful.

■ CODY

The Far West is full of "gateways," and one of the most famous and popular of these is Cody, "East Gateway to Yellowstone." There are rival gateways north, west, and south; but there's more to Cody than just a gateway. As the name obviously indicates, it is a memorial to the man who remains probably the most famous citizen of Wyoming—Colonel William F. Cody, or "Buffalo Bill." Although not the real founder of the town, and though he lived and worked all over the world during his active career, there can be no doubt of his total identification with his name-place. Scout and showman, buffalo slayer and friend of royalty, his stamp on the town is evident everywhere.

Cody was actually started in 1895 by a group of entrepreneurs near the De Maris Springs, a thermal display first described by John Colter in 1807, which has gradually lost its steam over the years. A company was organized to promote the town, and the organizers thought it might be a good idea to ask Cody, a friend, if he'd like to be president. He was traveling with his Wild West Show at the time and was the best advertised man in the West. Cody accepted and suggested that they name their new town after him. They agreed gladly, one reportedly said, "since this did no harm to us and highly pleased the Colonel." They moved the town up the Shoshone River and convinced the Burlington railroad to lay tracks to the town. When Park County was created in 1909, Cody became its seat. The first cabin there was built by a former Wyoming governor, Frank L. Houx, and well-known people have been flocking to Cody ever since. The first church was started with money raised at a poker game. The Colonel (so one story goes) sat in and won. The church's denomination was to be decided by the winner, and Cody said he guessed he was probably an Episcopalian since his folks had originally come from Virginia (though he was born in Iowa). So Episcopalian the church became.

From its beginnings, the town of Cody capitalized on its Western character, as did Cody himself. It has always been a tourist center. Being on the way to Yellowstone helped, as did the colonel's worldwide reputation. One of the town's principal monuments is the **Irma Hotel**, built by Cody and named for his daughter. It was decorated with Remingtons and catered to everyone of importance on their way through town. It has lost its Remingtons, but the great cherrywood bar still dominates the sumptuous dining room, still very active. Along with the Plains in Cheyenne, it's a souvenir of the days of Wyoming's great hostelries.

Buffalo Bill Cody with his family in front of the Irma Hotel in 1912. (Courtesy, Buffalo Bill Historical Center, Cody, Wyoming)

Nowadays, the principal attraction in town is a complex of museums under the umbrella of the **Buffalo Bill Historical Center**, which contains four separate exhibition halls. The center, which dominates the town at the western end of its main street, is now housed in a magnificent stone building with great, high-pitched roofs. The four very different, but equally fascinating, collections are housed in separate pavilions.

The most famous of the collections is the **Whitney Gallery of Western Art**, one of the most prestigious collections of its kind in the country. It was established by Gertrude Vanderbilt Whitney, whose Whitney Museum in New York did so much to foster the American realism movement that dominated the 1920s and 1930s. Like her New York museum, this one also fosters native Americana, specifically painting and sculpture associated with the Far West. The collection begins with earlier explorer artists, like Catlin and Miller, and the landscapists Bierstadt and Whittredge. It culminates in the later Remington and Russell, of which the museum has wonderfully representative selections. The art in the collection up through these masters is magnificent. Chronologically, under the influence perhaps of later patrons without Mrs.

Buffalo Bill's exploits inspired hundreds of pulp novels. (Courtesy, Buffalo Bill Historical Center, Cody, Wyoming)

An 1875 poster romanticizes Buffalo Bill's adventure-filled life. (Courtesy, Buffalo Bill Historical Center, Cody, Wyoming)

BUFFALO BILL CODY

For many people today, the name "Buffalo Bill" brings to mind a man who helped slaughter the vast herds of wild bison. But Col. William F. Cody cannot be so easily pigeonholed, for here was one of the most remarkable men of his or any other era, a man who almost single-handedly established the aura of the wild West. More than 800 books—many of them the dime-store novels that thrilled generations of young boys—have been written about Cody. In many, the truth was stretched far beyond any semblance of reality, but the real life of William Cody contains so many adventures and plot twists that it seems hard to believe one person could have done so much.

Born to an Iowa farm family in 1846, William Cody started life like many others of his era. His parents moved to Kansas when he was six, but soon his abolitionist father, Isaac Cody, became embroiled in arguments with the many slaveholders who were intent upon making Kansas a slave state, even if it meant killing those who disagreed. While defending his views at a public meeting, Isaac Cody was stabbed in the back and had to flee for his life. When a mob learned of his father's whereabouts, the eight-year-old Will Cody rode on his first adventure through enemy lines, galloping 35 miles (21 km) to warn of the impending attack.

Buffalo Bill poses in 1886 with eight Pawnee and Sioux chiefs. (Courtesy, Buffalo Bill Historical Center, Cody, Wyoming)

(opposite) Buffalo Bill in 1872. (Courtesy, Buffalo Bill Historical Center, Cody, Wyoming)

That winter, with his father ill, Will supplied food for the family by hunting birds and rabbits. Three years later, when Isaac Cody died of complications from the stabbing, the 11-year-old Will Cody became the family's breadwinner. There were four other children to feed. Will quickly joined the company of Alexander Majors, running dispatches between army supply wagons, with his $40 monthly wages going to his mother.

On his first long wagon trek west, the army supply wagons were attacked by Mormon zealots who took all the weapons and horses, forcing Cody to walk much of the 1,000 miles back to his Kansas home. It was apparently on this walk that Cody met Wild Bill Hickok, perhaps the best gunfighter ever. On one of these excursions, the impressionable young Will stopped in at Wyoming's Fort Laramie where he sat in awe as famed scouts Jim Bridger and Kit Carson reminisced. The experience was a turning point in Cody's life; he resolved to become a scout one day.

Cody's next job as a rider for the new Pony Express offered excellent training. At just 15 years of age he already was one of the finest horseback riders in the West, and a crack shot with a rifle. Cody's base was the Horseshoe Station, 36 miles (57 km) west of Fort Laramie. On one ride, he discovered that the man who was to take the next leg had been killed in a drunken brawl the previous night, and that he would have to continue on to Red Buttes, 85 miles (137 km) farther west. From there, he quickly turned back with letters bound for the east, covering a total of 320 miles (515 km) in just 21 hours and 40 minutes. This proved the longest ride ever for any Pony Express rider.

The Civil War had begun, and at age 18 Cody joined the Seventh Kansas Regiment, serving as a scout for the Union army. His adventures took him as a spy behind enemy lines in Tennessee on several occasions, and later back to Missouri to defend Pilot Knob. While working as a hospital orderly at the end of the war, Cody met Louisa Frederici. They were married the following year, a move that Cody would later regard as one of the biggest mistakes he ever made, for the two were as opposite as could be imagined. Louisa was a prim and proper young French girl who wanted a quiet home with a faithful husband. Will was generous, egotistical, and gregarious, the sort of man everyone loved to be around. Will wanted to become a scout, to roam the mountains and plains, to hunt buffalo, and to enjoy spending time with his many loud, heavy-drinking, gun-shooting friends.

After the Civil War, Cody briefly tried his hand at the hotel business, before heading west to briefly join General George Custer as a scout. In 1867, Cody found work hunting buffalo to supply fresh meat for the railroad construction crews, a job that paid a hefty $500 per month and soon made him famous as "Buffalo Bill." Cody was one of the best hunters in the West; in just eight months, he slaughtered 4,280 buffalo, often saving transportation by driving the herd toward the camp, and dropping them within sight of the workers.

After this stint, Cody finally got the job he wanted: chief scout for the U.S. Army in the West, a job packed with excitement and danger. The Indian Wars were on. Cody worked for General Philip Sheridan as scout, providing information on movements of the Indians, leading troops in pursuit of the warriors, and joining in the Indian battles.

During these campaigns, the writer/preacher/scoundrel Ned Buntline began writing of Cody's exploits for the New York papers, giving Buffalo Bill his first taste of national acclaim. Soon Buntline had cranked out many more romantic tales loosely based on Cody's adventures: *Buffalo Bill's Best Shot, Buffalo Bill, The King of the Border Men, Buffalo Bill's Last Victory*, and many others. America had a new national hero. East Coast and European gentry began asking Cody to guide them on buffalo hunts. Cody's incredible knowledge of the land and hunting greatly impressed the men, but they were stunned to also discover in him a natural showman whose wonderful stories and self-deprecating sense of humor made him a friend to all. In 1872, the Grand Duke Alexis of Russia came to the U.S. and was guided by Cody on a hunt that made national headlines and brought even more fame to the 26-year-old Buffalo Bill.

On a six-week trip to New York in 1872, Cody met Buntline again and watched a wildly distorted theater production called *Buffalo Bill.* Amazingly, Cody adjusted quickly to the new surroundings. Dressed in the finest silk clothes, but with his long scout's hair under a Western hat, Cody suddenly entered the world of high society. In a short while, Cody was on the stage himself, performing with Ned Buntline and fellow scout Texas Jack in a play without a script called *Scouts of the Plains.* Although meant to be serious, the acting of all three was so dreadful that the play had the audiences rolling in the aisles with laughter. A New York reviewer called the play "so wonderfully bad it was almost good. The whole performance was so far aside of human experience, so wonderful in its daring feebleness, that no ordinary intellect is capable of comprehending it." Audiences packed the theaters for weeks on end. But then, suddenly, Cody was called back to the West, for the Sioux were again on the war path after chafing under their forced reservation life.

Shortly after returning to guide General Eugene Carr's forces, they learned of the massacre of Custer's men at the Battle of the Little Bighorn. In revenge, Carr's men set out to pursue Indians along the border between Nebraska and Wyoming. Under Cody's guidance, they managed to surprise a group of warriors at War Bonnet Creek. Cody shot the chief, Yellow Hand, and immediately scalped him, raising the scalp above his head with the cry, "First scalp for Custer!" (Cody later claimed that he scalped the chief because he was wearing an American flag wrapped around his groin and had a lock of yellow hair from a white woman's scalp pinned to his clothing.) The battle did not last long, as the Indians immediately fled. If Cody had been famous before, this event propelled him to even more acclaim. It became the grist for countless dime-store novels, and was embellished in so many ways over the years that the true story will never be known. Today the impressive war bonnet of Chief Yellow Hand is on display in the Buffalo Bill Heritage Center in Cody.

Buffalo Bill's days in the real wild West were over, and he returned to staging shows, eventually starting his famed Wild West extravaganza. This was unlike anything ever done before. There were buffalo stampedes, cowboy bronc riding, Indian camps, a Deadwood stage and outlaws, crack shooting by Annie Oakley, and of course, Buffalo Bill. The Wild West Show was so successful that, at its peak in the late 1890s, it made Cody more than a million dollars in profits each year. The show triumphantly toured Europe, performing in England for Queen Victoria, who was enthralled by the shooting displays and performances.

Even Sitting Bull, who had led the Sioux against Custer, joined the Wild West Show, selling autographed photos of himself. Amazingly, Sitting Bull and Buffalo Bill became good friends. Cody, who had earlier bragged of his many Indian killings, changed his attitude towards them, eventually saying, "In nine cases out of ten when there is trouble between white men and Indians, it will be found that the white man is responsible. . . . The defeat of Custer was not a massacre. The Indians were being pursued by skilled fighters with orders to kill. For centuries they had been hounded from the Atlantic to the Pacific and back again. They had their wives and little ones to protect and they were fighting for their existence."

For the next decade the show continued to tour, gradually losing its originality as other forms of entertainment came along, especially movies. Cody used his money to buy the 40,000-acre (16,000 ha) TE Ranch in northwestern Wyoming. He helped establish the town of Cody, where he built the Irma Hotel in honor of his daughter. His hunting lodges of Wapiti and Pahaska Tepee (Pahaska was his Indian name) still stand today along the road to Yellowstone.

Unfortunately, Buffalo Bill seemed to have no comprehension of how to save money. He was a notoriously soft touch, and would give money to almost anyone who asked. As his fortune slipped away and his show became more dated, Cody was finally forced to join up with the owner of the *Denver Post*, H. H. Tammen. Tammen was a notoriously corrupt man who used the aging Cody's fame to attract people to his own circus. Eventually Tammen forced Cody's Wild West Show into bankruptcy, selling off the incredible collection of goods that had been amassed over the years, and leaving the workers to find their own ways home. Buffalo Bill was heartbroken, but still trusted Tammen and agreed to join his circus almost as a sideshow act.

Three years later, Cody died while visiting his sister in Denver and was buried on nearby Lookout Mountain. Cody had wanted to be buried on Cedar Mountain on his land above the town of Cody, but even this wish was denied by Tammen, who apparently paid Cody's widow Louisa $10,000 to be able to choose the burial site (and to use the funeral parade to the burial site as an advertisement for his circus troop).

Despite his pathetic ending, few individuals have ever lived such a diverse and adventure-filled life, and could count so many people as friends. He knew not only mountain men such as Kit Carson and Jim Bridger, but also President Theodore Roosevelt and writer Mark Twain. Cody's impact on American culture is still felt today, not just in the image of the West that he created and that lives on in hundreds of Western movies, but also in the Boy Scouts (inspired by his exploits), the town of Cody, and even in the dude ranches that dot Wyoming.

—Don Pitcher

Buffalo Bill's .44 Smith & Wesson revolver had a gold-plated cylinder and pearl grips. (Courtesy, Buffalo Bill Historical Center, Cody, Wyoming)

Whitney's acute and sophisticated taste, things go a bit astray. Much of the later painting, though always effective, dynamic, and above all colorful, is not on the same high level as the earlier work; notably a big area given over to an expert and rather meretricious *Saturday Evening Post* illustrator, whose works don't quite match those of the similarly featured Remington and Russell, with semi-reconstruction of studios, sketches, and painting gear. However, the total effect of the collection is so overwhelming, and so Western, that the slight post-Whitney decline doesn't make much difference—though a greater concentration of native Wyoming artists like Gollings, Will James, and Archie Teater would have been nice. Photographer Charlie Belden is in evidence elsewhere in the museum.

The **Plains Indian Museum** stunningly displays all kinds of brightly colorful, native arts and crafts.This section of the center alone is worth the price of admission.

Balancing the Whitney wing in front is the **Buffalo Bill Museum** collection, which ranges over the long and insanely active career of the great man, from his days as an adolescent but champion Pony Express rider, to his performances before crowned heads of Europe. It's gorgeous, funny, fascinating, and an outrageously glamorous panorama of the life of that extravagant, corny, and courageous figure.

A new wing opening in 1991 houses the **Cody Firearms Museum**, one of the largest of its kind in the world, and a mecca for gun lovers. (Until the new wing opens, the **Winchester Arms Museum** is in the basement.) There are also two small, beautifully landscaped side gardens, for resting the feet. Both are adorned with statues, the most conspicuous being one of Buffalo Bill by none other than Gertrude V. Whitney herself. It's a bit away from the museum in a separate, small park, to the north.

Wild Bill Hickok. (Courtesy, Buffalo Bill Historical Center, Cody, Wyoming)

The museum also has a big, cool cafeteria. The balcony around the entrance hall holds an entertaining exhibit of early views and memorabilia of Yellowstone Park. A happy full day could easily be spent in the center.

A pair of Best Western motels, the Sunset and the Sunrise, are right down the road, as it jogs temporarily south. They are both within walking distance of the Center, and in between is a stylish and good Sunset Cafe, with a glass-roofed front porch for dining.

Other sights of the town, which in itself is neat and nice but no longer picturesque, are the Irma Hotel and, out of town on the strip westward, a collection of pioneer relics housed in **Old Trail Town**. It's a bit off the highway, north, and can be missed amidst all that commercial crud, but a must for those going toward Yellowstone. It consists of a long street of rescued ancient cabins, stores, sheds, and buildings of all kinds, all original, and most of them full of fascinating memorabilia. One of the most historic buildings is the original Hole-in-the-Wall cabin, once used by Butch Cassidy and the Wild Bunch. Old Trail Town is a little run-down, but not to be missed.

Like Sheridan, Cody is also the town center for well-established dude ranches, so that along with cattlemen and cowhands, the population has for years been salted with distinguished dudes (like Mrs. Whitney), some of whom have bought ranches and settled; and also with well-known artists. The fact that Jackson Pollock, the famous abstract expressionist, was born there may be purely accidental, but it's not inappropriate. Like Sheridan and Jackson Hole, Cody also has that odd blend of worldliness and wildness so characteristic of the Far West in general, and Wyoming in particular. Wyoming has historically been tolerant of peculiarity, individuality, and varieties of humanity, from gunmen to European aristocrats. The smug, leveling intolerance of Main Street may influence some towns, but most of the state prefers to be as wide open socially as it is geographically.

John "Jeremiah" Johnson is buried in Trail Town cemetery near Cody. (Courtesy, Buffalo Bill Historical Center, Cody, Wyoming)

Cody Firearms Museum

The collections of the Cody Firearms Museum (formerly known as the Winchester Arms Museum) at the Buffalo Bill Historical Center in Cody are world-renowned for their diversity, breadth, and quality.

Although the nucleus of the collection is based upon the corporate collection of the Winchester Repeating Arms Company, founded during the 1860s by Oliver F. Winchester, the complete spectrum of American manufactured firearms is represented. Complementing the approximately 4,000 firearms in the museum are engineering drawings by Winchester, L.C. Smith, Hunter Arms Company, Hopkins & Allen, and Marlin Firearms Company.

The Cody Firearms Museum is housed in a new 47,000-square-foot wing connected to the historical center. The main exhibition area is divided into galleries which document the development of sporting arms from 1540 to 1980: American military small arms from the Colonial period to the present, and highly decorated arms of both American and European manufacture dating from the late sixteenth to mid-twentieth centuries. Additional exhibits include replicas of a Colonial gun shop, a Western Express or stage stop, a hunting lodge housing the Boone & Crockett National Collection of Trophy Heads and Horns, a Western gun shop modeled after John M. Browning's shop in Ogden, Utah, and a Connecticut valley arms factory outfitted with late-nineteenth century machinery.

Other galleries highlight the products of the following arms companies and inventors: Browning, Burgess, Colt, Evans, Fogarty, High Standard, Ithaca, Marlin, Remington, Savage, Sharps, L.C. Smith, Smith & Wesson, Spencer, Stevens, Weatherby, Whitney, and Winchester. Not only are standard production arms contained in these displays, but also prototypes and associated material such as advertising art, sales catalogues, and prize medals.

The lower level of the museum contains additional display space devoted to the museum's study collection. Here one may view the countless variations of Winchester firearms, a large number of more modern arms, foreign military small arms and various pistols. Also exhibited are two extremely large punt or market shotguns dating from the nineteenth century, and Tuft's revolving cannon built during the Civil War.

—Herbert Houze, Curator, Cody Firearms Museum.

(opposite) Guns are found not only in museums. Wayne Baker, owner of Freedom Arms, holds his .454 Casull, the most powerful handgun made.

FIRE LANE

■ THE ROAD TO YELLOWSTONE

The only road from Cody to Yellowstone is U.S. Route 20 (which includes routes 14 and 16). It's also the only highway crossing the mountains between Route 212 to the north, which wriggles along the Montana line, and Route 287 to the south, which runs between Jackson Hole and Lander in the Wind River Basin. From Lander to Cody as the crow flies is about 125 miles (200 km), and it's about 40 more (64 km) from Cody to Montana. This distance, crossed by just these three highways, is about enough to hold most of the Eastern seaboard between New York and Baltimore, and serves as another illustration of wide-open Western spaciousness.

Route 20 (14-16) goes up through the startling scenery of **Shoshone Canyon**, a sight of its own. It passes by Buffalo Bill Reservoir, a project sponsored by the colonel himself, and runs into the mountains along the rushing Shoshone River beneath fantastic, red-rock pinnacles with names like the Holy City, the Laughing Pig, and so forth. Despite these touristy names, it's hard to exaggerate the effect of them, especially against an intense, blue Wyoming sky.

The surrounding **Shoshone National Forest** is the oldest in the United States, created, like Devil's Tower National Monument, under that most ardently conservationist of all American presidents, Theodore Roosevelt. The fact that he was a notable slaughterer of game has been held against him by modern environmental purists; but big game hunters were early and active conservationists who fought to preserve animals for hunting.

Along this magnificent, forested valley, known as the Wapiti, are found a series of the state's best guest ranches. These are a cross between the old, established dude ranches (which never took people off the road without references) and tourist cabin camps (which do). The compromise of the guest ranch is one of the chief charms of Wyoming, combining the convenience and availability of overnight stays, hearty meals, and the pleasant surroundings of a regular dude ranch. Most offer comfortable, separate log cabins for sleeping and a big cabin for dining and relaxing. They have horses and guides for riding and fishing, and vary in style from comparatively modest to grandiose. One of the best, the Bill Cody Ranch Resort, was even founded by a descendant of the colonel himself. Another fine option is **Pahaska Teepee**, just before you reach the eastern gate of Yellowstone. Its great, steep-roofed, main building is made of logs, and once was a Bill Cody hunting lodge.

By the time you approach Yellowstone's eastern gate, the road is full of curves and slow traffic. It wriggles past Pahaska and into a final jam of waiting autos, indicating that you have reached Yellowstone National Park.

(previous page) Thomas Moran's etchings and paintings of Yellowstone Falls helped bring the park's remarkable landscapes to national attention. (Courtesty, Horace Albright Museum, Yellowstone National Park)

YELLOWSTONE

ROUGHLY 50 MILES (80 KM) WEST OF CODY you come to the east gate of Yellowstone National Park. Like the Absarokas, most of Yellowstone is wilderness, best seen and appreciated on horseback or afoot. The disastrous fires of 1988 burned hundreds of square miles of this wilderness forest, but the chief spectacles of Yellowstone were not touched and are abundantly accessible to the motorist.

Yellowstone Park, in fact, is an embarrassment of riches. There's so much to see there that a month would be too short a time to inspect everything, though much of this could be considered repetitive: hundreds of geysers and hot springs; dozens of waterfalls, canyons, and mountains; thousands of elk, bear, and bison, and even some museums. For the average traveler, a fairly complete—if crowded—survey of the famous sights can be made in two days (just!), around the two circuitous roads, Upper Loop and Lower Loop. This guide sticks to these loops. If you choose to stop en route and just gaze seriously at these sights, your two days will be happily filled. To do more requires more time, energy, and patience than a two-day round trip would allow.

If you want to stay overnight in one of the many and varied tourist facilities of the park, plan ahead and make reservations. A few of these lodgings are sights, practically natural wonders, in themselves. As you pass into the park at any of the five main gates, the ranger will be glad to hand you accurate and fairly detailed directions and data, and also to advise you on which facilities are booked up and which are possibly available.

■ YELLOWSTONE HISTORY

As Shoshone was the first national forest, and Devil's Tower the first national monument, so Yellowstone was the first national park. In this business of preserving land for the public good, Wyoming can smugly consider itself Number One. Wyoming is the birthplace of conservation (over, it must be said, the dead bodies of lots of its citizens, then and now.) With 2,221,773 acres (899,139 ha), Yellowstone is still one of the largest national parks in the country.

The first white man known to have seen it was the ubiquitous John Colter. He came west with Lewis and Clark, left their expedition on the way back from the Pacific in 1806, and went into the wilderness to trap and explore. His hair-raising adventures brought him into Jackson Hole from the south. He crossed the Hole and went over

Teton Pass into Idaho and Pierre's Hole. In 1807, he passed into the Yellowstone country from the south, where he saw Yellowstone Lake, the falls of the Grand Canyon, and various hot springs and geysers—but not Old Faithful and the main geyser basins, for which he was long given credit. The principal thermal display he seems to have described were the De Maris Springs, on which Cody was first founded. To the outside world, his descriptions were so unbelievable that he became known as a liar. Unlike other old-timers, like Jim Bridger, who rejoiced in this kind of reputation, Colter's feelings were hurt. He died before he could be vindicated, his name immortalized as Yellowstone's first sarcastic nickname: Colter's Hell.

As early as 1827, a member of the Rocky Mountain Fur Company visited Yellowstone and published in the *Philadelphia Gazette* a rather detailed account of what he saw. He mentioned a large freshwater lake on the south shore, along which springs of hot water and others "resembling a mush pot" were playing. Jim Bridger passed through sometime in the 1830s, but unlike Colter, he amused himself with deadpan fantasies, such as the wall of glass between him and an elk that stopped his bullets. (The elk was magnified by the glass wall, and was really 25 miles away.) He also described a canyon over which he walked on petrified air. This made Colter's Hell seem even more unbelievable, and confirmed the general impression that it was all a hoax.

In the 1860s and 1870s, serious expeditions were made or attempted (Raynolds in 1859-60, De Lacy in 1863, et al). In 1870 and 1871 occurred the two surveys that figuratively and literally put Yellowstone on the map. The official Washburn expedition in the summer of 1870 spent a month of careful, documented study, and made a report that "electrified the nation." For the first time, the public began to believe in Yellowstone. More decisive was the Hayden survey of the following year. This was the expedition that brought along William Henry Jackson and Thomas Moran, whose photographs and paintings of the beauties and wonders of Yellowstone so excited Congress that the park was created "for the benefit and enjoyment of the people." On March 1, 1872, President Grant signed the act of dedication.

It was some time before most Americans were able to enjoy their new park. Up to 1895, the annual visitor attendance remained less than 5,000. The park was still hard to get to, and hard to get *through*. Pack trips and stage coaches were the only means of transport, and holdups of the stages were routine. Before 1886, the park was run by a civilian superintendent and a few "scouts." The first of these superintendents was Nathaniel Pitt Langford, of the Washburn expedition. Then, for 30 years more, a U.S.

cavalry troop policed the area. Finally, in 1911, the Secretary of the Interior appointed a true superintendent, a corps of rangers was hired, and the park has been run under this system of management ever since.

The Northern Pacific railroad came to Gardiner, outside the park's north gate, in 1902. The Union Pacific arrived at West Yellowstone, outside the west gate, in 1907. The year 1905 brought some 25,000 visitors to the park, an early high point for tourism, but this was succeeded by an inexplicable nine-year slump. This slump was cured by the introduction of the first automobile in 1915, when the tally leaped to more than 50,000. By 1929, there were 260,000 visitors. Now the number is in the millions, which has caused massive problems, none of which has yet been solved. Cut the numbers? If so, how? Limit automobiles? Nothing has been done, and human erosion continues to be a severe problem at the major attractions. Crowds in Coney Island are not more dense in midsummer, and traffic near famous places crawls.

President Theodore Roosevelt and Major John Pitcher of the U.S. Army in front of Liberty Cap in 1903. (Courtesy, Horace Albright Museum, Yellowstone National Park)

■ The East Entrance

Coming from Cody, the first of these famous places is **Yellowstone Lake.** This is the largest, highest (7,731 feet/2,356 m), and one of the most beautiful such bodies of water in the country (of its kind, of course; it's not in the same league as the Great Lakes). On a clear day, with a vivid sky reflected on the still surface, the effect, especially on first sight as you descend from Sylvan Pass, is overwhelming. A viewpoint, **Lake Butte**, is reached by a short, steep road to the right, just before you reach the lake's shore. The view from above gives you a full sweep of the lake and a glimpse of the Tetons far to the south and west.

When the highway strikes the lake it curves along the shore in open meadows, decorated by lazy hot springs and grazing bison, till it reaches **Fishing Bridge**, which crosses the river at the lake's outlet. Once this bridge was lined with fishermen, but now fishing is prohibited. The stream is the true beginning, though not the source, of the mighty Yellowstone River, which rolls down to the Missouri and Mississippi rivers, and the Gulf of Mexico. Just beyond, the road merges into the Lower Loop.

The natural thing would be to turn south and continue the drive along the beautiful lakeshore; but in order to cover the whole circuit of the park without repetition, our route turns north.

> Standing near the margin and looking down the canyon, an immense chasm or cleft in the basalt, with its sides 1,200 to 1,500 feet high, and decorated with the most brilliant colors, the rocks weathered into an almost unlimited variety of forms and here and there a pine sending its roots into the clefts on the sides as if struggling with uncertainty for existence, the mind of the onlooker is seized with impressions of grandeur. Mr. Moran exclaimed with a kind of regretful enthusiasm that these tints were beyond the resources of human art. The waters of the Yellowstone seem, as it were, to gather themselves into one compact mass and plunge over the descent of 350 feet in foam as white as snow. Upon the yellow, nearly vertical western side, the mist mostly falls, and for 300 feet from the bottom the wall is covered with a thick matting of mosses, sedges, grasses and other vegetation of the most vivid green, which have sent their small roots into the softened rocks and are nourished by the ever-ascending spray.
>
> —Ferdinand Hayden, Geographical Survey, 1871

(opposite) The colorful walls of Grand Canyon of the Yellowstone.

■ Yellowstone Lake to Tower Junction

Heading north along the limpid and placid young Yellowstone River (once full of hip-booted fishermen, but now closed to fishing in this area), you come to **Hayden Valley**, a peaceful, wide, grassy meadow, and one of the park's beauty spots. In addition to its natural beauty, the valley offers thermal features and wild game. **Dragon's Mouth** and Mud Volcano are big water-and-mud hot springs that belch and roar and splash about and stink in a splendidly repulsive way, to the delight and horror of all children. The valley's buffalo population is a fairly recent phenomenon. The common roadside excitement used to be bear, but they became such a dangerous nuisance that the park service has persuaded them to move off the road and into the woods, where they belong, by moving feeding grounds and closing off garbage dumps. Bison, which used to be pretty much confined to the Lamar River Valley, have increased, and have now taken the place of bears as tourist pets and spectacles. Tourists used to be warned about the dangers of bears; now it's the dangers of bison. The only thing that hasn't changed is the idiocy of travelers who don't realize that wild animals are indeed *wild.* Meanwhile, the bird population of Hayden Valley remains spectacular. Not only such commonplace visitors from California and Utah as sea gulls and pelicans, but sometimes native rarities, such as wild swans. The valley is, of course, named for Ferdinand Hayden, whose 1871 expedition inspired Congress to create the park.

Soon, the pastoral serenity of the Hayden Valley gives way to dark canyon walls and rough water, and you come to the **Grand Canyon of the Yellowstone**, with its two spectacular falls. It's one of the world's colorful wonders, and enough all by itself to justify creation of a national park. The **Upper Falls** is the lesser of the two, but grand enough and more accessible. A path from the parking lot leads right to the point where the big, dark-colored power of the water topples over its cliff with a roar and spume of spray that catches the sun in rainbows. The **Lower Falls** is more spectacular, but best seen from a distance, looking up the multicolored canyon. You can drive down both sides of the canyon and get all sorts of variations of the beauties of this vista from lookouts labeled **Inspiration Point** and **Artist Point**. The Artist who first had the Inspiration and first painted the falls was, of course, Thomas Moran—and nobody since has done it better. Jackson took the first black-and-whites; splendid, too, but color is of the essence.

Canyon Village is a big, homely, modern center for everything from souvenirs to food and lodging. Built around a vast parking lot that has been much improved over the years by the growth of pines, it is, as usual, crowded in season. The cabins, in their pine-shaded "villages," are simple but comfortable and tasteful, if not luxurious. The food in the main restaurant is superlative, the shops enormous and richly stocked. It's all so large that it seems to be able to handle the huge crowds. But it can't be called "scenic." There used to be a beautiful hotel here, one of the most magnificent in the park, but the earthquake of 1959 damaged it (and it probably was losing money), so it was torn down just before the revival of art deco would have made it a historical monument. A great loss to architecture, and tourism, too.

At Canyon Village, you could go due west on a boring, straight road through timber and without sights to Norris Geyser Basin. But our route continues north on the Upper Loop, into open country after crossing **Dunraven Pass.**

Mount Washburn is the central feature of this new landscape, so much more decorative than the endless lodgepole plateau that occupies (or, before the fire, *occupied*) most of the southern half of the park. Washburn is only 10,317 feet (3,145 m) high, which in this part of Wyoming is just a hill. It is approached from the south by Dunraven Pass (8,859 feet/2,700 m), which also isn't much of a pass, but has fine mountain views south of still-unburned forests, though there is a considerable amount of burnt ground on the north side. Mt. Washburn balances Hayden Valley as a memorial to leaders of the seminal expeditions of 1870-71. Oddly enough, Mt. Washburn is one of the highest summits in the park that you can see from the road. For although the level of the park is high—most of it between 7,000 and 8,000 feet (2,100-2,500 m)—none of its peaks compare with the Absarokas to the east, or the Tetons, southward. A road goes part of the way to the summit from the north side, but the lookout on top is reachable only by trail.

Tower Falls is the next principal point of interest. Though less impressive than the falls of Yellowstone Canyon, it is attractive: a slender column of water emerging from a fantastic cluster of yellow rock spines. After falling 132 feet (40 m), it flows off in a sleek canyon to the deeper Yellowstone River canyon.

Shortly after Tower Falls, you come to the **Calcite Springs overlook.** The springs, down along the Yellowstone River, aren't much, but the gorge they are in, a second spectacular Yellowstone Canyon, is awesome—not colorful like the famous canyon, but grand, deep, somber.

(following page) The Lower Falls drops 308 feet (94 m) in its sudden descent into Grand Canyon of the Yellowstone.

■ Tower Junction to Mammoth

At Tower Junction, the Upper Loop turns west to Mammoth Hot Springs. To the right, due east, U.S. Route 212 goes over a spectacular pass and through the northeast gate toward Cooke City and Red Lodge, in Montana. Along the way the road passes the park's old buffalo range, the lush valley of the Lamar River. This area, especially around Cooke City, was devastated by fire.

These roads lead through open meadow and mountain scenery, ablaze with wildflowers in midsummer. Striking, odd-shaped peaks surround the valley on every side, most notably the jagged crags eastward toward Cooke City. Fortunately, the area to the west was only lightly touched by fire.

Along the road to Mammoth Hot Springs stands the comparatively ancient (1906) and honorable log cabin camp of **Tower-Roosevelt Lodge**, initiated by Teddy himself, and still retaining the air of a hunting lodge and dude-ranch outfit. There's a fine main lodge for meals, and many nice, smaller cabins for sleeping; but unfortunately it's comparatively small, popular, and hard to get into. Advance reservations are suggested.

Another park oddity is the **petrified tree**. It's just that—the remains of a whole tree trunk standing in a pretty, somewhat fire-scarred valley off the highway. There are other more extensive exhibits of the kind, notably one on the Laramie plains, but they are less accessible.

Farther along are the Wraith and Undine falls. **Wraith Falls** is a good half-mile (.8-km) trail trek south of the highway. **Undine Falls** is right on the road, to the north. Both are pretty, but Undine is a lot easier to see than Wraith.

Mammoth Hot Springs is the capital of Yellowstone. As park headquarters, there's a staid little village of old-fashioned stone houses where park personnel live under a canopy of old-growth trees, the whole resembling an old military post (which it once was). The vast Mammoth Hotel has been totally modernized, and is now very stylish-looking. Mammoth was the busiest entrance to the park when the railroad still brought a majority of visitors into it, before the automobile took over and the railroads ceased passenger service. A big, stone gateway at the north entrance celebrated its touristic preeminence, and the size of the Mammoth Hotel was accordingly immense. It is still enormously crowded and busy. Nearby **Horace Albright Visitor Center** is the central information source for the whole park; it's open daily year round.

The massive terraces at Mammoth Hot Springs front the hotel. Early this century,

(opposite) The travertine terraces of Mammoth Hot Springs.

these made Mammoth the park's foremost thermal display, as well as the premier tourist center; but things aren't what they used to be. Cutting off rail service is one thing, but worse is the slow death of the springs themselves. Instead of being a riot of colorful, steaming terraces, the springs today are a ghostly white, decaying monument to past activity. Though most of the terraces are dry or only faintly steaming, there are still two sufficiently active ones, **Minerva** and **Opal**. They are quite close together, on opposite sides of the highway going south as you leave the hotel complex. Opal is alongside the road to the east, a rather modest and low, but subtly colored effusion encroaching on the green lawns of Park Headquarters. Minerva is more like the old days—a fine, tall, fully flowing, multicolored terrace with hot water cascades. Paths and steps still lead all over the great white sepulchres of defunct terraces. The terraces have a melancholy grandeur and the springs show faint signs of residual life, but the walk is long and the steps are steep.

An automobile road, **Terrace Loop Drive** southward, gives a grand panorama of the springs, including one fairly active terrace on the very south end of the complex. Swinging into the woods, the road passes all sorts of fascinating, semi-defunct, curiously misshapen, separate outgrowths.

Albright Visitor Center, Mammoth Hot Springs

The Albright Visitor Center on Yellowstone's northern edge offers information about the park, ranger-led walks, films and videos, and exhibits about Indians and explorers who first came across the area's astounding sights. Notable are 23 watercolors by painter Thomas Moran, as well as his easel, chair, and painting accoutrements; and 26 photographs taken by William Henry Jackson in the 1871 Hayden Survey. Jackson's huge 8x10 camera, similar to the one used on the Hayden expedition, is also here, a reminder of how cumbersome it must have been to take these photographs.

■ MAMMOTH TO NORRIS

The 21-mile (35-km) road south from Mammoth to Norris is the homeliest stretch of travel in the park (except for the link from Canyon to Norris). In direct contrast to the road from Canyon to Mammoth, this one passes through forest and low hills, following the rather mousy Obsidian Creek through its willow valley much of the way. There are no particularly interesting or beautiful sights along the route, and even worse, it was more devastated by fire than any other section of the park visible from the loop roads. There are burnt patches at Dunraven Pass and elsewhere, but nothing quite like this complete holocaust. It's true that you can see the snow-capped Gallatins to the northwest, and that there are elk visible along the way; but the only two "sights," Obsidian Cliff and Roaring Mountain, don't really amount to much.

Obsidian Cliff, alongside the road to the east, is made of shiny black obsidian. People clamber about the base picking up pieces of obsidian, which is against park rules.

Roaring Mountain is a good deal farther south. It has long ceased to roar. When it blew up in 1902, killing lots of trees, it did roar and smoke; but now it's a big, bare, white sulphur cliff with two very feeble steam vents still active.

However, for thermal variety and profusion, nothing matches **Norris Geyser Basin**. Probably a full day could be happily spent looking and waiting for the eruption or mere bubbling up of each and every geyser and hot spring there. There are two large thermal areas at Norris: the Back Basin, south of the entrance near the visitor center, and the Porcelain Basin, to the north.

An ancient whitebark pine snag guards Dunraven Pass; Grand Canyon of the Yellowstone lies in the background.

The complete circle of **Back Basin** is longer, but it has fewer events spaced farther apart. They are big events however:

notably **Echinus Geyser** going off in a splendid, if diffuse, fashion about every 50 minutes. On the way there, **Steamboat Geyser** seems to perform modestly, but more or less continuously. However, it can erupt tremendously, as it did in May 1989, to become the tallest geyser in the park. On a shorter circle back to the visitor center, smaller **Pork Chop Geyser** has been ferociously blowing up without interruption for the last four years. The Norris basin has been active at all times through the years, but the program keeps varying dramatically. Former spectacles dry up, and new ones surge forth, especially geysers. Meanwhile, other less active springs and holes keep right on steaming and bubbling.

Porcelain Basin is far more crowded with thermal events (and people) than Back Basin. It's a wide pink-and-white valley where a constant, rather minor turmoil of spouting and steaming transpires. Printed guides are available in tin boxes near the visitor center, and rangers, mostly female, are very helpful.

At Norris, how much you see and how long you take is a matter of persistence, appetite, endurance, and time. If you're a thermal nut, this is the place. Otherwise the Echinus and a few others might suffice.

■ NORRIS TO OLD FAITHFUL

At Norris, the Upper Loop ends and the Lower Loop begins, and the dull 12-mile (20-km) umbilical cord to Canyon Village takes off east. The Lower Loop now goes down from Norris to Madison Junction, 14 miles (23 km) along the handsome gorge of the **Gibbon River**. It, too, has falls. However, this lovely area has also been devastated by fires and, in flooding rains, mud slides.

At Madison Junction is a small museum and campground. From there, a road runs west along the **Madison River**, one of the famous fishing streams of the West, and through mountain scenery to West Yellowstone, Montana. The Lower Loop continues south to Old Faithful, passing all sorts of pools and geysers en route.

Right beyond Madison Junction, before you get to these geysers, there's a short, scenic, one-way detour up the gorge of the **Firehole River**, with its fine cliffs, splendid rapids, cascades, and a big swimming hole in the river where kids rather surprisingly cavort. The chilly water temperature is supposedly modified by water from hot springs along the river.

(opposite) Winter turns Castle Geyser into an otherworldly masterpiece.

After this diversion and your return to the highway, it's hot water all the way. Among the myriad thermal features along this route, the most interesting are the Fountain Paint Pots, the hot-spring pools of Midway Geyser Basin and, finally, Old Faithful itself.

Fountain Paint Pots, in the Lower Geyser Basin, is sort of a *Traveller's Digest* of thermal phenomena. It has one or two of everything. There is one beautiful, blue, hot-spring pool; some hot, roaring steam vents, the Fumeroles; an area of pink, plopping mud-geysers; and several small but active water-geysers. Nothing stupendous, but a bit of everything. It could give a lazy tourist the opportunity to see all the main varieties of thermal display in one place.

Shortly beyond, a one-way road going back north called Firehole Lake Drive passes a **Great Fountain Geyser**. Farther on at Midway Geyser Basin are two immense, steaming, wonderfully colored, hot-spring pools. The one closest to the road, **Excelsior Geyser Crater**, was not so long ago a great geyser that blew up, leaving a deep cavity full of blue water. Behind, toward the hills, is the equally full and gorgeously colored **Grand Prismatic Spring**. There are many other smaller, less interesting pools, but these two great ones are the prime attractions.

Bison gather along Yellowstone's Firehole River during the winter.

(opposite) An enormous icecone forms at the bottom of the Lower Falls every winter.

The Biscuit and Black Sands basins are more of the same (except that thermal displays are never just the same). However, any attempt to list them all would lead to confusion and perhaps insanity, especially as they keep changing from year to year.

The supreme attraction of this whole thermal region is, of course, **Old Faithful**. This is undoubtedly the world's best-known thermal outburst. Though other geysers are, or have been, larger, nothing approaches the grandeur—or the familiarity—of aptly named Old Faithful. Though it is named for its regularity over the decades, in late years there has been a rather suppressed rumor of some fickleness; nonetheless, its regularity is still remarkable, and the always impatient expectation of hundreds of spectators during the season is faithfully rewarded by its 140-foot (43-m) explosions of roaring, steaming water, shooting up in a shapely fountain.

Old Faithful, however, is far from being the only spectacle in the vicinity. A rival in grandeur is the manmade **Old Faithful Inn**. This vast Hall of the Gibichungs, like some fairy-tale giant's castle, dates from 1903, and so is now approaching the status of an antique. It is still awe-inspiring, especially the six-story interior grand hall, with intricate log work and huge stone fireplaces. It claims to be the largest native-log structure in the world (designed by a R.C. Reamer of Seattle with something Swiss in

Old Faithful Inn is one of the world's largest log buildings.

(opposite) One of the most impressive sights in Yellowstone is Echinus Geyser in the Norris Geyser Basin.

mind); but is of course still very much an active hotel, with dining rooms, shops, annexes, and all sorts of accommodations at different price levels. The fire of 1988 came perilously close, but didn't touch the lodge, although some service buildings burned.

Roundabout the inn spreads one of the largest and most active of Yellowstone's geyser basins, Upper Geyser Basin. By comparison, Norris is profuse, busy, and cheerful; the Midway Basin pools calm and soothingly rich-colored. Old Faithful's Upper Geyser Basin is grand and awe-inspiring, a wide valley of white volcanic ash, full of gnarled cones of other punctually famous geysers, and studded with steaming hot springs. To catch some of these other geysers you may have to wait hours, weeks, months, even years. A few are seen only by greatest of good luck and planning. **The Giantess**, for instance, habitually waits six-to eight-month intervals before blowing up to 200 feet (60 m) in the air for four hours. Others are more amenable, such as non-eruptive springs named the Teakettle, the Pump, Spasmodic, and Summit. Long paths take you all about the basin and to other thermal areas, notably the nearby **Lone Star Geyser** and the far-off **Shoshone Geyser Basin** along Shoshone Lake to the south.

■ OLD FAITHFUL TO WEST THUMB

As you go over **Craig Pass** (8,261 feet/2,518 m) on the road to West Thumb, you get a glimpse of **Shoshone Lake**, far below to the south, looking as though it had been totally bypassed by the fire of 1988. The fire damage suddenly stops as soon as you leave Old Faithful, sparing a swath running southwest to northeast.

West Thumb, on Yellowstone Lake, is the place noted in the *Philadelphia Gazette* of 1827 with its accounts of active mud geysers. There are still hot springs along the lake shore and even *in* the lake itself, but here again, as at Mammoth, there has been a decline. The mud pots that used to pop and burble have subsided. An old sign once described them as being "likened to a bowl of porridge." The *Gazette* said the springs resembled a "mush pot." They no longer plop, but the residual springs are highly colored, and the wide, blue lake beyond is, when in a good mood, beautiful as ever.

These thermal areas are capricious. Earth tremors in particular, like the serious one in 1959 that killed people on the edge of the park, disturb geysers and upset springs. Also, they just get tired and fade away, as did the De Maris Springs, once active near Cody. On the other hand, Norris Basin seems feistier than ever.

(opposite) Roaring Mountain contains a steaming mountainside of hot rocks and fissures.

The Yellowstone Fires of 1988

The summer of 1988 will long be remembered as the year when Yellowstone was "destroyed" by fire. TV reporters flocked to the park, pronouncing the death of America's most famous national wonders as they stood in front of trees turned into towering torches and 30,000-foot clouds of black smoke. Newspaper headlines screamed, "Park Sizzles," or "Winds Whip Fiery Frenzy Out of Control," or "Firestorms Blacken Yellowstone." Residents of nearby towns complained of lost tourism dollars, choking smoke, and intentionally lit backfires that threatened their homes and businesses. Wyoming politicians berated the park service's "let burn" policy. President Reagan expressed astonishment that fires were ever allowed to burn in the national parks (a policy that had been in place for two decades). The media ate it up, with one headline reading, "Total Destruction: Intense Heat and Flames from the Fires in Yellowstone Left Nothing but Powdered Ash and Charcoal Near Norris Junction."

Unfortunately, the real story behind the fires of 1988 was lost in this media feeding frenzy. To understand what happened in Yellowstone, it is first necessary to look at the park's vegetation, its history, and the way in which fires help maintain the ecosystem. Although Yellowstone has large areas covered with sage, grass, and shrubs, these do not burn with the intensity of forested areas, and they recover rather quickly after fires. The focus of national concern, however, was the extensive Yellowstone plateau, where lodgepole pines dominate. These forests had burned many times since the last glaciers retreated more than 11,000 years ago. We could even count ourselves as fortunate to have been able to witness one of nature's most incredible spectacles. It may not occur again for another 300 years.

When Yellowstone National Park was established in 1872, most of the land was carpeted with a mixture of variously aged lodgepole stands, some established in big fires during the 1740s and 1790s, others from fires in the 1860s, and still others from the holocaust-like fires that burned in the 1690s and early 1700s. By the late nineteenth century the resulting vegetation was a mosaic of various age classes, with a predominance of younger trees. Under all but the most extreme weather conditions (such as in 1988), these younger forests are not as likely to burn as the older stands. During this century, however, these lodgepole forests grew older and began to fall apart. Fallen dead trees covered the ground and a "ladder" of young subalpine fir and Engelmann spruce helped carry fires into the crowns of older lodgepole pines. Fewer large fires, partly due to unusually moist summer weather conditions, and partly because of a fire suppression policy in effect until 1972, meant that by the 1980s, a third of the park's lodgepole stands were more than 250 years old. Yellowstone was "ripe to burn."

(top) The massive Yellowstone fires of 1988 burned across more than a third of the park land, attracting international concern. (Courtesy, Yellowstone National Park). (bottom) Fire intensity varied greatly during the 1988 fires, with some areas completely blackened and others burned only on the surface.

Since the early 1950s, the U.S. Forest Service's Smokey Bear drummed in an incessant message: "Only You Can Prevent Forest Fires." Forest fires were viewed as dangerous, destructive forces that must be stopped to protect our valuable public lands. Unfortunately, this immensely effective and generally valid ad campaign convinced the public that all fires were bad. Ecological research has shown that this is not only wrong, but that putting out all fires can sometimes create conditions far more dangerous than if fires had been allowed to burn in the first place. Fire, like the other processes that have affected Yellowstone—cataclysmic volcanic explosions, geothermal activity, and massive glaciation—is neither good nor evil. It simply is a part of the natural world that national parks are attempting to preserve. Unfortunately, national parks are no longer surrounded by similarly undeveloped land, so when fires burned in Yellowstone they also affected the surrounding towns and the people who make a living from tourism.

Fire has played an important role in lodgepole pine forests for millions of years, and as a result, the trees have evolved an unusual adaptation: resinous cones that only open under the heat of forest fires. The parent trees are killed, but a new generation is guaranteed by the thousands of pine seeds (20 seeds per square foot) that are released to the bare, nutrient-rich soil underneath the blackened overstory. Within five years this blackened landscape is dotted with thousands of young pine trees, competing with a verdant cover of grasses and flowers for sunlight. Although some animals are killed in the fires (including, in 1988, 257 elk out of a Yellowstone population of 32,000), and others die from a lack of food immediately after a fire, the early decades following a fire create conditions that are unusually rich for many animals. Wildlife diversity in lodgepole forests reaches a peak within the first 25 years after the fire. Woodpeckers, mountain bluebirds, and other birds feed on insects in the dead trees, while elk and bear graze on the lush grasses. As the forest ages, a dense stand of trees forms, keeping light from reaching the forest floor and making it difficult for understory plants to survive. These trees eventually thin themselves out, creating openings in the forest, but after 250 to 300 years without fire the lodgepole forests become a tangle of fallen trees, susceptible to attacks by bark beetles, creating even more potential fire fuel.

The cause of Yellowstone's 1988 fires is not just the heavy fuel loading from an aging forest, but weather conditions that were the driest and windiest on record. The winter of 1987-88 had been a mild one, and by spring there was a moderate to severe drought in the park, lessened only by above-normal rainfall in April and May. Since 1972, when Yellowstone officials first began allowing certain lightning fires to burn in backcountry areas, there had been hundreds of small fires along with a few large ones. The total acreage burned by these fires during the first 15 years totaled less than two percent of Yellowstone's 2.2 million acres. (Mistakenly called a "let burn" policy, the natural fire program actually involved close monitoring of these lightning-ignited fires to determine when and if a fire should be suppressed. All human-caused fires were immediately suppressed.) When the first lightning-ignited fires of the 1988 season began in late May, those in the backcountry areas were allowed to burn, as fire management officials anticipated normal summer weather conditions. Many fires went out on their own, but when June and July came and the rains failed to materialize, the fires began to spread rapidly. Alarmed park officials declared them wildfires and sent crews to attempt to put them out.

As the summer progressed, more and more firefighters were called in, eventually totaling more than 25,000 personnel. The effort would cost $120 million and involve 51 spike camps, 150 helispots, 1.4 million gallons of fire retardant dropped by dozens of helicopters and planes, 665 miles (1,070 km) of hand line, and 32 miles (51 km) of bulldozer line in the park.

This enormous expense was, in large part, a waste; the fires were far beyond any human effort to control, and only nature could stop what it had started. By mid-August, more than 25 fires were burning simultaneously all over the park and surrounding national forests, with many joining together to create massive complexes. The fires had become so large that they started making their own weather, throwing ash thousands of feet into the air and creating a thick layer of ground smoke that made it impossible to see where the actual firefront was. Fighting fire under these conditions was nearly impossible, and in many instances firefighters retreated to the developed areas, circling the wagons around structures in an attempt to save them. On a single day, September 7, more than 100,000 acres (40,470 ha) burned and 20 buildings in the Old Faithful area were destroyed (out of more than 400). The fires seemed poised to burn the remainder of Yellowstone, but four days later the season's first snow carpeted the park. Within a few days firefighters had the upper hand, though the last fires were not declared out until early December.

More than 793,000 acres (320,927 ha; 36 percent of the park) had burned. Visitors to Yellowstone today will see enormous blackened expanses in some parts of the park, especially along the highway south of Grant Village, while in other areas they find a complex mosaic of burned and unburned forest land.

—Don Pitcher

From West Thumb, the Lower Loop Road turns north along the shore of the lake toward the junction at Fishing Bridge. This particular stretch of shoreline was completely spared by the fire and is its old pristine self. Sights include a **natural bridge** to the west. One of the remaining grand hostelries of the park, **Lake Hotel**, still stands on the shore at Lake Village. Far from being Nordic or Western in style, it's the model of a Great Lakes-style, yellow, early 1900s, neo-Colonial inn. It has an especially comfortable, delightfully old-fashioned atmosphere, though recently it's been tastefully redecorated. You can imagine evenings sitting on a front veranda, the ladies rocking, the gentlemen smoking pipes, and someone strumming a mandolin.

West Thumb to Jackson Hole

Just south of West Thumb, on a short detour east, is **Grant Village**, with its handsome new marina and campground. It was desperately threatened by fire in 1988. Then you begin a gradual decline from the Pitchstone Plateau, which occupies most of the southwest corner of Yellowstone, passing **Lewis Lake**, a favorite fishing place, and somber **Lewis Canyon**. These are the principal sights en route, along with pretty little **Lewis Falls**, close to the lake's outlet. Unfortunately, this area is far from untouched by the fire: Lewis Canyon, in particular, has been devastated, and much of Lewis Lake's shoreline was ravaged, though the stretch along the roadside miraculously escaped the flames. This area was the first to burn.

Finally, you exit Yellowstone through the south gate onto the **John D. Rockefeller Jr. Memorial Parkway**. Its name recognizes in a special way one of the most extraordinary and generous conservationist efforts in the history of America—the rescue of the floor of the valley of Jackson Hole from predatory commercialism by the timely purchase of private lands for their inclusion in a national park. Local activists (who thought of the idea), Horace Albright (who got Rockefeller personally involved) and, eventually, the governments of the state and nation, brought about the creation of Grand Teton National Park in 1950.

The result of this long effort lies at the end of the memorial highway. The first upsurges of the Tetons come into view as soon as you leave Yellowstone, becoming more and more visible and exciting as you head south. When you reach the extremely long Jackson Lake itself, you have entered Jackson Hole, though the valley proper doesn't begin till you reach the Snake River below the dam.

(opposite) Snowmobile police bundle up for a day on the drifts. Wintertime temperatures in Wyoming regularly plummet to sub-freezing temperatures; the coldest recorded temperature was –66°F (–54°C).

SPEED
LIMIT
15
SPEEDGUN
AFS

(top) For many years, Menor's Ferry offered one of the only ways to cross the Snake River in Jackson Hole (courtesy, Jackson Hole Museum and Teton County Historical Society). (bottom) Beaver Dick Leigh and his wife Jenny with their children in Jackson Hole. Leigh and Jenny lakes are named for them (photo by William H. Jackson, courtesy, Horace Albright Museum, Yellowstone National Park)

JACKSON HOLE

ALTHOUGH JACKSON HOLE LIES IN THE FLATS THAT BEGIN where the Snake River flows south from the Jackson Lake Dam, the term describes the whole of the mountain area surrounding the valley, including the Teton and Gros Ventre (pronounced, and sometimes spelled, *Grovont*) ranges. By that larger measure, the Hole begins where the Snake runs into Jackson Lake, at Grand Teton National Park's northern boundary.

Jackson is the name of the lake and town, Jackson Hole the valley. No wonder some people get confused. It's all perhaps too much of a memorial to David Jackson, an early local trapper who is not otherwise distinguished enough for that much honor.

■ HISTORY

All of Wyoming was involved in the fur mania, but no section more so than Jackson Hole. The first white man to see it was John Colter, a trapper, of course. Up through the 1840s, traders and trappers bustled through the Hole like today's tourists. This same Colter, whose tales of the Yellowstone were not believed, probably passed through in 1807. Although Colter himself kept no records, a map printed in Nicholas Biddle's history of the Lewis and Clark expedition, published as early as 1814, has a dotted line across a map of the area marked "Colter's route in 1807," and Jackson Lake is labeled "Lake Biddle," after the author of the book. (Not really the author so much as the transcriber-editor, since the material was based directly on the original writings of Lewis and Clark.)

Jackson Hole became the crossroads for trappers coming and going between Wyoming and Idaho from the 1820s through the 1840s. David E. Jackson frequented the region for years, though nobody can be quite sure when his name was first attached to it. William Sublette supposedly christened it in 1829. It was probably called "Jackson's Hole" even before then. It appeared so in a book dated 1837.

All this activity simmered down when the fur trade died. The beaver were then left in peace, and for more than 40 years the valley was relatively empty of humans except for Indian summer camps (of which teepee rings still exist as evidence) and fall hunting. White hunting parties came through later, but the first permanent homestead was not established until 1884. By 1889, some 40 settlers were living in the valley, and in the fall of that year the first wagon train of five Mormon families crossed Teton Pass bearing members of the Wilson family. The community of Wilson at the foot of the pass was for decades the valley's "second city," after the metropolis, Jackson.

Teton Pass remained an adventure for many years, particularly after snowfall, until the mid-twentieth century. Nowadays, thousands of cars stream over it, but fewer than over the other highways opened more recently. The Hole now regularly fills with a transient population greater than its permanent population, in both the summer and winter seasons. Jackson Hole can no longer be called lonely; but beautiful it certainly still is.

■ Along Jackson Lake

Traveling from Yellowstone down U.S. Route 191 (and 89), the first impact of the Tetons, rising sheer across the water, is from the north shore of Jackson Lake. Among the most familiar of all American photographs, by William Jackson, is that of Mt. Moran reflected in Jackson Lake. This combination of names ought to celebrate the friendship of the two artists who first put this corner of the state on canvas and film (or rather, on plate)—Thomas Moran and William Jackson. A pity the lake is named for the wrong Jackson.

The road then passes the well-known Flagg Ranch and Leek's Camp, two old and indigenous fishing, hunting, and overnight camps, before hitting the big, handsome Rockefeller complex of **Colter Bay**. Centered around a marina and a street of stores, a splendid restaurant and cafeteria, and other conveniences are an extensive camp of old cabins moved from older resorts around Jackson Hole. Colter Bay even has a small museum (mostly Indian artifacts) and an outdoor church stadium, where weekly services are held by young students attached to the Christian Ministry in the National Parks. In the late 1980s, the complex was temporarily disturbed by the rebuilding of the Jackson Lake dam, and the consequent lowering of the water level, which put the marina out of business. The dam is now repaired, the water has risen, and the marinas have resumed business.

The dam was built under difficult conditions in 1910-11 on the site of a feeble earth dam. The tale of its building is grippingly and amusingly told by Eliot Paul in his somewhat fictionalized *Desperate Scenery* of 1954, an overdramatized account which is much too pro-dam and anti-native; but it certainly gives a vivid picture of the engineering feats of the dam's construction by a superb writer who just happened to be there. Locals, particularly conservationists, were violently opposed to the project. For one thing, the

GRAND TETON NATIONAL PARK
YELLOWSTONE NATIONAL PARK
JOHN D. ROCKEFELLER JR. MEMORIAL PARKWAY
FLAGG RANCH
N
GRAND TETON NATIONAL FOREST
TETON NATIONAL FOREST
TARGHEE NATIONAL FOREST
JACKSON LAKE
TWO OCEAN LAKE
EMMA MATILDA LAKE
COLTER BAY VISITOR CENTER
BUFFALO ENTRANCE STATION
CHAPEL OF THE SACRED HEART
SIGNAL MOUNTAIN LODGE
MORAN JUNCTION
MOUNT MORAN (12,605 FT.)
SIGNAL MTN. (7,593 FT.)
GRAND TARGHEE RESORT SKI AREA
LEIGH LAKE
TEEWINOT MTN. (12,325 FT.)
TO DUBOIS AND TOGWOTEE PASS
STRING LAKE
HIDDEN FALLS
MOUNT OWEN (12,928 FT.)
GRAND TETON (13,766 FT.)
JENNY LAKE
CUNNINGHAM CABIN HISTORIC SITE
MIDDLE TETON (12,804 FT.)
BRADLEY LAKE
TRIANGLE X RANCH
SHADOW MOUNTAIN
SOUTH TETON (12,514 FT.)
ANTELOPE FLATS RD.
DEATH CANYON
TAGGART LAKE
TETON SCIENCE SCHOOL
HOLE
PHELPS LAKE
IDAHO
WYOMING
GROS VENTRE RIVER
KELLY
BLACKTAIL BUTTE (7,688 FT.)
GROS VENTRE
GROS VENTRE SLIDE
JACKSON HOLE SKI AREA
TETON VILLAGE
JACKSON HOLE AIRPORT
RENDEVOUS PEAK (11,092 FT.)
SNAKE RIVER
NATL. ELK REFUGE
TO GRAND TARGHEE
JACKSON NATIONAL FISH HATCHERY
MOOSE-WILSON RD.
TETON NATIONAL FOREST
REFUGE VISITOR CENTER (WINTER ONLY)
TETON PASS (8,431 FT.)
WILSON
WEST GROS VENTRE BUTTE
EAST GROS VENTRE BUTTE
JACKSON
INFORMATION CENTER
JACKSON
SNOW KING MOUNTAIN SKI AREA
TO PINEDALE
89
191
287
26
22
0
5 mi
0
5 km

The Creation of Grand Teton National Park

Unlike most Western national parks that were created from wilderness by the government, Grand Teton National Park was a home-grown product, the result of local effort.

After World War I, it became obvious that the beauty of the old, secluded Jackson Hole was being tarnished by the booming commercialization of the Roaring Twenties. A group of Jackson Hole idealists, violently opposed by a group of local entrepreneurs, began to discuss ways of preserving the valley from exploitation. It became obvious that the only agency powerful enough to provide that sort of protection was the National Park Service.

Yellowstone Park was a next-door neighbor, but Yellowstone was exactly what the idealists did not want. A meeting at Menor's Ferry (now Moose) in 1923 with the then-superintendent of Yellowstone, Horace Albright, confirmed that Albright just wanted to extend Yellowstone's boundaries to include the Hole. The locals hated the Yellowstone spectacle of yellow buses, gaping tourists, and huge hotels. They just wanted to keep the Hole the way it had been—a place of untouched natural beauty, with a small population of ranchers and sympathetic summer visitors.

What stood in the way of a takeover by the park service was the amount of privately owned land, mostly ranch holdings. When the idealists sought some benefactor to buy up these lands and turn them over to the National Park Service, the most obvious choice was John D. Rockefeller, Jr. Rockefeller had already demonstrated an incredibly generous interest in land preservation, as exemplified by his contributions to the Acadia and Great Smoky Mountains national parks. When J.D. Rockefeller visited Yellowstone in 1926, Horace Albright seized the opportunity to show him around Jackson Hole, and to point out examples of the progressive deterioration there—dead timber on the shores of Jackson Lake, cheap commercial excrescences around Jenny Lake, and uncontrolled, messy automobile camping sites. John D. Rockefeller got the message.

A camouflaged company called the Snake River Land and Cattle Company was organized to buy up properties in the north end of Jackson Hole. No one was supposed to know who the buyers were, as the very name of Rockefeller would, of course, boost prices. Against the advice of the project's initiators, the Rockefeller organization chose as their purchasing agent the most prominent local banker. He was in some ways the obvious choice; he knew the local real estate situation, since so many local ranchers were deep in debt to his bank. Unfortunately, he was also a leader in the local movement against conservation and for "progress."

All the bank's outstanding ranch mortgages were cleared up in no time. Then the banker resigned as agent and publicly exposed Rockefeller and his plans. Prices immediately rose, and a very active and vocal resistance to the plan emerged. The matter became one of local, then national, politics. Everyone got into the act, and the explosion nearly destroyed the whole project. For 20 years the battle raged. U.S. senators came to investigate, constant hearings were full of bitter debates between local pros and cons.

Since the actual Teton range itself was already in the national forest, it was easy enough to convert it into a Grand Teton National Park in 1929. This preserved the peaks and the lakes from any further exploitation, but the valley floor was still threatened. In 1943, Franklin D. Roosevelt created a Grand Teton National Monument, which took in the whole upper valley, including many of the by-now Rockefeller-owned properties. J.D.R. was becoming impatient. Horace Albright, now director of the whole National Park Service, and Harold Ickes, Roosevelt's Secretary of the Interior, were hard at work influencing the president and trying to keep Rockefeller from getting discouraged and selling out his holdings.

The move of creating a monument, however, roused a real storm of fury. National monuments could be created by direct presidential fiat, unlike national parks, which were created by Congress. But national monuments were *supposed* to be *small* sites, not thousands of acres of rangeland. Anti-Roosevelt politicians, who had no particular interest in conservation, took the opportunity to create an anti-Roosevelt crusade. The fact that they had some justification made the battle especially furious.

When the national monument was turned into Grand Teton National Park in 1950, the battle was won. Rockefeller donated his lands, the Park Service took over. A grim vision of what the valley would be like now if the conservationists had not won can be seen today south of Jackson. Rockefeller and Albright get the praise that they richly deserve for this salvation. The locals who started the whole idea are forgotten.

(following pages) Looking west to the Soda Fork Meadow in the Teton Wilderness. The Tetons are visible on the horizon.

water didn't help Wyoming at all. It was piped to Idaho's potato farmers. For another it ruined the shores of one of America's most beautiful big lakes for years and years. Dead timber, killed by the rise of the water, disfigured the lake until the Civilian Conservation Corps came along and cleared away the debris in the 1930s. Now it's beautiful again, if not quite natural, and there are beaches for swimming and water activities; especially since the marinas at Colter Bay and Signal Mountain Lodge are back in business. Just the same, Jackson Lake is, and always will be, an ambivalent example of exploitation on a grand scale. Potatoes are a good thing, and the lake is still beautiful. But.

Just before you get to this dam, up on a bluff with an overwhelming panorama of the Tetons, is **Jackson Lake Lodge**. This grandiose Rockefeller enterprise belongs in spirit to the similar great hotels of Yellowstone, like Old Faithful. It is, however, very much in the modern style, with an enormous plate-glass expanse in the main lobby looking out on lake and mountains, a huge dining room, luxurious cabins furnished in attractive Western style, and even a big swimming pool, opened to the public for a fee. Also a snappy new bar with a Teton view. It is not what in the West is called "rustic"—that is, built of logs, homey, and primitive. J.D. Rockefeller himself liked to contemplate the scenery from a little knoll north of the lodge, **Lunch Tree Hill**, to which a trail leads. It is marked by a memorial plaque.

The road forks south of Jackson Lake Lodge. The main highway, U.S. routes 26 and 287, goes east towards Moran Junction, Togwotee Pass and Lander. Teton Park Road, which runs down the west side of Jackson Hole, follows along the lake shore, past **Signal Mountain Lodge**, one of the more attractive lakeside resting places. Shortly beyond, a side road cuts east, rather steeply up **Signal Mountain**. From the top of this isolated foothill peak are epic views north, east, and south. Particularly vivid at sunset, the wide, gray, sagebrush valley floor stretches south on both sides of the wriggling course of the Snake River, and the great heights of the Gros Ventre (Grovont) mountains loom eastward. It was from Signal Mountain that Jackson took the first photograph of Jackson Lake in 1877. The photograph was dimmed by the residual smoke of a great forest fire, and burnt trees on top of Signal Mountain were visible in the photograph. That was more than 110 years ago.

(opposite) The Grand Teton rises behind the fall colors of Grand Teton National Park.

■ THE LAKES AT THE FOOT OF THE TETONS

Teton Park Road soon leaves the timber and starts across the sagebrush flats toward the Tetons. Again, from this angle are new, spectacular views of the principal peaks at their most pointed. From every direction, the Grand Teton (13,766 feet/4,196 m) changes character. From this northern side, it is a sharp spire; from due east, a rather smoothly shaped but elongated half-dome; from the south, a hulking, almost square-topped, rugged mass. The fact that Gannett Peak in the Wind Rivers beats out the Grand Teton as tallest in the state by a mere 38 feet (12 m) is a bitter pill for local chauvinists, sweetened by the knowledge that the Grand is world-famous and universally photogenic, whereas it's hard to pick out Gannett from the surrounding mass, and nobody has ever heard of it outside of Wyoming anyway.

At the foot of the abrupt wall of the Tetons is a chain of glacial lakes, each one different, which are among the park's chief glories. Leigh, String, Jenny, Bradley, Taggart and Phelps lakes are all preserved in their virgin state from the fate of Jackson Lake—but only because of the vigilance of local people who found out and exposed plans to desecrate them by dams; and from 1929 onward, by the park service. Leigh, String, and Jenny are approached by a one-way detour road that cuts west from Teton Park Road at North Jenny Lake Junction.

Trails from the parking area at String Lake lead to Leigh Lake and up toward the mountains. **String Lake** is something of a misnomer, since it's not really a separate lake so much as the somnolent outlet of Leigh Lake, suitable for canoeing. You lose the crowds quickly as you walk north toward Leigh Lake. **Leigh Lake** is the most beautiful of all the park lakes, with many timbered bays and promontories reachable by trail, and magnificent views of the peaks, especially Mt. Moran.

The detour road continues south, passing the handsome **Jenny Lake Lodge**. Once the Tony Grace dude ranch, it is now a luxurious Rockefeller cabin-camp with the best restaurant in the valley attached to it (not cheap or easy to get into; reservations recommended). The road then goes alongside **Jenny Lake**—round, deep blue, right under the Grand Teton—the most accessible and frequented of these smaller lakes. This area was devastated by a freak cyclone from the mountains a few years ago, but now has grown back. Facilities include a campground, store, docks, and boat service across Jenny Lake. There, you can hike to **Hidden Falls**—rushing, white, ice-cold, but these days anything but hidden.

Reaching the two smaller lakes farther south, Taggart and Bradley, requires a certain amount of tramping, particularly Bradley. **Taggart Lake** suffered a fire about its eastern approaches in 1985, and the area now gives the hiker some idea of just how slowly fire-damaged forests recover. The blackened timber, mostly lodgepole pine, remains grimly erect overhead. But undergrowth is green and burgeoning—sometimes head-high aspens and stream-side bushes, sometimes a vast carpet of baby lodgepoles. One odd advantage of the fire damage is the extensive new views of the nearby Tetons and the farther Gros Ventre peaks. Luckily, Taggart's shores remain almost totally untouched, and the fire didn't get to Bradley.

Bradley Lake is really "hidden" (as the aforementioned falls is not), secluded in its own cup of forest foothills, separated from Taggart by a high, wildflower-covered moraine. The trail to the lake is moderately steep and requires some stamina, and like all park trails is clearly marked, with mileages.

All these trails continue up into the mountains behind. Miles of scenery; views of the valley below and the peaks above; tumbling, icy mountain streams cascading down from hidden, small glacial lakes, and all sorts of flowers and growth alongside the trail are revealed to travelers on foot or horseback as they climb above the cliffs and canyons. Then come the peaks themselves, and the world of mountain climbing. The Grand Teton is the prime target here—one of the safest, and in its way easiest, of Teton climbs. That doesn't mean it's a boulevard for wheelchairs; but the routes and variations are thoroughly worked out. Properly guided, no one is at risk. This can't be said of some other peaks, and foolish people who scorn guides and don't follow instructions fall off every year.

Phelps Lake, southernmost of the chain, is semi-private. The land around the outlet is the J Y Ranch, first dude ranch in the valley (circa 1907), and for years one of the most prestigious. It now belongs to the Rockefeller family. Park trails go up along its northern side and into **Death Canyon**. This most conspicuous of the Teton Range's canyons leads up from the west end of Phelps Lake, and is a favorite camping and packing area. The name seems appropriate to the great, solemn cliffs at the entrance, which look like Hittite or Egyptian gods. But no one really knows for sure what the name signifies. There are old tales of mysterious noises—horses running where there were no horses—and rumors of rustlers ambushed and killed; but nothing worthy of the setting and the name. Nothing sinister has happened up there lately.

Altogether the Tetons and their lakes, trails, canyons, and climbs are enough to keep a healthy hiker or horseback visitor happy for weeks.

■ Moose

The Jenny Lake detour joins Teton Park Road at South Jenny Lake Junction. Passing along an odd, forested protrusion from the flats called **Timber Island** (where it's quite easy to get lost, despite its narrowness), Teton Park Road crosses Cottonwood Creek and goes down a bench to Moose. Here, it crosses over the Snake River to join U.S. Route 191, which has been running down the east side of Jackson Hole.

Moose was once the crossing point of the old Menor's ferry (pronounced MEE-ners), for years the only way across the Snake between Wilson, way to the south, and Moran, way to the north. The Snake River at this particular point is, for a change, concentrated in one smooth, deep channel. Besides the ferry, there was a store and a few cabins. Now it's the site of the Moose Post Office, official headquarters and chief visitors center for Grand Teton National Park, with a tourist desk and a big exhibition area. Along the river are preserved mementoes of the old days. Of these, the most popular is the pretty little log **Chapel of the Transfiguration**, with its plate-glass window framing the Grand Teton behind the altar. This was copied from the famous mission church at Ethete,

John Jakubowski and Shanna Driscoll enjoy amenity-free country living in their small Wilson cabin.

(opposite) A rainbow arches over Rosie's Ridge near Moran.

on the Wind River Indian Reservation; but it must be admitted that the scene so framed is far more dramatic in Moose. The summers-only congregation is not Indian, but a total spectrum of visitors passing through, of nearly every Protestant denomination. You no longer see horses tied to the fence outside as you did in bygone days, when some prestigious dude ranches, now defunct, were nearby. A trail leads from the church's crowded parking lot to the river, where is preserved the old Menor cabin and a replica of **Menor's ferry**. Two cantankerous bachelor brothers, Bill and Holiday, lived on opposite sides of the river and refused to speak for years. Bill operated the ferry.

Nearby is also preserved the **Maud Noble cabin**. Miss Maud was a Philadelphia spinster of high degree and great presence, who ran away west with the family coachman, Sidney Sandell. He was a lively little Cockney, who for years ran the store at the ferry. She always called him "Sidney." He always called her "Miss Noble." She looked like George Washington, with snow-white, cropped hair and severe black riding clothes. The cabin is preserved not so much in memory of this odd companionship, as it is for the site of a seminal meeting in 1923. Horace Albright, then superintendent of Yellowstone Park, and a group of local conservationists got together to try to work out a plan of action to preserve the valley. Albright simply wanted to extend the boundaries of Yellowstone. The locals objected strongly. They didn't want to see their valley become another mass tourist attraction, with big hotels, yellow buses, and fat ladies in knickers and golf caps—which was the distinguishing dress of the touristic fat femme fatale in those ancient days. (It can't be said that things are any better now.) They had in mind some sort of preservation of Jackson Hole, exactly as it had been before the contaminations of the Twenties—a "museum on the hoof"— a romantic and impractical hope of preserving the past into the present. The meeting was a failure, but these former antagonists got together later on, and in a battle that lasted for decades finally saw the creation of the enlarged Grand Teton Park in 1950.

Though Grand Teton is no museum on the hoof, but rather a big, crowded national park, there still is a difference between it and Yellowstone. Yellowstone remains strictly a mass operation. Grand Teton is much more individual, informal, intimate, and oriented toward youth, action, nature study, science, and art. People aren't just crowding around geysers. They climb mountains, watch birds and big game, ride horses and hike on trails, and raft down the Snake. Just the same, it's a big bustling park, and not what the idealists of 1923 had in mind.

A big bridge, no longer a ferry, now crosses the Snake at Moose. On the other side is **Dornan's**, a private enclave founded and owned by the daughter and son-in-law of

Joe Jones, one of those local dreamers. There is a picturesque, outdoor chuckwagon eating place, adorned with teepees for bad weather, with the river alongside and spectacular views of the Tetons to the west. Stores carry sundries and specialties, and a most pleasant bar has an open deck on top.

■ The Back Road from Moose to Teton Village

The Moose-Wilson Road turns southwest from Moose, back up the bench and down the west side of Jackson Hole to Teton Village and Mosquito Flats, below the park boundary. It's a narrow road, paved only part way, between the river and the foothills, going through aspens, willows, and pines, and past various hidden ranches, including the JY. It's a road that can be recommended scenically, but not as a traffic artery. Too many people use it for slow-going comfort, and curves threaten collisions.

When you emerge into the sunlight, you are faced by the grandiose, absurdly neo-Swiss compound of **Teton Village**, full of broad, overhanging roofs and balconies. This importation of the spirit of Colorado (á la Vail) into Wyoming is Jackson Hole's principal ski resort, with lifts (including a famous year-round one to the top of the foothills), runs, and Alpine hotels. It is all very modern and rather awful, but also amusing and very successful, especially in winter. In summer, it's very active, too. The hotels cater to different budgets, with varying degrees of competence. There are shops and condominiums. The principal summer attraction is the Grand Teton Festival Orchestra and its solid, two-month-long schedule of musical activities, ranging from full orchestral concerts each weekend to a great variety of chamber and solo performances during the week. Famous soloists, visiting orchestras (the New York Philharmonic performed in 1989), and choruses diversify the summer programs. Under the long-time direction of conductor Ling Tung, this musical attraction has become one of the chief pleasures of the valley's summer life.

South of this enterprise, with its restaurants, famous chair lift, concert hall, and mosquitoes, lies a sort of super-strip of other attractions—some cheap in every way, some very elegant. Along the river, you still see beautiful, big private ranches, green with hay, aspens, and cottonwoods. But on the right, under the mountains, there are all sorts of developments. Most elegant of these is the public **Jackson Hole Racquet and Tennis Club**, which operates a choice restaurant. It is one of the nicer additions to the new Jackson Hole—albeit very un-Old Time.

(following pages) Old wagons age gracefully at Triangle X Ranch, with the sharp-edged Tetons as a backdrop.

Still farther down the road is a brand-new, billion-dollar extravaganza called Teton Pines. Brought seemingly intact from Hollywood, this development has as much to do with the Hole as any other movie set. Its enormous main building looks like a beautifully decorated airport, with a beautifully decorated restaurant overlooking beautifully decorated condominiums. You could fly in from L.A., play golf, fly out, and never know you'd left home. There is, of course, a fine view of the Tetons—which in this setting look like photographs of themselves. This is the most extreme manifestation of the new Jackson Hole—of far-flung movie moguls and millionaires from all over, who have built massive mansions and swimming pools so that they can enjoy the simple life of the Old West. Fortunately, many of them are full of local spirit and support for conservation, the arts, and everything worthwhile. It's all rather breath-taking and confusing. Things sure ain't what they once was.

■ Teton Pass

The Moose-Wilson Road comes to an end as it runs into Wyoming State Highway 22, after a good deal more roadside development—some of it pretty tawdry. Highway 22 runs west from Jackson over **Teton Pass**, which at one time was the one viable way into the Hole and the only real link with the outside world. Teton Pass was famous for its difficulties. Nowadays, it leads easily up over the tail-end of the Tetons to Victor, Idaho, once the train station for Jackson, but now a farming backwater town. This route is also the only link with an odd little lost fringe of Wyoming that lies on the west side of the Tetons. From Victor, take Idaho State Highway 33 due north, then turn east after Driggs, Idaho, to the secluded resort of **Alta**, Wyoming, nestled under the *west* side of the Tetons in the Targhee National Forest. Alta is a world-class ski resort and the view of the Tetons from the back, so to speak, is pretty striking, too. It was from this side that Moran did his sketches of the Teton range—the first in history—but not of his own Mt. Moran.

Back on Highway 22 at the eastern end of Teton Pass—in Jackson Hole—is the small community of **Wilson**. Named for the family that moved here en masse in 1889, the town is still a small center for neighboring cattle and dude ranches, and has a bar and stores. Its permanent population is surpassed even by the temporary populations of Teton Village and Colter Bay, but it has always been the "other town" of the Hole from the earliest days. A fascinatingly detailed history of Wilson and the Teton Pass by Doris B. Platts traces the story from trapper days up to 1940, with biographies of

Movies Made In Wyoming

Wyoming has been a setting for movie-making from the industry's earliest days. Some more recent films have celebrated such far-flung locales as Devils Tower (*Close Encounters of the Third Kind*) and Hole-in-the-Wall (*Butch Cassidy and the Sundance Kid*), but the principal location has been the exceptionally photogenic scenery of Jackson Hole.

Some of these Jackson Hole films have been easily forgettable horse operas, or silly romances such as *The Cowboy and the Lady* of 1922, starring the ill-fated Mary Miles Minter. She reclined in a sort of Arabian tent at the foot of the Tetons and received the peasantry there with royal condescension. Tom Mix's oater of 1925 was no more memorable. Much less forgettable, in Jackson Hole at least, was *The Big Trail* of 1930, an epic production that turned the economics of Teton County upside down, and was a major flop. However, it served its purpose. It introduced to the public the handsome, if not very animated, features of John Wayne. The West and Wayne were pals from then on.

Shane starred Alan Ladd and was shot in Jackson Hole in 1951. During the same summer as *Shane*, two other films were made in the Hole: *Jubal*, with Glenn Ford, and *The Big Sky*, with Kirk Douglas. These three rather exceptional shootings were balanced by the egregious *Spencer's Mountain* of 1963, which attempted to graft an Appalachian tale full of moonshiners and religious revivals onto Wyoming scenery. Henry Fonda did his best in this one.

The roster of male stars who have worked in Jackson Hole also includes such stars as Charlton Heston, Clint Eastwood, and Wallace Beery. Among heroines, only Jean Arthur seems to have made much of a hit in the Hole. It is a man's world, from the movie-making point of view. A nice little TV series, *The Monroes*, was shot on the shores of the Snake in 1970.

Somewhat different was the presence in the Hole of western comedian Wallace Beery, who became an annual summer visitor and obtrusive local personality in Jackson bars. He arrived by plane on the flats near Jenny Lake in the late 1930s and put up at a raffish pseudo-dude ranch called the Elbo, where he chased the cook around the kitchen. He then settled into his own summer place on Jackson Lake, where he made various forgettable films. His most spectacular public appearance was a much photographed ride across the flats to protest the creation of Jackson Hole National Monument, in 1943. This was supposed to be in defense of the rights of the range.

A complete filmography is available from the Wyoming Tourism Association.

(following page)The aerial tram offers unparalleled vistas on its 4,139-foot (1,261-m) climb up Rendezvous Peak at Jackson Hole Ski Resort.

JACKSON HOLE

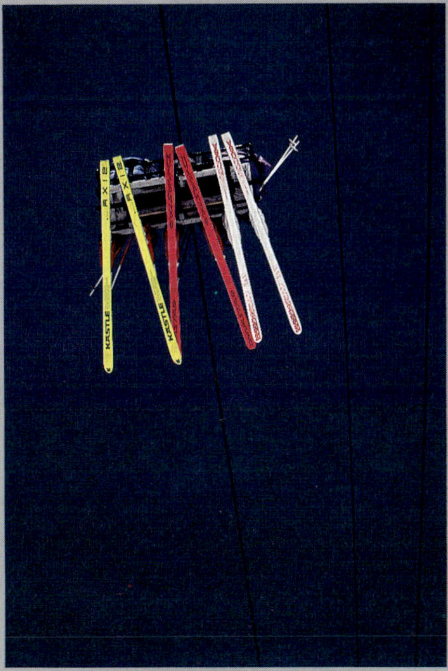
KÄSTLE

ATOMIC
ROSSIGNOL
BLIZZARD
HEAD

settlers and endless anecdotage. Longtime residents of the Hole have special feelings about the pass, not all necessarily kindly.

■ JACKSON

Going east from Wilson, the road soon reaches the outskirts of Jackson and its present day welter of commercialism. For years, since its founding at the turn of the century, Jackson was a dusty little cow town built around a dusty open square surrounded by a fence, to which were hitched dusty cow ponies (covered in mud and snow during the winter). No longer. Now it's a little metropolis overwhelmed by tourists. The town's central square has become a green, tree-shaded oasis, with **elk horn gates** leading into it, and surrounded on all four sides by a medley of shops—a few still in the old buildings, but transformed—and with the old plank sidewalks intact. The shops house everything from hardware to art galleries, but the effect is overwhelmingly that of expensive tourism.

Jackson in 1907 consisted of little more than a couple of farmhouses and shops. (Courtesy, Jackson Hole Museum and Teton County Historical Society)

(previous page) Jackson Hole Ski Resort is one of the premier ski areas in North America, a true "skiers' mountain."

Away from the center of town, south toward Snow King and its ski lift, Jackson's original character and charm abound in the casually mixed, old residential section, with its residual log cabins, such as the excellent **Public Library**, and old houses hidden in big trees, with bright flowers out front. However, farther south of town is the horrendous strip of rampant, unregenerate commercialism. There, modern times have conquered, as the founding fathers of the Grand Teton Park feared they would, all over the Hole, with the usual mix-up of supermarkets, stores, and motels run riot. In South Park, site of the valley's principal ranch and hay fields, new tract houses disfigure the landscape with brown suburbia. This is entirely the product of Wyoming's latest and only present boom: tourism. Like other booms, it too is hard at work disfiguring Wyoming's most precious asset—scenery—but with much, *much* less excuse than coal, oil, or reclamation dams.

However, in central Jackson you can certainly enjoy yourself, and it does have a wacky charm—half genuine Western, half bohemian pseudo-Western. Many of the restaurants are good, ranging from plain fare to the superlative, and the shops are enticing, if not cheap. There are summer theaters that put on spoofs of old musicals, and the **Silver Dollar Bar** of the handsome Wort Hotel still has its namesake coins imbed-

Jackson's 1920 local election created the first all-women town government in America. (Courtesy, Jackson Hole Museum and Teton County Historical Society)

COWBOY BAR
MILLION DOLLAR
Cowboy BAR
9PM
5 TO 7
ED THRU SAT

ded in the bar. Nightlife riots at the Wort and elsewhere roundabout, though the open gambling of the Thirties and later has gone—some think to the detriment of atmosphere (if not of pocketbooks). Things are still going on in winter during the skiing season, so the town jumps both day and night, summer and winter.

There are some 40 art galleries (so-called), and this phase of Jackson life has gotten rather out-of-hand. Lots of galleries are full of junk, not art, but many are serious and have choice objects—at a price.

There are also real museums. One of these is the **Wildlife of the American West Museum**, on the northeast corner of the town square, which has a stylishly hung and well-cared-for permanent collection of wildlife art, as well as temporary exhibits. The museum is famous for its landscapes by Carl Rungius, and also features works by Russell, Schwiering, Catlin, Ernest Thompson Seton, and John Clymer. Also fascinating, with far more local emphasis, is the **Jackson Hole Museum**, much better organized and displayed than most places of its kind (every town in Wyoming has one), with strikingly presented local history ranging from prehistoric days to the present. It's now on the corner of DeLoney and Glenwood streets, right in midtown, but plans to move into a newer, bigger, fire-proof building; one hopes it won't lose its present charm and

Christmas lights dress up the famous elk antler arches of Jackson's town square.

(opposite) Jackson's famed Cowboy Bar attracts both locals and tourists.

character in the process. This museum is a one-man foundation by old-timer Slim Lawrence, who collected most of the material himself and founded the museum. The present superb display is that of later hands. Both museums have entrance fees.

There is also a small **Teton Historical Society** with exhibits, free, located at the far (which isn't very far) northwest of the town at Glenwood and Merrill streets. You can also find two good bookshops. Essentially, however, Jackson is now very much a good-time town, and culture merely a by-product.

Jackson to Moose

Heading north again from Jackson on U.S. Route 191 (which is also routes 89 and 26), you pass along the west edge of the **National Elk Refuge**, where the local elk are fed in the winter. The adjacent bird sanctuary occasionally has rare wild trumpeter swans on its waters. A handsome, modern visitors center en route has a respectable collection of paintings of Jackson Hole.

After passing a smattering of gas stations and stores across the road, the highway rises and leaves Jackson and all its works, good and bad. You are back out on the flats. The Tetons command the view from now on, and soon you re-enter Grand Teton Park. Numerous turnouts along the road permit you to gaze and photograph. Then

you cross the **Gros Ventre River**, flowing down from the northeast. Right after the bridge, there's a crossroad known as Gros Ventre Junction.

One road goes northeast to the site of the **Gros Ventre Slide** and its residual lake. This dramatic cataclysm of 1925 was, first, a great landslide down the rump of **Sheep Mountain.** Named for its mountain sheep, but nicknamed the Sleeping Indian because of its profile, Sheep Mountain is the principal protuberance of the Gros Ventre Range. A huge mass of earth slid across the Gros Ventre River and swooped up the opposite side, forming a lake. In 1927, this lake burst through its dam and roared downstream in a flood that destroyed the little town of Kelly (since rebuilt), devastated ranches, took out bridges, and drowned several people. What was left was the huge gouge of the slide, the remains of the dam, and its reduced lake. The road goes up along all this, and then rather precariously on into the secluded valley beyond, with its few choice ranches and surrounding wilderness. (Incidentally, *Gros Ventre* means "big belly" in trapper French, while *Teton* means "tit." Though the names are totally appropriate to the shape of the two ranges, if hardly poetic, they were originally derived from the French names for two local Indian sub-tribes.)

A second road at Gros Ventre Junction takes off *west* from the highway to another of the Hole's modern Shangri-las. This is **Jackson Hole Golf and Tennis Center**, sponsored by Rockefeller interests, with a beautifully manicured golf course, big swimming pool, tennis courts, and a fine restaurant, the Strutting Grouse. These facilities are generally open to the public (notably the wonderful restaurant)—at a price. Around and amid the wanderings of the green golf course are various developments called "estates" (of a few acres), with sumptuous, modern villas on them. Once again, the new Jackson Hole with a vengeance.

Of these villas, the most astoundingly beautiful is that of the well-known artist, Joanne Hennes, one of the key figures in Jackson's hyperactive art world. As it's her showroom and studio, as well as her home, you can visit it; and it is certainly one of the most fantastically and originally landscaped garden spots in Wyoming, or anywhere. Once-humble ranch ditches have been converted into a paradise of pools, fountains, small waterfalls, bridges, groves of trees, lawns, and flowers, native and exotic. To find the villa, take Spruce Drive west from the south side of the clubhouse complex. Larkspur Drive is the second road to the left, and the studio is at the end.

The road past the center follows and crosses the Gros Ventre River, and then heads through still unspoiled **Spring Gulch** and its fine ranches. On top of the big butte east is yet another Shangri-la, Spring Creek Ranch. On top, there is no ranch at all, of

(opposite) Slide Lake and the devastating Gros Ventre Slide of June 1925. (Courtesy, Jackson Hole Museum and Teton County Historical Society)

course, but a collection of Scandinavian-style condominiums, and another restaurant, The Granary, with one of the most astounding views of valley and peaks in the Hole. The restaurant is worth the trip, particularly at sunset.

Returning to Gros Ventre Junction and to real life, the main highway continues north, past the airport, and back to Moose.

■ Moose to the East Gate

The road from Moose to Moran Junction follows along the top of the bench above the Snake River, with turnoffs all along. Here are probably the most spectacular series of roadside views of the Tetons, across the river and the flats beyond, each with its slightly different aspect of the mountains. Little dirt roads take you down to the river and boat landings at various points. Fishing is popular here. Guides lead rubber raft floats down the river. In the old days, people drowned trying it on their own.

Along with the view of Mt. Moran reflected in Jackson Lake, another famous photograph of the Tetons, this one by Ansel Adams, shows the pointed peaks rising over

Barry Richardson unhitches a team of work horses from the hay sleigh at Jackson Hole Hereford Ranch.

(opposite) The view across Antelope Flats to the Tetons.

the bend of the Snake River at **Deadman's Bar.** Unlike Death Canyon, the story behind the sinister name is common knowledge. A group of German strangers came to the bar, a flat place in the curve of the river on the west side, looking for gold. They dug sluices, traces of which still remain, kept to themselves, and then suddenly disappeared. Grisly remains of three of the gold seekers were found in the river. The fourth was eventually arrested in southern Wyoming, and in one of the most notorious miscarriages of justice, even for Wyoming, was set free due to "lack of evidence." He was never heard of again.

Now the view over Deadman's Bar is internationally familiar. A giant blowup of the scene even appeared as an advertisement over Times Square, in New York, a few years ago. Things sure have changed from the days of the murdered gold miners.

Then the road descends, leaving the bench to curve through hay fields and meadows, and crosses Spread Creek and Buffalo Fork. At **Moran Junction**, the official east gate of the park, the highway splits, with one road returning to Jackson Lake and Yellowstone. This guide, however, follows U.S. Route 287 (and 26) east over Togwotee Pass, and down into the Wind River Basin.

■ POSTSCRIPT

The tourist season in Jackson Hole lasts from early summer into fall (fishing, hunting) and winter (skiing, snowmobiling). In late winter and early spring, the natives get a chance to catch their breath.

In the old days, those who wanted to stay in the valley for a long summer would check into one of the many area dude ranches. Starting with the J Y, and growing over the years to include a group of others, the Hole was one of the principal centers of dude ranching. In those days, visitors came by train to Victor, and stayed for weeks. Teton Pass was the only safe way in, and even that wasn't too safe. The valley was nearly empty above Menor's Ferry, the lakes pristine and unvisited, fishing in the Snake world-famous (for a few), and the surrounding hills ideal for pack trips. Everybody who wasn't on a dude ranch was a cattleman or worked in Jackson.

Then, beginning in the late 1920s, came the automobile, and what were derisively known as "tin can tourists."

The automobile did not really take over until World War II, however, and the dude ranch world still dominated the thoughts and feelings of visitors until the 1950s. Now, the great flood of car travel has pushed the earlier way of life and conception of Jackson Hole into a reclusive, but still active, corner. The remaining dude ranches still flourish. Many of the long-time settlers and ranch owners were once dudes; but the new Jackson Hole, south of the park, is for the most part ignorant of that whole way of life and feeling.

Golf courses, fancy restaurants, and condominiums were not part of that bygone era, and these amenities were and are despised by those who once loved and still love the old Jackson Hole. A good dude ranch still remains the best way to get away from that brand-new way of life and the explosion of summer tourism, and to find out what Jackson Hole used to be like. The moral in back of this, however, is universal. A day's drive through the Hole or any part of Wyoming is just a glimpse, a taste. However you manage it, you have to stop and stay and poke about and discover for yourself (or with the help of experts) what you can never see from a passing automobile.

> Young man after young man, coming west with the intention of curing his passion for alcohol, opened a dude ranch. And young women, not so alcoholic but equally irresponsible, did the same. The mountain fastnesses are still filled with them, and in their not so tender keeping the dude is still breaking bones and getting lost. Strange that you would trust yourself in a lonely, and always potentially dangerous, country, if you don't know what you are doing, with anyone but an expert! It all looks so simple, but it isn't. . . . And my advice is that if you want to go to a dude ranch, find out first the history of the man who runs it. A college education doesn't necessarily make you good in the mountains.
>
> —Struthers Burt, *Powder River, Let 'Er Buck*, 1938

INDIAN LAND

THE ENORMOUS WIND RIVER AREA, EMBRACED BY FREMONT and Sublette counties, poses a special problem for the traveler because of the rugged nature of the Wind River range. There's no real way to get through it. Between the Wind and Green river basins, there's no direct road.

These two sides of the Wind River Mountains are directly accessible for most travelers from the south, through Rawlins or Rock Springs, across vast stretches of semidesert. Far more beautiful and impressive is a round-trip starting and ending in Jackson Hole: a great loop going over Togwotee Pass to Lander, around the south end of the mountains up to Pinedale, and back. It's better done as a two-day trip. From Moran Junction to Lander is 128 miles (206 km), a good morning's drive. Settled at Lander, the afternoon can be profitably spent on the Wind River Indian Reservation. After Lander the trip back up to Jackson Hole, via South Pass and Pinedale, is full of scenic and historical rewards.

■ TOGWOTEE PASS TO DUBOIS

Togwotee Pass (pronounced toegatee) crosses the Continental Divide between Jackson Hole and the Wind River Basin. It was used by Indians, by Colter and fellow trapper-guide John Hoback about 1810, and afterward by numberless other trappers and explorers. After the period of the trappers, it was more or less forgotten and not really rediscovered until 1873. Then, an army surveyor recommended it as a possible military road, but Congress was not interested. In 1898, however, a military road was finally built. It was declared by its builders to be a "model road," but since wagons had to be let down the west side by ropes and winches, one wonders. It wasn't till 1922 that a barely passable auto road evolved from the wagon trail. Until very recently, the pass was famous for corkscrew curves, steep grades, and exciting views west. Now, of course, you can sail over without a thought and miss half the charm and all the excitement. It's still surpassingly beautiful, however, especially through the lush meadows at the top, often decorated by snowbanks into July, and by wildflowers well into August. There are still fine views of the Tetons to the west, and a big pull-off at the top, indicating that this is the Continental Divide—9,658 feet (2,944 m) high.

(opposite) A dancer sits on the sidelines at Fort Washakie's Eastern Shoshone Indian Days Powwow.

A brief detour to the left, as you go down the east side, takes you to secluded **Brooks Lake**, surrounded by odd, steep-sided, white mountain mesas, and green vales. This was once the site of a famous dude ranch, the Diamond G, now a nice camp, picnic area, and fishing site. Continuing east, with a wide panorama of the valley ahead and startling views north of the white, pinnacled Palisades, you pass the Falls Campground, eventually leaving the timber and crossing the infant Wind River.

Before reaching Dubois, you pass a conspicuous monument celebrating the tie-hackers of the Wind River Basin. It has a fine view down the valley from its site on a roadside hillock. Tie-hackers were lumbermen who cut track ties for the railroads. The forests to the west were the scene of their activities from 1914 until the 1950s. The peak year was 1947, when some 700,000 ties were cut; but with the decline of the railroads, the business declined, too, and died. It is now romanticized as a special, macho John Bunyan sort of profession. At the time, ranchers and conservationists looked at it all with dismay—the slaughter of trees and choking of mountain streams, including the Green River, with lumber floating down at flood time toward the Union Pacific. Now, however, it has become part of the historical heritage of the upper Wind River valley.

Dubois is the first town on the drive from Jackson, and another Western cow town raped by highway expansion through its main street. Yet, it still retains some of its old quality as a center for cattle and dude ranches for a wide area of the mountain-bordered valley.

The fairly new **Dubois Museum and Visitor Center** on the western outskirts of Dubois celebrates the tie-hacking profession and other aspects of local and natural history. These displays provide colorful, instructive, and even amusing historical detail. Almost every town of any size in the state now has a historical museum, but the Dubois Museum is especially nice.

■ Wind River Reservation: Historical Overview

Southeast from Dubois, the country opens and dries up progressively as the highway travels downstream through spectacular red badlands, with high peaks in the distant background. Soon the road enters the Wind River Indian Reservation, one of the largest in the West, and the only one in Wyoming. It covers a green, flat valley that gradually broadens out into the central plains of the Sweetwater River.

The Wind River Reservation differs from some others, notably the Sioux reservations of the Dakotas, in that it was more of a reward than a punishment. It was given to the

Shoshone in recognition of the friendship of their great Chief Washakie with the white settlers. Whereas the Sioux chiefs, like Red Cloud, were shipped to the Dakotas as a penance for their wars against the whites, Washakie saw the future, having lived the past; and though he didn't necessarily like it, instead of aggravating the United States government, he decided to cooperate. Whether, in the end, he and the Shoshone fared much better than the warlike Sioux will always be a matter of dispute. It is impossible to get a truly impartial, wise, all-knowing opinion on any matter of any kind involving Indian-white relations. Bias emerges inevitably. Suffice it to say that Washakie was the U.S. government's favorite chief in Wyoming, and that in giving his tribe this passably fertile and well-watered land, officials believed they were rewarding him.

Just after you pass into the reservation, about ten miles (16 km) beyond Dubois, you cross Dinwoody Creek, which flows down from the Dinwoody lakes in the foothills. On the **Upper Dinwoody Lake** is one of the most important prehistoric sites in Wyoming: a series of abstract pictographs, different from other Plains work. Unfortunately, they are not readily visible. The tribal agency has closed the area to protect the pictographs from vandalism, and they are reachable only by a very rough road not suitable for ordinary cars. Anyone with serious interest and credentials, however, might arrange a special visit by calling the agency's fish and game department.

Chief Washakie, longtime leader of the Shoshone and a friend of the U.S. government. (Courtesy, Wyoming State Museum)

Along the river, some ten miles (16 km) farther south, is a striking butte with a flat top, called **Crowheart Butte**. This was the legendary site of a single-combat fight between the Shoshone and Crow chiefs. The Shoshone, supposedly Chief Washakie himself, won and celebrated his victory by eating the heart of his enemy. This was not too outrageous by Indian standards, since eating the heart of something brave, say a bear, gave you the victim's courage. Everyone in the region was brought up on this story, and it is indeed an excellent example of the superiority of Memorable Myth over Fussy Facts. No one could possibly forget the heart-eating story. Unfortunately the Fussy Facts—the probable facts, as prominently presented by a detailed historical marker on the road opposite the butte—confirm these details: the battle took place in March 1866, with the Shoshone and Bannocks fighting the Crows over the perennial issue of hunting rights. Chief Washakie sure enough conducted the battle and won, but the battle was just in the neighborhood, near Black Mountain. Nobody fought on top of the butte; indeed it would have been a scramble to get up there (although teepee rings show that people did reach the top). And nobody ate a heart. Chief Washakie merely "displayed a Crow warrior's heart on his lance at the war dance after the battle."

This is a flawless example of the relative value of myth versus fact. No one would give two cents for the truth (if it is truth) of this story, interesting though it may be. But the myth is unforgettable and appropriate for this striking landmark. At sunset, the butte is a mythical blood-red; at noon, a factual drab tan. Take your pick. (It may be that the myth is true. Washakie himself never denied the story. In fact, when quizzed about the incident by an old-timer, he replied cautiously, "When you are young and full of life, you do strange things.")

The badlands country in the western part of Wind River Indian Reservation is some of the most dramatic in Wyoming.

All Wyoming is saturated with such myths, a good many of them bloody. Some are more true than others; but true or not-so-true, they have become an integral part of the state's personality. To ignore or downgrade them is to dismiss a basic part of the Wyoming character, which has always been prone to tall tales. So take the stories as repeated in this work with the same grain of salt as you would the tales of any Wyoming old-timer.

After you pass an irrigation dam (Bull Lake), the road forks. Continue on U.S. Route 287 toward Lander. **Fort Washakie**, 16 miles (26 km) from the junction, is reservation headquarters, and named for the great Shoshone chief "in whose teepee never hung the scalp of a white man."

The Shoshone were by no means blindly loyal to the whites. There was an uprising in 1861-62, but most of the country was then involved in the Civil War, so the government appeased the tribe with vague promises of huge grants of land—most of southwest Wyoming. In 1868, out of friendship for Washakie, the tribe was promised the entire lower Wind River Basin, at that time called the Popo Agie after the river flowing across the southern border. (Opinions on pronunciation vary widely, but you won't

Sharply folded beds of purple and black shale create a lunar landscape behind the lush Wind River west of Crowheart.

go wrong with "po pashia.") This was the richest, wettest land in the whole area, so the Shoshone were gradually pushed north by eager, illegal settlers. Sioux, Cheyennes, and Arapahoes kept invading, and in 1869, Red Cloud killed 30 Shoshone (and two white women), and stole their horses. In protest, Washakie refused to occupy the area without U.S. military protection. He eventually trekked south to the Green River area, and wouldn't come back until a treaty was signed in 1872. However, he settled for less than what he wanted, giving up some 600,000 fertile acres (240,000 ha) of the Popo Agie valley for $25,000 and a promise of protection. The reservation was now confined to the north part of the basin, spilling over eventually into the Big Horn basin, and the government established Fort Brown for protection. The name was changed to Fort Washakie in 1878.

After a defeat by the joint forces of the Shoshone, Crows, and U.S. troops in 1876, the Arapahoes were settled on the east side of the Shoshone Reservation. One story goes that the Shoshone wanted to keep an eye on these troublemakers. There was a long history afterward of suits and counter-suits by both tribes. By now, the two tribes are more or less blood brothers in the common cause of protecting Indian rights and resources on the reservation. The ancient hatchet appears to have been buried.

The U.S. government wanted to abandon Fort Washakie, along with its other old Indian war forts, at the end of the nineteenth century. But Washakie was still alive to object until his death in 1900, and out of respect, the post was not closed till 1909. Now, the fort's many buildings have been turned into the tribal agency headquarters. Instead of being a carefully embalmed but empty historic site, it's full of life and occupancy, and probably gives a truer idea of what such a living fort may have been like in earlier days.

■ Lander

Just four miles south of the reservation border on Highway 287 is **Lander**, the seat of Fremont County. With a population of 7,800, it's a prosperous-looking, settled, civilized place—old cattle, old oil, with residential sections more like an older New Jersey suburb than anything Wild West, far less Shoshone. The town's chief attractions include the once-famous **Noble Hotel**, tree-shaded side streets and a pretty town park on the Popo Agie River. In its day, the Noble was full of handmade furniture and decorated with Indian designs, while the lobby walls were hung with mounted game heads and

Pioneer Museum, Lander

The Lander Pioneer Museum is worth visiting for its impressive Indian collection, which preserves buffalo robes, beaded gloves, painted buffalo hides, and a squaw saddle. For something completely different, peek in the tiny wedding chapel, a popular place for spring nuptials. Another room, the One-Shot Antelope Hunt Memorial Room, is devoted to this rather bizarre sport with its own celebrities. Out front is the obligatory sheepherder's wagon, an older version of the RV, still used by those who spend months at a time alone with their flocks of sheep.

Indian trophies. Anybody of importance who came to the reservation put up there. No more. Now the motels and roadside eateries have everywhere taken the place of such grand old Wyoming hotels. The loss in atmosphere is total; the loss of the convenience of a downtown location is likewise considerable; but in comfort, cleanliness, and quiet, the good motels are certainly improvements on some not-so-good hotels of yore.

The newly enlarged **Pioneer Museum** is full of souvenirs from the good old days; which in Wyoming means almost any time before 1920. At the north edge of Lander is a little, modern **Indian village**, with teepees, a store, and a center where various dances and celebrations are put on by tribal youngsters.

A circle tour is the best way to take in the sights of the reservation, if you can make camp in Lander early enough to have a free afternoon. A visit to Fort Washakie and the three missions—St. Stephen's (Arapaho and Catholic), St. Michael's (Arapaho and Episcopalian), and the Reverend Roberts' Episcopalian girls' school (Shoshone)—will give you a survey of this special and curious area.

■ St. Stephen's

Big, wide Wyoming State Highway 789 leaves Lander heading northeast, immediately after crossing the Popo Agie on the south end of town, and passes some messy old oil works toward Riverton. At **Hudson**, a quaintly derelict cow town (where there is a famous old restaurant, **El Toro**, specializing, of course, in beef), turn left on State Highway 138, clearly marked, which takes you directly to the St. Stephen's Catholic mission.

St. Stephen's is a big establishment, with rather grandiose Victorian and early twentieth-century buildings, and a proper air of some papal pride and grandeur. Its old school is now gone, but as you drive up the long entrance road south from Highway 138 to the mission itself, you pass an almost equally grandiose new public school, its gymnasium peaked with a teepee-shaped roof. This impressive new building keeps to the spirit not only of St. Stephen's, but of the reservation as a whole. Quite a few strikingly designed modern buildings, most of them devoted to various aspects of the agency's public business, are equally impressive. They contrast with the modest private dwellings on the reservation.

St. Stephen's was started in the 1870s by Jesuits and nuns (German and Irish), who ran the school for boys and girls, and started a long tradition of preserving Indian arts and crafts. Most of the religious personages have gone since the schools secularized (with the establishment of public education). The big Victorian nunnery, which once housed the sisters, is vacant. The pride of the mission now is its comparatively new (1928) **church**, combining Catholic ritual with Indian decor. Vivid native patterns decorate the church inside and out. Details—like a huge log-stump support for the christening font, a small teepee for an altar tabernacle, and Indian figures in the Stations of the Cross—all give the large, airy, handsome building a special atmosphere. The church seats a congregation of 700.

But probably the most interesting and exciting aspect of the present-day mission, reflected in the excellent museum and store, is the continuing work in local craft and art. Such products are displayed, along with some wonderful old photographs of Arapahoes, in the main church office building. An older building east of the church shows further evidence of this renaissance. Local Arapaho artist Bob Spoonhunter is actively promoting the rebirth of reservation arts and crafts, combining tradition with sophisticated modern styles and techniques. It's hard to resist purchasing some of the beautiful jewelry and other art work. This program is still in its early stages, and the plan is to take over the entire old building with permanent and changing exhibitions, studios, workshops, and lecture rooms.

(opposite) Flat Top Mountain juts above the scenic Green River Lakes in the Wind River Mountains. (photo by Martin Vidak).

■ Ethete to Fort Washakie

St. Michael's Episcopalian mission is in Ethete, right in the center of the southern, settled part of the reservation, between Riverton and Lander. It was the principal school for Arapaho children, and consists of red stone buildings, most of them built around a circle by Bishop Nathaniel Thomas of Wyoming, beginning in 1913. The most famous and attractive building is the mission church, **Our Father's House**, a log building, dark and rather low, in direct contrast to the church at St. Stephen's, but also full of Indian motifs—a big drum for an altar, an elk-horn bishop's chair, and more. Behind the altar is a picture window with a view of the Wind Rivers, celebrating the glory of God in nature as being especially appealing to the Indian parishioners. (This idea was copied in the Chapel of the Transfiguration at Moose, in Jackson Hole.) The once-flourishing school is now used as a community and mission center.

Driving west on State Highway 137, cross over U.S. Route 287 at the tiny settlement of Wind River and continue west to the **Roberts' Mission**, founded in 1889 as a girls' school and religious center for the Shoshone. The founder, Reverend John Roberts, was a Welshman and Oxford graduate, who came in 1883 and did not die until the 1940s. Chief Washakie urged Roberts to concentrate on the young, whose ears were open, since the old were set in their ancient ways. Ironically, Washakie himself was converted just before he died. This mission school, like the others, was absorbed into the public school system, and the charming old pink Victorian building is shut. But there is a small, active church (also with picture window) and a busy parish hall. The atmosphere on the edge of town is that of a peaceful, old, somnolent, and neglected English country churchyard. On weekdays, it's all green, shady, silent, nostalgic.

The famous **grave of Sacagawea** lies up the small road north of Reverend Roberts' school grounds. Born a Shoshone, Sacagawea was kidnapped in an Indian raid and sold as a wife to Toussaint Charbonneau, a fur trader along the Missouri. The two were engaged by Lewis and Clark as guides, and Sacagawea went on to become a heroine of historical romance. She survived the 3,000-mile (5,000-km) trek with the expedition, along with her infant son, Baptiste. After many incidents, including the adoption of a nephew, Bazil, she finally returned to her Shoshone people, where she died and was buried, here, in 1884. The graves of relations and descendants, including Bazil, flank her handsome tombstone. Baptiste caught the attention of a German prince, who took him to Europe for a formal education. Though he was buried somewhere in the wilds of the Wind Rivers, a monument to him stands next to his mother's.

(top) Indian teepees surround the powwow grounds in Fort Washakie, on the Wind River Reservation. (bottom) Sacagawea, the young Shoshone girl who served as a guide on the Lewis and Clark expedition, is buried on the Wind River Reservation.

The graveyard is dominated by a small log building, where one of the first Episcopal services and baptisms of the area was held in 1873 by Bishop Randell of Colorado, Wyoming, and New Mexico—a sizable diocese. Many graves are adorned with fancy bedsteads, and more genuine Indian names than the military cemetery at nearby Fort Washakie, where Chief Washakie himself lies.

Sacagawea has become one of Wyoming's great heroines (along with Calamity Jane and Esther Hobart Morris), and there are memorable statues of her, notably one in the Cody Museum garden, and another on the campus of Central Wyoming College in Riverton. Most who lived on the reservation, like Sacagawea and Washakie, were eventually converted by one of the missions.

The **military graveyard** where Washakie is buried is located just outside the Fort Washakie compound. Like the civilian graveyard where Sacagawea lies, this graveyard is not a place of grace and charm. Both are totally bare and indiscriminately covered with bouquets of artificial flowers, with no attempt at planting. Still, behind Sacagawea's tomb is the grand swell of Wind Rivers, while the military cemetery is framed by trees and nearby buildings. Nonetheless, the atmosphere is evocative, if desolate.

Many of the plain wooden crosses are without dates, but some stone monuments were erected as late as the 1970s. Washakie's memorial is the most substantial, a gray granite oblong, with inscriptions on its side. Washakie was nearly 100 years old at the time of his death in 1900. (His tombstone gives his birth as 1804, but who was around then to check dates?) His youngest son, Charles Washakie (1873-1953), is buried just behind. Other, older monuments of flaking yellow stone mark the graves of soldiers stationed at the fort and their families. There are almost no Indian-sounding names, except for Raymond Shoulderblade and his kinsman Raymond S. Blade.

It can't be said that the reservation gives one a sense of great individual prosperity. Most ranch and farm houses are small, and some rather derelict; others, however, are spic-and-span new. It is rather the collective busyness and impressive new buildings at Fort Washakie that seem to indicate the tribe's communal prosperity and activeness. The contrast is interesting and provocative.

■ LANDER TO SOUTH PASS

The only way around the Wind Rivers without returning to Jackson Hole is by way of South Pass. The ordinary route from Lander is via U.S. Route 287 and Wyoming State Highway 28, a wide, easy, rather scenic thoroughfare across the final foothills of the Wind Rivers. More exciting and adventurous, however, is a less civilized, but far more picturesque, road from the center of Lander across the southern tip of the mountains. It's not a time-saver by any means, but will give a glimpse of the forest and lake country of the Wind Rivers that you won't otherwise get by car.

Well-marked Wyoming State Highway 131 leads west from Lander's center, following the Popo Agie River upstream for nine miles (15 km) to the chief natural curiosity of the region, a phenomenon called **the Sinks**. The Popo Agie, dashing down from the mountains in its rugged canyon, is suddenly swallowed up by a sinister black cave at the bottom of a cliff. A few miles farther down at **the Rise**, the water oozes out from the bottom of another cliff into an equally sinister, big, dark, calm pool. The whole is preserved and protected by a well-kept state park with a fine visitors center.

Just below the Rise is a tiny sample of **prehistoric pictographs**. A big ditch flows along the north side of the road. There's a little gravel pull-off, and what looks like a steep little spillway of white concrete. This path, or scramble, leads up to the edge of the ditch, across which you can clearly see the two small, red, vaguely animal-like designs. Since pictographs are so hard to get at, even such a tiny, though vivid, sight of them is worthwhile.

Up the canyon beyond the west boundary of the park, past the road to nearby Popo Agie Falls, the paved highway turns into a good gravel road. Soon leaving the rush of the river, it zigzags up the bare side of the mountains to the south. There's plenty of room to pass, and the view back down into the valley becomes increasingly spectacular. This road is easy to drive in ordinary weather conditions, but be sure to check at the visitors center before you start up.

Once you get to the top, you're on a great, forested plateau studded with small lakes (Frye, Fiddlers, Christina, Louis), the goal of campers and fishermen. **Louis Lake**, shadowed by some peculiarly foreboding, tall, rocky cones that look like piles of coal, has a pleasant log lodge on its shore, with overnight cabins.

Shortly beyond Louis Lake, the road emerges at last from the almost continuous timber of **Shoshone National Forest** (marred by extensive lumbering operations), with occasional glimpses of great, snow-capped peaks to the west. It then emerges onto open, hilly, sagebrush range, with scattered pine copses and queer, piled-up castles of gray-brown rock, much like the Vedauwoo near Cheyenne.

Finally, you reach the junction with Wyoming State Highway 28. Turn left to get to the gravel road that leads to Atlantic City, passing en route the gigantic Atlantic City Mine Company.

(top) Hidden away throughout the Wind River Reservation are countless petroglyphs of unknown origin and age. (bottom) Harvey Morgan was murdered in 1870 by Indians, one of many casualties of the battles between invading whites and the Indians. (Photo by Dr. George Gill)

■ South Pass

Atlantic City is not really a ghost town. Its picturesque remains are still inhabited, and there are signs of arts and crafts, and a certain bohemian touch. On the road west of town, a handsome, old two-story log cabin, the Miner's Delight Inn, continues its tradition of hospitality from the days when Atlantic City was a solvent gold town.

It's called Atlantic City not because of the ocean, obviously, but because it's on the Atlantic side of the Continental Divide, over which South Pass crosses. On the other side, Pacific Creek flows down toward the Green River, accompanying the Oregon Trail onward.

Atlantic City was a mining suburb of **South Pass City**, a former boom town which lies a few miles west along a big, dusty road. Like Atlantic City, it too is nestled in a bare, open canyon, with rugged brown hills about it; but unlike Atlantic City, South Pass City is now entirely a restoration, not a living community.

The South Pass area, with its two little towns (one still alive, the other carefully embalmed), is yet another memorial to one of Wyoming's boom-and-bust cycles, the state's only significant gold strike. Tales of gold were circulating as early as the 1840s, but not confirmed till 1867. The population suddenly leaped to 2,000. Stages ran north from the distant, brand-new Union Pacific railroad. The town then boasted of five hotels, 13 saloons, bowling alleys, beer halls, lawyers and doctors, and a school that was rated one of the best in the state. It was here in those palmy days that Esther Hobart Morris—whose memorial stands in front of the capitol in Cheyenne—was sworn in for eight months as the first woman justice of the peace in the universe.

South Pass was the county seat of the new, now-extinct Carter County, which took up most of western Wyoming, within the Dakota Territory. When the present Sweetwater County, which at first included this area, was finally created in the 1880s, South Pass was already well on the decline. South Pass tried valiantly to retain the honor of county seat, but the Wyoming territorial government peremptorily threatened suit and transferred the seat to the city of Green River. South Pass and its surrounding mines, bowling alleys, and bars simply died out altogether. What's there now is a small, evocative restoration—a street of fixed-up or reconstructed business and residential buildings that once operated there. A nice, modern museum concentrates on mining, and the restored houses give you a strong flavor of what the town might have been like; except, of course, for the now-missing crowds and bars, the bustle and excitement. Particularly nice is a law office that acted as the town hall, which has information on the complicated issue of the South Pass City bid for county seat. Also notable are the refurbished two-story hotel run by one Widow Sherlock, with parlor below and bedrooms above, and the choicely decorated cabin of Esther Morris.

Here again, one of Wyoming's good myths takes a beating. A marble memorial slab from the 1930s proclaims Esther's involvement in the Woman's Suffrage Act passed by the territorial legislature in 1869 as the first of its kind. Next to the marble monument is a later myth-destroying marker, indicating clearly that Esther had nothing to do with this seminal legislation; though she was undoubtedly justice of the peace in 1870. So be it. It's certainly more fitting that a woman should be remembered in this nationally important first, even though the true bill-proposer, William Bright, a South Pass saloon-keeper, and another man active behind the scenes, Edward Lee, have been unjustly ignored.

South Pass City is a state park, with a nice place to picnic in back of the restored houses, alongside the aptly named Willow Creek. There you are very likely to see someone panning gold, for people are still at it. This whole effort of the state is splendidly done; but it's hard to imagine 2,000 people crammed into this narrow, now peaceful valley.

The gravel road continues north and west to rejoin paved Wyoming State Highway 28.

Of all the many souvenirs of the Oregon Trail, **South Pass** is the most significant. From the earliest days of trapper exploration, the pass was famous as the one truly open and easy way to cross Wyoming, avoiding the unbroken belt of mountains north and south, with good water along the way. South Pass thus became a goal of all immigrants along the trail.

As a pass, it's certainly not very impressive—nothing to compare to Teton, Togwotee or Hoback. But historically, it's a pass over which historians pause with reverence. Now open range, it's almost impossible to tell exactly when and where you cross the divide. This pass was once key to the whole settlement of the northern Far West. Old wagon tracks made by thousands who passed over the years have visibly scarred the dry soil of the barren sagebrush-dotted hillside.

TRAPPER LAND

WYOMING STATE HIGHWAY 28 GRADUALLY DRIFTS down from South Pass, with the brown cliffs of the Antelope Hills to the south and the Wind Rivers beginning to emerge in the northeast. Ahead lies nothing but vast rangeland. For the more adventurous, a rough gravel road takes off to the north, at the feet of the mountains, along one of the tributary forks of the Sweetwater, toward a dot on the map called Big Sandy.

The highway zooms down some 40 miles (60 km) alongside the invisible Pacific Creek to another dot on the map, **Farson.** North of Farson lies the Big Sandy Reservoir and Recreation Area, a most unlikely water resort in the desolation of this basin. Water from the reservoir is used to irrigate the area around Farson and Eden (a bit farther south). These are the only civic centers of any size from Rock Springs, in the south, to Boulder and Pinedale, in the north. **Eden** has pretty, tree-shaded picnic nooks, and gurgling ditches. If you need gas, stop at Farson, which consists of a fine, rather derelict brick building of oddly distinguished architecture, and nothing much else. Then, our route heads north.

■ WIND RIVER VISTA

Now really begins one of the great mountain-viewing experiences of the Far West. For over 60 miles (100 km), U.S. Route 191 takes you north along the western flank of the tremendous Wind River Mountains, the highest and most rugged, not only in the state, but in the Rocky Mountain West, except for the great congeries of 14,000-foot (4,250-m) peaks scattered across central Colorado. This view—one of America's most bleak yet sublime panoramas—displays the entire west side of the range, lined up for inspection at one glance, for miles and miles. There's nothing between the road and mountains except areas of rolling range with sheep, cattle, and antelope in shining, evasive numbers. Every time the road rolls and rises to another higher crest, the mountains approach and grow larger: from south to north, Wind River Peak (13,200 feet/4,023 m), Mt. Washakie (12,524 feet/3,817 m), Fremont Peak (13,745 feet/4,189 m), Downs Mountain (13,341 feet/4,066 m), and Gannett Peak (13,804 feet/4,208 m), highest in Wyoming. True, the Wind Rivers don't have the jagged edges and individual outlines of the Tetons, their nearest rivals in the state. But as you come closer and closer to them, they grow in grandeur and solemnity.

Meanwhile, other lower mountain ranges begin to crowd in: the tail end of the Absarokas in the north, the top end of the Wyoming Range far to the west. It's a magnificent vision any way you come, but much more exciting heading north, particularly when there's lots of snow.

■ Green River Rendezvous

Highway 191 takes you right on up to Pinedale and constantly closer to the mountains. At the risk of breaking that gradual mountain-range crescendo, a detour along Wyoming State Highway 351 is highly recommended. It goes smoothly due west across this northern apex of the Green River Basin, to a point just above the settlement of Big Piney, an old cattle town which hasn't much to offer. The attractive heights of the **Wyoming Range** tower straight ahead. The road crosses two big rivers: the New Fork (of the Green), and then the **Green River** itself. Turning north on U.S. Route 189, through varied country of rangeland, pink badlands, white alkali flats, and constant cattle and sheep, you approach Daniel, 19 miles (32 km) north of the Big Piney junction.

Big-sky country near the tiny settlement of Big Piney.

(opposite) The mighty Wind River Mountains rise more than 7,000 feet (2,100 m) above the sagebrush-covered plains to the west.

Daniel itself lies in a broad cottonwood valley where Horse Creek and the juvenile Green River meet and mingle. Horse Creek was the site of many of the most important trappers' rendezvous of the 1830s and 1840s.

On the still-bare heights, before you descend into this valley, is the so-called **Prairie de la Messe**, where the indefatigable Father De Smet celebrated the first Roman Catholic Mass in the state, in 1840. A historical marker on the right side of the road gives no indication of where the De Smet monument is. Next to the marker, however, a big sign reads DANIEL CEMETERY, and a little gravel road goes east up the bank to a high, deserted, sagebrush plateau. (The road goes straight ahead to the cemetery, despite a rather misleading arrow that seems to point leftward.) A bit beyond the cemetery, you come to the **De Smet Memorial**. For all the the fuss that's been made about it, with annual celebratory masses, etc., you'd expect that there would be a big arena and a high altar. On the contrary, the De Smet Memorial is a pretty little shrine, not much taller than a man, on a promontory with magnificent views over the river valley and to the numberless mountains all about. The shrine may not be grandiose, but its location is exotic.

Beside the De Smet shrine is an odd, small gravestone dedicated to Pinkney Sublette, one of the many brothers of the famous fur trader, William, after whom Sublette County is named. What Pinkney is doing here one can't imagine. He was supposedly killed by Indians after the Rendezvous of 1828, and somehow what remained of him was interred on this high bench. He was then removed and taken East; but by Act of Congress (it says here), he was brought back and reburied in 1936. Why? William shed brothers like leaves. Another fell sick at the more permanent shelter of Fort Laramie, but suffered so from his infections from an amputated leg that he doped himself with liquor and supposedly died of delirium tremens.

Down at **Horse Creek** stands a stone memorial to Narcissa Whitman and Eliza Spalding, the first white women to cross the American continent. That, and a big historical highway billboard, are absolutely all there is on this site, except lots of nice, big cottonwoods. But the memories for those interested in Western history are as thick as the cottonwoods.

The untiring Narcissa, with her husband and the Spaldings, attended the rendezvous here in 1836. On arrival, as soon as Narcissa alighted from her horse, she was "met by a company of mature native women, one after another shaking hands and saluting me with a most hearty kiss." Present at this particular affair were, as usual, Jim Bridger, who managed to make almost every one of the rendezvous, and also Captain Nathaniel

Wyeth, an active fur trader and ancestor of famous illustrator N.C. Wyeth (prominently represented in the Cody Museum), whose son was the famous painter, Andrew. Doctor Whitman had removed an old Indian arrowhead from Bridger's back at the rendezvous the previous year, so Bridger greeted him with special warmth. On July 9, the local Indian tribes gave a final parade for the ladies, singing, dancing, and cavorting. All were painted and dressed in bright animal skins. The warriors wore little else but paint, and gave startling equestrian performances. On July 18, the sacred quartet left, accompanied by a Mr. Drips, and went on to many excruciating adventures.

The monument to Jim Bridger at Kansas City's Mount Washington Cemetery. (Courtesy, Buffalo Bill Historical Center, Cody, Wyoming)

Another festival in honor of ladies was much less well received. Four missionary wives of a less amiable sort were serenaded at the Popo Agie Rendezvous of 1838. One of the serenaded wrote, "Last night disturbed by drunkards. A large company arrived under the command of Capt. Bridger. A number of them came to salute us. One man carried the scalp of a Blackfoot. The music consisted of tambourines accompanied by an inarticulate sound of the voice. They fired guns and acted as strangely as they could." A companion, Myra Eels, was even more shocked. "Twelve white men . . . dressed and painted Indian style . . . gave us a dance. No pen can describe the horrible scene they presented. Could not imagine that white men, brought up in a civ-

ilized land, can appear to so much imitate the devil." So much for hospitality, trapper style. Victorianism continued West with the ladies.

The last rendezvous was held in 1840. The American Fur Company, sponsor since 1836, closed them down. During the 16 years of these rendezvous, Jim Bridger seems to have missed only a couple. One of the more memorable was in 1837, when Sir William Drummond Stewart, the itinerant Englishman, presented him with a suit of ancient English armor (Jim wore it at the rendezvous). Most of the rendezvous, from the first down on Henry's Fork of the Green in 1825 to the 1840 Horse Creek affair, were held in Wyoming. Of these, six were held at Horse Creek. The well-known 1833 rendezvous, with some 250 whites and 250 Indians in attendance, was described by Washington Irving in his *Adventures of Captain Bonneville* (1837). Though Irving himself never attended a rendezvous, Captain Bonneville gave him detailed descriptions. William Sublette was at this one, too. So were Bridger, Wyeth, and many others.

Horse Creek is handy and accessible, and it's a pity something more isn't done with the site to memorialize these raucous but significant affairs. The best contemporary tribute is the annual Rendezvous celebration, held every July in nearby Pinedale, which celebrates most, but definitely not all, of the rendezvous' characteristic events.

Daniel, the small community immediately north of Horse Creek, retains a good deal of Old West cow-town charm, despite the best efforts of the highway department.

■ PINEDALE

Unfortunately the same can't be said of Pinedale. Its wide central street is designed to encourage you to speed through without a glance. To prevent this, there are dips in the road at every street crossing. But even so, like Dubois (Pinedale's "twin city" to the north), the old-time charm has been obliterated.

However, it would be a pity to go through Pinedale without stopping, since both the town and its environs have a lot to offer. Pinedale is the most accessible, civilized starting point for a trip to the Wind Rivers. The town is a center for shopping and entertainment, the smallest county seat in the state (population 1,000), and the highest, at 7,178 feet (2,188 m). The superb and elegant, yet also very Western, **Magruder's Pub**, in the 1905 Pinedale Hotel building, is one of the best restaurants of the state.

Pinedale and its neighbor to the south, **Boulder**, stand out among modern

(previous pages) Alfred Jacob Miller's famous painting, Green River Rendezvous, *hangs in Laramie's American Heritage Center. (Courtesy, American Heritage Center, University of Wyoming)*

Wyoming towns for their deliberate attempt to keep the tradition of the log cabin. New log cabins are still being built there; and very good-looking and appropriate they are, too. There are motels, like the squeaky-clean Wagon Wheel, and the whole town offers a refreshing sense of peace and order compared to frenetic Jackson, the next major stop on the road west.

WIND RIVER EXCURSIONS

Pinedale is above all a center for excursions into the rather formidable but gorgeous Wind Rivers. The more adventurous can pursue an infinite variety of horseback riding, backpacking, mountain climbing, skiing, and snowmobiling opportunities. A series of foot and horse trails leads through the entire length of the range. The fishing on the outskirts of Pinedale is famous, and the local Chamber of Commerce on the main street will be glad to help you make arrangements.

One easy excursion from Pinedale takes you to Fremont Lake, practically in the suburbs of town. The road starts at the east end of the main street, passing near the large new **The Museum of the Mountain Men**, full of souvenirs not only of trappers but of local life, particularly as portrayed in wonderful photographs of early Wyoming life.

Back on the road to **Fremont Lake**, you pass over a summit, where you get a stunning view up the long lake to the distant mountains, 16 miles (26 km) away. That, unfortunately, is about it. You can get the same view from the lake shore, where a cutoff to the left leads to a pleasant log lodge with an extensive marina, cabins, and food. From there you can arrange for a boat to take you to the far end; there are no direct roads. The east shore is bordered by a popular, tree-shaded campground. The opposite shore is occupied by a grim, bare butte, whose cliffs slope precipitously into the water. A roundabout road takes you to the north end of the lake, but it's not very inviting country around the south end, a dreary and gray stretch of badlands. But that one grand vista looking to the north is worth the trip.

Another destination from Pinedale is the view of the faraway **Green River lakes**, reached by Wyoming State Highway 352, which takes off from the west side of town. **Cora** is the only settlement on the road, and consists of a quaint old log store and post office. That's about it. Don't try to find Cora city center or you'll just bump into ranch gates. The highway continues north over rolling sagebrush range, with the magnificent Wind Rivers visible to the east. Crossing a minor pass, you enter a broad valley of the

Green River. All the way along are the gates of big ranches, and the valley below is full of them.

At a scattering of pleasant summer cabins, where the Bridger-Teton National Forest begins, the paved highway turns into a white gravel forest service road, at first wide, then gradually narrower, alternating between smooth and tooth-shattering. The road veers east as the valley narrows, following the delightful Green River all the way up its open, pleasant course. Along the way are off-road campsites and historical markers, one describing the tie-hacking that once flourished here. Another points out the site of the Gros Ventre Lodge, a hunting camp that opened as early as 1897, and closed in 1906. It catered mostly to Eastern and English big game hunters, but folded when game laws became more strict. While there's no sign of it now, the lodge may have been the state's first unofficial dude ranch.

The end of the line is the beginning of the Bridger-Teton Wilderness Area, where you can camp for a fee. Trails lead up to the nearby Green River lakes. The lower lake, long, blue, and dominated at the end by the striking monolith of **Square Top Mountain** (11,670 feet/3,557 m), is without doubt one of the state's most beautiful lakes. Totally unspoiled, although much visited, it's certainly worth the long motor trek to get there, and the trek itself is beautiful, too. This end-of-the-lake spot is ideal for a picnic. Nearby is a small, coarse-sand beach. Trails continue on both sides of this lake to the upper lake. Weather, however, is crucial. The road can be difficult in wet weather, and the lake gloomy under clouds. Fishing is choice all along the upper Green River.

The oddity of the river is that it comes right into life full-grown, so to speak—a wide, smooth, clear stream from its very beginning, which flows unchanged all the way to Pinedale (or its vicinity) with the same width, depth, and character, gliding or gamboling over stones on its long way toward the awesome Flaming Gorge and, eventually, the Gulf of Mexico. In the days before the Flaming Gorge was dammed, the trip down its rapids was considered very dangerous indeed.

The expedition to the lakes is beautiful and rewarding, but it is something of a relief to get back to the paved road again.

(opposite) The modern-day mountain men rendezvous attracts an unusual cross section of people such as Swamp Fox, with his fox headgear.

■ PINEDALE TO JACKSON HOLE

The highway between Pinedale and Hoback Junction, at the south tip of Jackson Hole, traverses 64 miles (107 km) of increasingly exciting scenery. First, open sagebrush range stretches toward low, pine-topped ridges, surrounded by distant peaks. The timber and hills soon close in, and you cross a divide with wide, wonderful views into the watershed of the Hoback. The road then travels up the Hoback Valley, open and green, with big hills about, and mountains to the north. **Bondurant**, a small summer-cottage and ranching center, lies in the middle of this valley. Then gradually, the walls of **Hoback Canyon** struggle to contain the increasingly rough water of the river.

This spectacular canyon is named after trapper-guide John Hoback, who guided W.P. Hunt's company through the region as early as 1811. Hoback Canyon and the more difficult Togwotee Pass have long been the two main east entrances to Jackson Hole.

Religion got an early start here, too. On August 23, 1835, the Reverend Samuel Parker preached the first Protestant sermon in Wyoming near the river's banks. Parker was an associate of Dr. Whitman. These religious firsts seem to have had little effect on the tone of the region's future moral scruples.

Along the canyon, some ten miles (16 km) before the Hoback joins the Snake River, the sizable **Granite Creek** comes down from the north. A road follows it through an especially beautiful valley to **Granite Recreational Area**, and a hot spring open to the public. Bathing hours are posted at the junction.

The highway gradually emerges at the south end of Jackson Hole, where the Hoback joins the Snake as it rumbles off into its Grand Canyon, and Idaho. **Hoback Junction** offers a rash of tourist facilities and traps. The **Teton Mystery**, a small frame building on a steep slant, causes participants to experience thoroughly unsettling and inexplicable gravitational upsets. Probably the explanation is in fact simple, but the effect is not. This is a good stop, especially for children.

This ends the big circular tour of the Wind Rivers. You can either return to Jackson, 13 miles (21 km) north, or head south into Star Valley.

STAR VALLEY

OF ALL THE REGIONS OF WYOMING, STAR VALLEY IS MOST deserving of the rather un-Wyoming term "pretty." It's peaceful rather than grand—though the surrounding mountains are grand enough. It's not knee-deep in historical gore. It's famous for cheese. The trip south from Jackson Hole does, however, begin with the grandeur of the 3,000-foot-deep (900-m) **Grand Canyon of the Snake River**, a gorge of white water, where early attempts (like those of the Hunt party) to raft down into Idaho met with trouble. A spectacular yet amiable road in the canyon alongside the river eventually crosses the state line at Alpine Junction.

Alpine Junction is not a town so much as a clump of tourist facilities at the point where the Snake River roars out of its canyon to an abrupt halt in the big **Palisades Reservoir** in Idaho. The principal attractions at Alpine are water sports: white-water rafting in the canyon, or calm-water playing on the reservoir. You can go riding, hiking, and fishing in the mountains roundabout, and partake of all kinds of winter sports when snow flies. To cater to all this, motels have congregated. Most striking of such hostelries is an immense and elegant neo-Swiss hotel called the **Alpen Haus**, obviously built with Swiss winters in mind. It is beautifully done up with luxurious quarters, and dining and lounge rooms. Walls are decorated charmingly with Swiss-style painting, mottoes in German, and eighteenth-century peasant touches. A fancy, terraced esplanade in front, with a fountain, carries on the illusion. It's all very spectacular, if somewhat peculiar.

■ STAR VALLEY

From Alpine Junction, U.S. Route 89 heads straight south, first through a low, wooded pass, and then the pastoral and Mormon-settled farmlands of bucolic Star Valley. It could be called a "hole" like Jackson's—that is, it's totally surrounded by mountains. But it isn't so called.

The chief occupation of the valley is dairy farming, and products like cheese and butter are produced by ranchers, handled by cooperatives, sold to tourists, and shipped out over the whole northwest.

A most pleasant vacation from purposeful, big-highway travel is to spend time just wandering back and forth on small roads crisscrossing the valley, admiring the moun-

tains from one side and another, and letting the peaceful farm greenery soothe you. There's nothing else in Wyoming quite like it for spacious, pastoral greenery and sheltering hills.

Though the first non-Indians to see Star Valley were trappers and a rather off-course trickle of Oregon Trailers trying a shortcut northward, the area was deliberately colonized by Brigham Young in the late 1870s. His delegate, the Apostle Moses Thatcher, is supposed to have exclaimed on his first overview, "I name thee Star Valley because it is the star of all valleys." This is contradicted by a tale that it was originally called "Starved Valley," because of the hard winters endured by the first settlers; hard to believe now.

Settlement was accelerated by Mormon reaction to the Edwards Anti-Polygamy Act of 1882. Star Valley was a remote refuge beyond any attempts to enforce this law, since Idaho police couldn't cross the state line, and Wyoming lawmen didn't care. It was too remote. Settlers arrived with their plural families and have created many more families since. The valley is 80 to 90 percent Mormon, and the general feeling is that a century after settlement, all the descendants of the older families are at least second cousins.

Unlike most of Wyoming (except around equally farm-oriented Torrington), Star Valley is studded with little old farming villages (Etna, Freedom, Thayne, Bedford, Auburn), most of which have either been eviscerated by Highway 89, or dwindled away in the age of the motor car, in favor of larger centers, notably Afton. A sad example is the town of **Freedom**, south of Alpine and right on the state border. (One side of the principal street is in Wyoming, the other in Idaho.) It is the oldest settlement in the valley. The name celebrates the joy of immigrants in 1879, escaping to the safety of Wyoming from persecution in Idaho. Unfortunately, there's nothing much left of the town now except the usual substantial, red-brick, Latter-day Saints church—another small community whose life has been all but drained away by the automobile and the proximity of larger centers.

Bedford is an exception. It lies off to the east, in a separate, secluded nook of the valley, the most beautiful part of it. The town is very small, but famous for flower gardening. It's well worth a detour, especially if you want to buy some plants or garden supplies.

Another specialty of the valley is the big cheese emporium at **Thayne**, north of Afton. Here you can sample and acquire a bewildering variety of the native Star Valley Swiss Cheese and other products. It's tourist-crowded, but the cheese is good. You can eat, drink, and buy many a postcard.

(opposite) Bridger-Teton National Forest is one of the largest in the lower 48, with hundreds of lush mountain meadows popular for pack trips.

■ Afton

Afton (population about 1,400) was casually named by some poetic wanderer after the old British song:

Flow gently, sweet Afton
Among thy green braes.

Afton was a stream, of course, not a town. The Salt River, which flows through Wyoming's *town* of Afton, does indeed flow softly among its green braes.

Afton is a marketing center for dairy and farm products, also for religion. Moses Thatcher, the founding father, supposedly struck the ground with his cane and said (more or less), "This is the place!" The town is still dominated by the high steeple of the unusually original and handsome big LDS mother church of the valley. (LDS or Latter-day Saints is the name most Mormons prefer for themselves.) Built of yellow stone sometime around the turn of the century, it has been remodeled most tastefully in a style that blends a touch of New England severity with Mormon solemnity. It is surrounded like a hen by chicks with all sorts of up-to-date school and church edifices. Impressive, beautiful, interesting, dominant.

A surprising early phase of the town's history was its use as still another hideaway for outlaws, like the inevitable Butch Cassidy. They holed up in this rustic sanctuary between jobs, and patronized a barroom reputed to have been papered with stolen bank notes. Nothing like that in town nowadays.

Unlike surrounding small villages, Afton is anything but decadent. It's as spic-and-span a community as Wyoming, or any other state, could be proud of. It has the air of a county seat, but it isn't. Kemmerer down south still dominates Lincoln County. One suspects the people of Star Valley wish it were otherwise. The wide main street, Washington, is spanned by an **elk horn arch** and lined with well-kept stores. You feel you could eat off the sidewalks. Flawless lawns and neat flowers surround the snug houses on the east side of town, along streets named after the earliest U.S. presidents, from Washington to Monroe (two Adamses might be an embarrassment). If the town has a fault, it is that those fine streets are too wide and handsome; good for traffic but producing a sort of lonely, empty effect, which tends to contradict the cozy households on either side. This is a general fault of Wyoming towns: there's already enough wide-openness all around, and towns ought to try for intimate compactness. Afton has motels as spic-and-span as everything else in town, notably the neat, pleasant, log-cabin Corral Court, as well as equally spic-and-span eateries, such as the spacious Elkhorn

Cafe on Washington Street, right at the elk-horn arch. One can sleep, eat and no doubt live well, if simply, in Afton.

■ The Periodic Spring

The principal sight of Star Valley, in the mountains east of Afton, is a phenomenon called the Periodic Spring. When it's functioning properly (late summer and early fall), it gushes out of a cliff face for 18 minutes, then shuts down for an equal length of time. This particular oddity is caused by a subterranean water chamber behind the cliff face. In dry seasons, the chamber empties to the extent that the flow stops; then subterranean springs refill it and the overflow begins again. Supposedly there are only two other such phenomena in the world. This is the only one in America. All very curious; but there are other reasons for going to see the spring. After all, the spring is more or less inactive most of the year, especially in spring and early summer. If that were all there was up there, the trip might be a disappointment; but it isn't.

Getting there is half the reward. Start from the north end of town on Second Avenue, heading east. The street becomes an unpaved road which goes into the hills along **Swift Creek**, in its rugged canyon. Never was a stream more aptly named. It dashes down between high cliff walls studded with peculiar yellow towers and pinnacles, and serrated walls. It's slightly macabre, but most arresting, notably the **Balancing Rock**, which teeters over the road to the left, seemingly about to crash onto the passing car. To the right, the almost hidden, delicate **Shawnee Falls** streaks the high cliff face. Lush vegetation and massive, leaning firs and spruces line the creek, as well as a modest pipeline, which conveys water to Afton. The road only permits a speed of about 5-10 mph (8-16 kph), so you get plenty of time to admire the scenery.

From the ample dirt parking lot 5.5 miles (9 km) up the creek, the trail to the spring takes off along the north side of the towering heights. It's well marked, tended, and graded, but is definitely designed as a horse trail, not for pedestrians. It proceeds for three-quarters of a mile (1.2 km) up the canyon, as the scenery becomes more and more wild and glorious. This trail leads farther into the mountains, and to a view of the Periodic Spring's white cascade of water foaming down the high cliff (in season, of course). But to get down to the spring's outlet, you have to take one of two slippery little cutoffs (sliding on the bottom is sometimes appropriate), until you reach the rushing swift creek.

At the bottom of the canyon, and past a small concrete tank with odd water spouts coming out of it (*not* the Periodic Springs), rustic bridges lead across the roaring water to the trail that takes you up to the spring itself. Early in the year, when there is nothing periodic going on anyway, a big, picturesque arch of frozen snow blocks the way up, with the cascade roaring down through the center—a grand enough sight in itself.

This whole trip and the setting of the spring's cascade down the cliff is as romantic as anything in the Alps. In fact, there's a curious Germanic fairy-tale quality about the whole canyon, its sheer cliffs, magic springs, wild waterfalls, and great, leaning, shaggy spruces—a setting for gnomes and water sprites like Undine.

An added spectacle is a tall, narrow landslide down the opposite side, below the springs. It makes a sinister gash in the cliff and forms a sickly, poisonous-looking lake at the bottom.

■ Greys River Road Detour

Greys River Road is a far more adventurous alternate route south to lower Star Valley from Alpine Junction. Well-marked by a Forest Service sign, the road takes off in an

Sherman Lainhart rakes mozzarella curds at the Star Valley Cheese factory in Thayne.

(opposite) Roger Preston bags wool on the Preston Ranch in Bedford.

easterly direction, and before you know it you are in Bridger-Teton National Forest. Be sure to check at the nearby ranger station at the beginning of the trip for road conditions.

For the first 35 miles (56 km), the highway is wide, two-lane, and gravel. After a junction with the road east to Merna, Daniel, and Pinedale, things get rougher. The principal danger all along the route is the big logging trucks that command the highway and raise great clouds of white dust in dry weather. In wet weather, don't go. In any case, go slow, stay alert, and pull to the side when the trucks hurtle by, then wait for the dense dust cloud to subside.

There are all sorts of delightful picnic turnoffs along clear, rushing Greys River, and it remains a fisherman's delight as well as a constant refreshment to the eye (except in dusty conditions). Being an open and easy passage from the Green River to the valley of the Snake, Greys River was a favorite route for early trappers.

Greys River exactly parallels the Salt River. Between them are the also-parallel Salt River Mountains. The Wyoming Range is on the eastern side. Both ranges are rugged enough, especially the Salt Rivers; but the total effect of the scenery is cheerful and comfortable, rather than stunning like the Tetons, or grim like the buttes and breaks farther south along the Green River. The only habitations are some tucked-away guest ranches and hunting lodges, notably the Box Y, nestled in a beautiful meadow across the river.

After the junction with the Merna-Pinedale road, marked with a big directional sign, things change for the worse. The road first passes through a wide, willowy meadow where elk sometimes graze. Then it goes into timber marred by a recent forest fire. Logging off the burnt area has not improved its looks. Big cliffs frown overhead. The road is definitely a single-lane, dirt logging road by now; but once past the fire damage, the scenery gets more attractive, and the road easier. The river begins to shrink into a brawling creek, the timber opens up, sagebrush hills and ridges emerge; and also the feeling of drier country, farther to the south. Finally, you come to a big, wide, handsome, empty valley that tips southeast toward La Barge on the Green River.

To return to Star Valley, a good side road peels off southwest, then north to Smith Fork pass. Gradually the road descends along water and willows to the valley. Particularly memorable are the views of the valley northward as you return to it; truly a glimpse of a "promised land of milk and honey," sheltered by its friendly hills. When you strike busy Route 89, you can return north through **Smoot**, named for a famous Mormon senator and apostle, to Afton for rest and recuperation, or turn south toward Kemmerer.

FOSSIL COUNTRY

YOU'VE NOW LEFT WYOMING'S NORTHWEST CORNER, with its peaks, lakes, streams, forests, and numberless beauties, and are back once more in the world of dry, open spaces. Wyoming's southwest corner, however, is not really plains. Bits of national forest encroach on it. There are lots of irregularities—plenty of cliffs, buttes, ridges, and breaks, full of fossils—but no real mountain ranges. True, the massive Uintas loom to the south, whose peaks are as high as some in Wyoming; but they're in Utah. Although the Bear River crosses through the far corner of the state, watering farms and ranches en route, the prevailing colors of this part of Wyoming seem to be tan and gray, with dashes of red.

It's an important area for stock raising, intensive coal mining, and oil drilling. Still, it seems largely uninhabited outside its valleys and towns. The principal attractions for visitors are Fossil Butte and Fort Bridger. The only real urban centers are Kemmerer, the seat of Lincoln County, with over 3,000 people; and Evanston, seat of Uinta County, with about 6,500. Lyman has a bit more than 2,000 inhabitants, but the other communities are villages, even by Wyoming standards.

■ SOUTH FROM STAR VALLEY

As you come down to all this dryness from the lush, secluded, picture-postcard charms of Star Valley, the contrast becomes more and more vivid. Trees become sparser. **Cokeville**, in the wide, green, almost treeless Bear River valley, has the reputation of being one of the foremost stock-shipping centers in the state. Cokeville boasted that during World War I, it was the richest town per capita in Wyoming. Not many capita, however. The incongruity of the name "Cokeville" for a place so obviously not devoted to coal is supposedly explained by a mistake. The Oregon Short Line of the U.P. goes right up the middle of the valley, and some confused railroader mixed up his station signs, Sage and Cokeville. Sage was supposed to go here, and Cokeville was supposed to go down toward the coal-mining town of Kemmerer, but he switched them by mistake.

■ Fossil Butte

Fossil Butte is a noted quarry of ancient sea creatures. During the Eocene Age, some 50 million years ago, it was the sediment-covered bottom of a tropical freshwater lake. In the usual course of geological time, it dried up, was thrust up, and eroded. Now the lake bottom lies on top of buttes which contain many remains of ancient fish and plants that died, settled on the bottom in the mud, and now are preserved in incredibly delicate detail on easily detachable, flat slabs of fragile oil shale.

Founded in 1972, **Fossil Butte National Monument** is still in its infancy, and has barely been developed. A brand-new park center and picnic ground may be built in 1991, but until then, a trailer-sized museum holds a fine, small collection of the local fish fossils, with commentary. There are rough picnic tables out front, privies out back, and that's it. A two-mile foot trail leads up onto the bare, grand Fossil Butte. There's a deserted quarry on top from which fossils were once crudely dredged, and a fine view over the desolate, rugged landscape.

Far more interesting and rewarding is a private establishment down closer to the road and on the south side of the railroad tracks. This is **Ulrich's Fossil Gallery**. Started in 1947, this by-now famous gallery displays and sells the diggings of Carl Ulrich and his assistants from private quarries on high buttes to the south. This process involves clearing off the topsoil and rubble to reveal the flat substratum of oil shale. Carefully extracted, the fossils are taken to the Ulrich's three-story wooden castle, a contemporary romantic, irregular structure with laboratories below, display area above, and living quarters behind. When properly salvaged and mounted, these fossils are presented not just as specimens, but as natural art objects. They range from tiny to enormous, and are now in museums, galleries, and private collections all over the world. You can admire and buy them here, along with many other useful and ornamental objects and books.

If by any chance you can observe the actual digging up of one of these fossils, it is an emotional experience. Imagine standing on top of a steep butte with a panorama of the august country roundabout, antelope skipping across the slopes, and even an eagle nesting in the canyon nearby, as workers carefully lift out a brown slab of fragile stone with a 50-million-year-old black fish perfectly preserved on it. Almost anything in the area seems anti-climactic by comparison.

(opposite) The cliffs of Fossil Butte National Monument contain countless numbers of fossil fish.

■ KEMMERER

About ten miles (16 km) east on antique U.S. Route 30 is the only really flourishing town in the area, Kemmerer. The names of its satellite towns—Diamondville, Opal, and Cokeville—testify to Kemmerer's origins as an old-time mining center. Most of the original mines have been exhausted, however, and the area is full of memories of extinct ghost towns, mostly vanished—Cumberland, Ham's Fork, Sublette, Fossil, Blazon, and Brilliant. Even Kemmerer's city streets are mineralized (Pearl, Emerald, Diamond) and testify to the town's basic interests.

A coal vein was opened near Kemmerer in 1897, backed by a Mahlon S. Kemmerer, of Mauch Chunk, Pennsylvania (the town was later renamed Jim Thorpe, after the famous Indian football player). Mauch Chunk was also into coal. Kemmerer's right-hand man was an Irishman, Patrick Quealy, whose name is also dotted about the area, and whose descendants are still prominent in town. Here was still another Wyoming boom and a polyglot influx of miners, as at Newcastle; but nowadays Kemmerer seems to have settled down as a regional shopping center and county seat of big Lincoln County. Its odd claim to fame is that a resident, Mr. James Cash Penney, opened his first store there in 1890, and went on to father the ubiquitous chain store that carried his name all over the globe.

Kemmerer has an oddly picturesque site, with remnants of big old houses on the upper slopes, and a green, triangular city park oasis at town center. In the middle of this refreshment is a small log-cabin **visitor center** and **historical museum**, and roundabout are the principal stores, the old hotel (closed, but possibly being revived), and the souvenir of Kemmerer's peculiar claims to national prominence: the first store and the early house of J.C. Penney. Unfortunately, **The Golden Rule Store**, as it is known, is not preserved in its original form, except on the outside. It's just an ordinary shop, not worth visiting unless you need to buy something. But the old, small, white homestead of J.C. Penney, also on the Triangle, is full of memorabilia of Penney's extraordinary rise to success. The fact that it all started here in this isolated corner of Wyoming is an economic fairy tale, thoroughly documented and illustrated by souvenirs and photos in the homestead.

Another object of interest, farther up the hill above the Triangle, is the **County Courthouse**. This is a pretty special, domed building, designed in a combination Native American-Art Deco style, very original and colorful, and well worth the walk uphill. A splendid Italian restaurant in Diamondville, Luigi's, should complete your appreciation of this odd, curiously pleasant, and quirky representative of Wyoming's early coal days. Nowadays, there's oil roundabout, though coal still persists.

Evanston

The next logical destination on this tour of Wyoming is Evanston, tucked down almost in Utah, in the very southwest corner of the state. It's an almost empty drive from Kemmerer on U.S. Route 189, with not a settlement of any kind on this 50-mile (83-km) route. Of course, it's range for cattle (and antelope), and many oil roads lead off it into the surrounding hills.

The trip begins with a grand, faraway panorama of the great Uintas to the south, but the hills around Albert Creek soon enclose the road and block this mountain view. "Beautiful spaciousness" again takes over, in this case enlivened early in the summer by an odd phenomenon: great swatches and pools of brilliant, violet-blue flax flowers along edges of the highway for miles and miles.

Interstate 80 looms inevitably. To go either east (to Rock Springs) or west (to Evanston), you have to take it whether you like it or not. It's as truck-choked here as everywhere, but the scenery—though not as handsome as the stretches around Laramie—is rather impressive for Interstate 80: great rolls of land swooping up and down, rocky prominences, groves of odd, stunted, wind-combed aspens, and occasional stirring vistas of the Uintas to the south. Evanston, 11 miles west, is the gateway to that range and its camping and fishing opportunities. For Wyoming, it's the end of the line.

Evanston is a Mormon farming center along the Bear River. It's on the Union Pacific railroad line to Salt Lake, but that doesn't mean what it once did. Like its sister cities along the line to the east, Evanston was settled by the Union Pacific railroad building crews in 1868. Some 600 Chinese workers were soon brought in to break a strike. Unlike Rock Springs, where a similar action caused an infamous, bloody riot, nothing that violent seemed to happen in Evanston. A Chinese temple, called Joss House, was erected, but unfortunately burned down in the 1920s. One famous citizen named Chinese Mary survived all sorts of vicissitudes and lived to be well over 100.

Evanston is the seat and hub of Uinta County, which stretched right up to Montana from 1869 to 1872. Then Yellowstone was cut out of it. In 1911, Lincoln County broke off from Uinta; and in 1921, Teton from Lincoln. It's surprising Star Valley hasn't managed to secede from Lincoln as well.

(top) For many people, visiting Wyoming means a long drive across the state on Interstate 80. (bottom) For several hundred miles in all directions, signs proclaim the distance to Little America, home of the world's largest gas station.

Like other up-and-coming Wyoming cities, there are two Evanstons. The first, reached by Exit 6, is an area of unbridled commercialization—garages, motels, shopping centers. It's very dreary, though useful. A bridge then crosses the Bear River to old Evanston, which can be reached directly from Exit 7. Up a slight rise behind the center of town lies the shady, pleasantly old residential section. It's altogether a model small Wyoming city.

Old Evanston has a fine central shopping area, concentrated along Front and Main streets, the latter lined with trees. The chief attractions of this part of town include the Uinta County Courthouse and the depot area. The old, original **courthouse** at Ninth and Main is not at all distinguished, but around it has been wrapped, with marvelous architectural ingenuity, a brand-new section of very modern construction, where most of the civic offices now are located. In back, separated by a planted walk elevated over parking spaces, is one of Wyoming's most spacious and well-organized public libraries.

The depot area, near Tenth and Front, has a prime Chamber of Commerce information center, and a two-room museum combined under one handsome roof; the building was once the Carnegie Library. The Union Pacific depot itself is quite handsome, but not functional. Evanston seems to be full of such substantial, turn-of-the-century civic buildings, no doubt expressing the then-great size of Uinta County and Evanston's grandiose ambitions as the future capital of western Wyoming. Today, the depot area is the focus of a planned visitor area that may include a rebuilt Joss House.

It's doubtful that this kind of tourist development will solve the problems of Evanston and similar Wyoming towns. Places that once prospered on the proceeds of coal, oil, uranium, or the railroad now don't prosper, except as perennial stock-shipping centers. Tourism constitutes the present boom in Wyoming. Evanston is right on Interstate 80, where tourists presumably pour along by the thousands. How to capture the overflow and siphon some of it into Evanston? A bilious outbreak of billboards, reminiscent of the 1920s, disgraces the interstate, proclaiming motels, syndicated fast food joints, et al. When you take Exit 6, they are there alright, but in an ugly environment no different from 100,000 other such American towns. Not a trace of Wonderful Wyoming there. What other real reason is there for a tourist to stop in Evanston, except to see a nice specimen of urban Wyoming, and to eat and sleep?

There are, of course, events. There is a Wyoming Downs race track, and the usual rodeo and fair. But as nice as older Evanston is, what's so special about it? Will a Joss House be enough? This remains the present predicament of those Wyoming towns that, having lost whatever real tinge of Old West character they might once have had, now have nothing to attract tourists except facilities—nice motels and good restaurants. They are refuges for the night, and centers for expeditions roundabout, but they don't really offer much during the day. Too bad, because as towns go, they are often pleasant. Nice places to live, but not much fun to visit.

■ FORT BRIDGER

For the very first time, this tour turns for good eastward. Before you leave Uinta County, however, Interstate 80 takes you past the most interesting historic center of Wyoming's southwestern corner. This is Fort Bridger, now a registered historical site and museum some 34 miles (57 km) east of Evanston.

Fort Bridger was established in 1842 along Black's Fork of the Green River, one of the few green, shaded areas of the lower county. It is not too far from the site of the first annual trapper rendezvous, on Henry's Fork in 1825.

Fort Bridger bears the name of the most constant attender of these riotous occasions, which developed into real extravaganzas attracting as many as 1,500 Indians, traders, trappers, and travelers. The old system of using military or trader forts as gathering places for fur trading proved inconvenient, since they weren't near fur-producing regions. General William Ashley instituted the tradition of holding annual rendezvous in various locations, a practice continued by later fur-trading companies. Many trappers went for months alone or with only a few companions, and had lots of steam to let off. Gorging, drinking, dancing, singing, fighting, games, sex, story-telling, and athletics went on for days. In the whole West, at this early date, there were no gatherings more famous.

As the fur boom died, Bridger established his so-called fort as a trading post for the swelling flood of immigrants on the Oregon and Overland trails. All routes converged at the crossing of Green River, funneling west past Fort Bridger. It flourished for awhile, but trouble began when Mormons established themselves on Willow Creek, 12 miles (20 km) to the south, the very first agricultural settlement in Wyoming. Unfortunately for neighborly harmony, they opened a rival trading post. Bridger claimed the Mormons were driving him out of business, and sold out. A Mormon eventually took over his fort, but tension between Mormons and others evolved into a miniature war, during which the original fort was burned and the Mormons were driven back to Utah. Their Willow Creek settlement was also destroyed. In 1857, Bridger's fort was rebuilt to serve as a military base. The army closed it in 1890.

Now preserved and refurbished, Fort Bridger is perhaps not as authentic as Fort Laramie, as naturally evocative as Fort Fetterman, or as beautiful as the site of Fort Kearny. It is, however, far more completely and elaborately restored than any of the others, and its site in a lush valley, with willows and grass, is in itself a relief after so many miles of semidesert.

As at Fort Laramie, one is astounded by how big these military installations were. Working quarters, offices, horse corrals, a blacksmith shop, guard house, and other structures give you a complete picture of the total activities of such a place. The original **commandant's house**, on the east side of the parade ground, is stylishly furnished as of the 1880s. Nearby in a low log house are the bachelor officers' quarters, amusingly restored as though occupied by two very different officers. Their contrasting characters are portrayed through furnishings and decor. One is an earnest young post-Civil War science buff, full of high thought and neatness, his bedroom dominated by the portraits of his stern parents. The other is an older, raffish Civil War veteran, whose bed is unmade and whose dining table is littered with the debris of last night's poker and drinking party. The restored **trading post** was originally managed by a sutler named William A. Carter, who went on to become a successful entrepreneur and judge. The original (now vanished) Carter County, with its seat way up in South Pass City, was named after him. He is much memorialized here, and is buried in a pleasant little family graveyard next to the commandant's house. Bridger's own old log-palisaded post, where all of this started, is reconstructed, but does not seem to be regularly open to the public.

The center of attraction in the fort, at the western edge of the parade ground, is a large **museum and store** full of Indian, trapper, and military information. Chief Washakie is prominently noted, as is the creation of the Wind River Reservation after many adjustments and treaties.

Altogether, Fort Bridger is an oasis of historical interest and greenery along the grimness of Interstate 80.

■ Flaming Gorge

Unless pressed for time, one can avoid the interstate in favor of taking a long, worthwhile detour south to Flaming Gorge and back via either Green River or Rock Springs. This trip is one of the most spectacular of Wyoming's Happy Surprises.

(following pages) Sheepherder Pedro Gonzalez watches over 1,800 sheep in the Firehole Canyon section of Flaming Gorge National Recreation Area.

S4

From Interstate 80 near Fort Bridger, Wyoming State Highway 414 heads south to Mountain View, which initially doesn't have much of a view, since it is down on the flat bottomland. Farther on, the Uintas are indeed beautifully visible. The scenery changes continually, but never less than handsomely. You go through pink-and-white badlands, broken-up range country, and several tiny dots on the map—Lonetree, Burntfork, McKinnon—but no real settlement other than ranches. Wider vistas open as you near the semidesert country around Flaming Gorge. Black timberland topped by distant snow peaks encroaches on the southwest, and the road finally crosses the state line into Utah.

At Manila, in Utah, you can recoup with gas and food, if necessary, and make a choice of return routes north. Directly up from Manila, Utah State Highway 43 almost immediately recrosses the state line and becomes Wyoming State Highway 530. It proceeds along the west side of the Flaming Gorge Reservoir to the town of Green River. This is an interesting if somewhat bleak trip. It provides not only glimpses of the blue reservoir, with its striking red-cliff shores, but it gives easy access to marinas and camp sites near the water. Information is available at Manila.

A far more exciting motor trip detours through Utah around the south end of the gorge and up the other side to Rock Springs. This is altogether one of the more spectacular drives in the state. Unfortunately for this guide, however, the climax of it belongs to Utah, not Wyoming.

Utah State Highway 44 heads south from Manila, beginning a long, rather hair-raising, but exalted ascent on a fine, wide road. It eventually reaches a forested plateau that broods high over Flaming Gorge to the north. Unfortunately, the Ashley National Forest's insatiable lumbering operations have devastated the looks of this entire section of the Flaming Gorge National Recreation Area. Evidently "Recreation" does not provide the protection that is furnished by national parks and monuments.

Halfway along Highway 44, you come to a short, well-marked road leading north to a series of sensational viewpoints. From the top of the 1,000-foot (300-m) cliffs above the reservoir, you can look dizzily down the flaming red cliffs to the jade-green water below. "Spectacular," "sensational," "awe-inspiring"—all these well-worn words are inevitable at this point.

The road then proceeds east to join U.S. Route 191. Here it goes across the dam at the end of the reservoir, past a camp area with the picturesque name of Dutch John. Shortly thereafter you are back in Wyoming, and bowling along on yet another of the state's Happy Surprises. This smoothly paved and beautifully engineered highway swoops through and alongside some of the state's most colorful and intimidating scenery. You are now on the east side of Flaming Gorge, but too far away to see it. What you do see is the desolate and marvelous expanses of Sweetwater County, a great, empty country, uninhabited and more or less impenetrable except for those who know what they're doing. Stock graze there and pipelines have crossed it, but mostly it's all bare wilderness. To the left, a paved road leads west through Firehole Canyon to the more remote east shore of the reservoir.

Flaming Gorge is one of the most conspicuous, famous, popular, beautiful, and intensely controversial of Wyoming's many dams and reservoirs. It provides a great source of pleasure and recreation in an area that has precious little of the kind. However, the waters engulfed one of the most spectacularly famous gorges in the West, the Grand Canyon of the Green River, with consequent loss of a natural wonder (and no agricultural gain to Wyoming; only to Utah). The fact that this wonder was almost inaccessible to any but hardy rough-water boaters (like the indomitable John Wesley Powell, who first navigated it in 1869) does not mitigate this environmental crime of major proportions. The harm is done now, and the benefits are universally available.

The Powell expedition of the Green River in 1870. (Photo by E.O. Beaman, U.S. Geological Survey. Courtesy, Green River Museum)

GEOLOGY

The geology and topography of present-day Wyoming are a result of relentless geological processes that uplifted land into hills and mountains, while concurrently washing them away, depositing the sand and silt into lake bottoms and rivers. Direct evidence gathered, from small pockets of very ancient rocks to the deposits which are forming today, indicate that these processes cover a time span of three billion years.

However, most of Wyoming began forming about 250 million years ago, when the area was covered intermittently by a shallow inland sea. Into this sea great depths of sediments were deposited.

Around 70 million years ago, part of this land began to rise, forming the Rocky Mountains, while large rivers eroded the mountains away, depositing vast areas of sedimentary rocks.

Thirty-five million years ago, Wyoming was covered by huge deposits of volcanic ash carried eastward by the prevailing winds from the violent volcanic activity to the west. The amount of ash and debris was so copious that it obliterated valleys and mountains. Today this vulcanism is still active in the Yellowstone area.

Six million years ago the old mountains began to rise again and rivers deeply eroded the landscape, washing away much of the volcanic ash deposits and exposing the older rocks that were underneath.

While all this was taking place, valuable minerals were

Devils Tower National Monument is one of the strangest geological formations in America.

slowly deposited in the rock formations. As a result, the state has petroleum and natural gas deposits and many operating mines that produce gold, uranium, iron, soft coal, and phosphates. Wyoming also mines important industrial and construction materials, such as gypsum, bentonite, sand gravel, and some marble. In several areas, gem-quality agate is found, and Wyoming is famous for its jade.

The state is also noted for some unusual fossil sites. Dinosaur remains have been found in abundance in several areas, notably at Como Bluffs. The Green River Formation is world-famous for its 50-million-year-old fossil fish preserved in remarkable detail in a fine silt deposit. Not only fish are found there, but an occasional insect, a tiny frog, and the oldest known bat. In the Absaroka Mountains whole forests are petrified *in situ* by the slow process of mineral grains replacing the wood.

Parts of Wyoming took millions of years to form, while three minutes took care of one geological phenomenon. Well-known landmarks, such as the Devils Tower and the geysers and hot springs of Yellowstone, result from long-term volcanic activity. At the other end of the spectrum, three minutes was all that was needed on June 23, 1925, for a gigantic landslide to drop 37 million cubic meters of rock down Gros Ventre Mountain, creating that huge scar on the landscape.

—Peggy Cross

. . . There was a Green River Basin in Wyoming that was not to be confused with the Green River Basin in Wyoming. One was topographical and was *on* Wyoming. The other was structural and was *under* Wyoming. The Great Basin, which is centered in Utah and Nevada, was not to be confused with the Basin and Range, which is centered in Utah and Nevada. The Great Basin was topographical, and extraordinary in the world as a vastness of land that had no drainage to the sea. The Basin and Range was a realm of related mountains that all but coincided with the Great Basin, spilling over slightly to the north and south. To anyone with a smoothly functioning bifocal mind, there was no lack of clarity about Iowa in the Pennsylvanian, Missouri in the Mississippian, Nevada in the Nebraskan, Indiana in the Illinoian, Vermont in the Kansan, Texas in the Wisconsinan time. Meteoric water, with study, turned out to be rain. It ran downhill in consequent, subsequent, obsequent, resequent, and not a few insequent streams.

—John McPhee, *Basin and Range*, 1980

GREAT BASIN

THE TOWN OF **GREEN RIVER**, WHICH YOU WILL MISS if you take the long detour from Fort Bridger to Rock Springs, is the first real civic center along Interstate 80 since Evanston. Though very much a mining town, it has an attractive site on the river under a dominating Castle Rock. It is in a way older than any other southern Wyoming town, since at this site, or near it, all the covered wagons came together to camp and celebrate their passage across the plains.

Green River is a typical railroad city, laid out in 1868. By September of that year it had 2,000 settlers. It now has over 12,000, which by Wyoming standards qualifies it as a city. It claims to have one of the mildest climates in the state.

Green River is a mining town, but it's a bit unique because the treasure is neither coal nor oil, but something called trona, on which Green River seems to have a monopoly. In fact, two-thirds of the world's supply comes from here, and it's very much the Trona Capital of the World. Trona is the ore from which white soda ash is produced, and white soda ash is used to make products as varied as glass and baking soda; so trona is a good thing for Green River. The city is lightly powdered with white dust.

It's sort of a nice town, too.

■ ROCK SPRINGS

Rock Springs is 15 miles (24 km) east of Green River and the real metropolis of southwest Wyoming. It's big, for Wyoming, with about 20,000 people, putting it in a class with Laramie, and just below Cheyenne and Casper. Nobody ever described it as a nice town. It's a place that is, and always has been, devoted to energy; first coal, then oil, then uranium; and it has always been a rough, tough town, as rocky in its character and situation as its name implies. Not cowboys, but miners, prospectors, engineers, and entrepreneurs have roamed its streets and filled its bars, and even the look of Rock Springs is not a bit like the wide-open gridirons of most of Wyoming's townscapes.

Though only a short distance from Green River, Rock Springs is quite opposite in character. Green River has scenery, the river, and Castle Rock looking benignly down from above, not to mention stability (trona). Rock Springs doesn't. It's in a grim gorge, where the railroad was put through, and trees struggle to survive.

Like Green River, Rock Springs began as a stage station, but along the Overland (rather than Oregon) Trail. This Overland Trail was created in an effort to avoid Indian attacks; but though safer, it was never a real success. The country was rough, arid plains, lacking in water. The railroad made the town Wyoming's first great coal-shipping depot, controlled by and dependent on the Union Pacific. It was the urban center for miners from the nearby pits.

The usual polyglot population of such mining centers settled here in exaggerated diversity. Some 47 different nationalities and ethnic groups are represented. French bakeries, Greek confectioners, Chinese restaurants, and German beer gardens have been traditional in the town since it started, and the mixed atmosphere still lingers. Beginning in 1924, an international festival has been celebrated by all these different groups.

This does not mean that the history of Rock Springs is one of unblemished toleration. As in Evanston, a group of Chinese workers was brought in by the railroad to break a miner's strike in 1878. By 1885, over a thousand were living in the segregated, close-packed, shanty complexes characteristic of these railroad "Chinese company towns." A mob attacked these Chinese, considering them strike-breaking scabs. Thirty were killed, and an attempt was made to drive the rest out of town. Troops were called in to protect them and stayed till the end of the nineteenth century. Chinatown was rebuilt after being gutted by fire, and carried on life and customs for decades, including an annual dragon procession with firecrackers. Nowadays, this has all disappeared—except for the modern Chinese restaurants.

The name of the city was derived from a spring discovered in 1861, which became an oasis and stopover for the Pony Express and stagecoaches. The random building of miners' houses later on, and mine pits right in the middle of the town, caused the streets to wander and to be built up densely, so that the confusion of a European street plan exists downtown, unlike the monotonously rigid pattern of most settlements west of the Alleghenies. Nobody, however, can claim that Rock Springs ever was "charming" or "quaint." It is, however, picturesque in its rugged way, with nice residential streets scrambling up the heights south of the city, and lots of life in the crowded downtown. In later years, while there was still an energy boom, various intellectual, collegiate, and even artistic plans were made on a large scale; but it would seem that the oil collapse of the 1980s has rather dimmed these bright prospects. When you went into a public place in the seventies, it was full of wild, rugged characters, male and female, who looked like extras in a TV shoot-'em-up spectacle: handsome but desperate. Things are quieter now.

Green River and Rock Springs are by general consent (except for their chambers of commerce) not really tourist meccas. They are, as has been noted, of special interest as centers for the production of energy and the study of geology that goes with it. The best recent book describing this is John McPhee's *Rising from the Plains* (1986). He gives a vivid and somewhat horrifying picture of what's been going on around this area in the last years: enormous mining and energy producing developments, none of which is visible from any of the roads recommended or mentioned here. In fact, the great energy development and spoliation of the state is something of a hidden secret. This is probably just as well, at least from a tourist's point of view. Still, the energy industry is an important part of modern Wyoming. The boom of the seventies and its partial collapse in the eighties had a traumatic impact on the whole state.

■ Great Divide Basin

From Rock Springs to Rawlins, it's Interstate 80 all the way for 110 straight miles (177 km) of the most desperate scenery in the state. If you can think clearly about what you're seeing as the trucks rush by, however, it's certainly curious enough.

Lunchtime at the FMC trona mine near Green River, the largest trona mine on earth.

The Great Divide Basin, through which the interstate passes for much of this journey, is a huge depression where all the streams sink into the ground and the continental divide makes a big corral around the 6,000-foot-high (1,829-m) total desolation. No trees, no farms, no people—in an area about 100 miles (160 km) from east to west, and 50 miles (80 km) north to south. Except for little dots on the highway, relics of old U.S. Route 30, or defunct railroad stations, there is not a habitation north or south, except some ranches, from the Colorado border to the central belt mountains. Point of Rocks (an old stage station and railroad stop), Bitter Creek and Table Rock (old Union Pacific stops), Red Desert (a big service station), Wamsutter (which actually has 600 people in it), and Creston Junction (which does not)—these are the names that try to fill up the empty map.

This stretch of Interstate 80 has given all Wyoming a bad name. The typical, snide crack that "Wyoming is nothing but Yellowstone and Grand Teton, and Rock Springs in the rearview mirror," comes from the unimaginative tourist exposed to this almost unavoidable stretch. More cross-continental travelers pass over it during the year than through any other part of the state—even Yellowstone. Most of them, of course, are on their way somewhere else.

Sweetwater County, which contains almost all of this landscape, is the largest county of the state, and most of it is not only the least inhabited, but the most completely uninhabitable section of Wyoming. No name could be more ludicrously inappropriate than "Sweetwater." For one thing the Sweetwater River, that savior of immigrants, is located north, across the central belt mountains in Fremont County. In the second place, once east of the Green River and its few tributaries, Sweetwater County has hardly any water at all.

There are, however, those who love it—absolutely uninhabited space—and even those who live off it. It's considered good winter sheep range for ranches to the south. Geologists love it passionately. It's full of game: antelope in great numbers, of course, and one of the largest herds of wild horses in the country, carefully watched by the government. The inevitable inbreeding caused by isolation is cured by periodic importation of new, vigorous stallions from other western herds.

It was a cold, dark night, so I hunted around and scraped up enough sagebrush to build a fire beside the tracks. Then we set hunkered over our fire for quite a while, somewhere out there on the Red Desert, before we saw a light coming down the track from the west. That headlight was sure a welcome sight to us; as it belonged to a passenger train which was coming along slow, with our brakeman standing on the cow catcher looking for our caboose. The brakeman told us that he and the conductor'd been asleep too and when they woke up they discovered that the caboose'd been lost off the train, so they'd started out with their lanterns, one going each way along the track, to flag down the first train that came along.

The passenger train pushed our caboose on east, and pretty soon we met the engine of our train backing down the track looking for us. When our engine crew had noticed that their caboose was gone they'd pulled the train in on a siding, unhooked from it and started back along the track. They hooked us on again, waited for the passenger to pass, and went on towards Laramie.

Shortly before daylight that morning the train stopped somewhere west of Laramie, and I got off and went up to the front end of the cattle cars to look at our steers. Before I had time to start back to the caboose the train began to roll. By the time the caboose came along I figgered the train would be going too fast for me to get back on so I climbed up on top of the car next to the engine, thinking I could walk the top of the train back to the rear end.

By then we were heading down the east slope of the mountains and, for the first time that night, that train was getting up some speed. I'd tied my bedroll and saddle on top of one of our saddle cars and by the time I got to them those cars were swaying and bucking along so rough that I couldn't stay on my feet any longer. I got down behind my bed and saddle and hung on. A cold east wind was blowing and the smoke and cinders was something fierce up there. When the train pulled into Laramie at nine o'clock I was about froze to death.

—A.B. Snyder, *Pinnacle Jake,* 1953

(opposite) Old City Hall in Rock Springs now houses the local museum.

CITY HALL

COPPER COUNTRY

BY THE TIME YOU REACH RAWLINS YOU HAVE ALMOST completed a total tour of Wyoming—if by any chance you had the pertinacity to follow along the path laid out by this particular guide. When you cross the Sweetwater County line, some ten miles (16 km) west of Rawlins, you are back in Carbon County and the southeast corner of Old Wyoming again.

For anyone heading east, the normal and natural thing to do would be to speed right along Interstate 80 back to Laramie and Cheyenne. Since this guidebook has so far not included this particular piece of highway, it would presumably be new territory; and it happens to be the best-looking part of Interstate 80 in all of Wyoming. It skirts the northern edge of the Medicine Bows and Elk Mountain. To the northeast, the Laramie plains stretch out grandly, and it is altogether a splendid change from the preceding Great Divide Basin.

■ RAWLINS

Rawlins, with a population of about 11,500, is a frontier town on the edge of that long stretch of desolation, westward. To the east lies increasing settlement. Despite its fairly dour surroundings, Rawlins itself is a nice, clean, well-watered town, rather on the order of such old railroad cities as Laramie or Evanston. Its chief claim to fame is not a capitol or a university, but a jail. In such a way were territorial and state plums parceled out when these railroad towns were young. From 1903, when the prison was built, till 1982, when a new one went up south of Rawlins, the handsome, castellated old prison was the town's chief attraction—though in some cases involuntarily. The **old prison** is indeed a fine castle, pretty well-aged for Wyoming, surrounded by nice planting. It's now on the National Register, and is open to visitors in summer. Many old-timers in the state spent vacations there in former times.

Like all these southern belt towns, Rawlins was a Union Pacific creation of that busy year, 1868, and went through the obligatory Hell on Wheels stage. Criminals not only were hanged, but it seems actually *skinned.* That's what happened to the town's most serious outlaw, "Big Nose" George Curry. Various items made of his hide were available as souvenirs and as a warning to other malefactors. Things, as usual, quieted down. Today, Rawlins is a generally prosperous center for stockmen and the various surrounding energy producers.

■ East of Rawlins

From Rawlins, Interstate 80 takes you back to Laramie. Just east of town, and a bit off the Interstate, are three very different sites of some interest.

Sinclair (once called Parco) is a town that was built all at once during the oil boom of the 1920s, in the then-popular Spanish style. Its many pseudo-adobe cottages surround a handsome 80-room hotel resembling a Spanish mission. In fact, it is modeled on the monastery of Montesion in Barcelona. In its palmy days, it was a welcome refuge for motorists along the Lincoln Highway. Long in decline, it is by now pushing its seventieth year, and if it survives will no doubt be rescued as "historical." Seventy-five is *old* in Wyoming.

Nearby, to the southeast, is the site of **Benton**, a mushroom town on the Union Pacific. In 1868, it was considered the first real city west of Laramie. The railroad brought its usual hectic prosperity and high jinks. Within two weeks after it was founded, Benton had a population of 3,000. The great institution of Benton was the Big Tent—100 by 40 feet in diameter (30 X 12 m), covered with canvas (as were most of the buildings of Benton), and floored for dancing. The usual end-of-the-line rabble rejoiced, drank deep, shot one another, and departed. Nothing remains of Benton except the faint, rancid perfume of its rowdiness.

By contrast, **Fort Fred Steele**, farther east along the highway and beside the North Platte River as it flows north, is now in pretty good shape—what's left of it. It is surrounded by a well-kept picnic area and a small, restored, historic site by the water. As early as 1843, blood was shed there, by accident. Cheyennes saw Lieutenant Frémont and his group camped there drying buffalo meat, and thought they were an enemy tribe. They attacked, but quickly made peace when they saw their mistake.

The army established a fort there from 1868 to 1886, to safeguard Overland Trail immigrants.

■ Over the Sierra Madre

There is a long, beautiful alternate route from the Great Divide Basin to Laramie, which takes you away from this last mad dash eastward, and into a whole separate region of southern Wyoming that includes some of its most fascinating country and history.

The detour begins 27 miles (43 km) west of Rawlins off Interstate 80, from a no-place on the map, Creston Junction. Almost as soon as you turn due south on wide, smooth, straight Wyoming State Highway 789, things begin to change for the better. Though for another dozen miles (20 km) the road still runs through the Great Divide Basin, the landscape begins to ameliorate. It's still vast, wide-open rangeland, but more and more you perceive the gradual emergence of the Sierra Madre Range. There is, once more, that typically Wyoming excitement of unobstructed plain and approaching mountains.

Imperceptibly crossing the continental divide, you strike an actual water course, Muddy Creek. When it does have water in it, it flows into the Little Snake River, crosses into Colorado, slips into the Yampa, then the Green and the Colorado, and so to the Gulf of California. The idea of such rivers, often so paltry in Wyoming, and their incredibly distant and various ocean-ends in the Pacific and the Atlantic, takes on a certain glamour. Muddy Creek needs all the glamour it can get.

There's no settlement for 50 miles (80 km). Ranch houses are visible, gravel roads

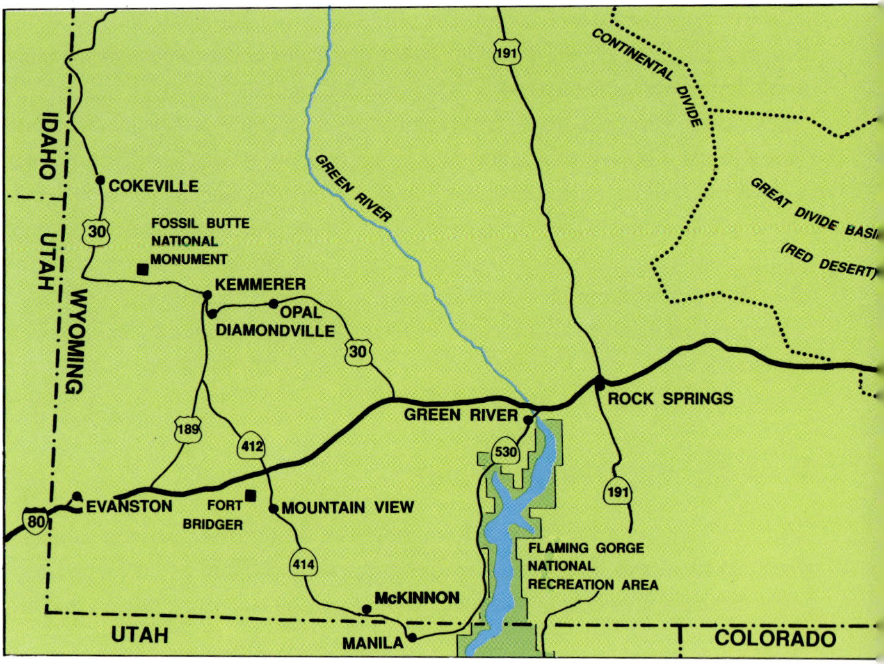

stray off on either side, cattle, sheep, and antelope (your by-now familiar travel companions) appear as usual. Eventually you get to Baggs.

Baggs is an old cow town, once totally isolated from any other settlement of any size. It's still pretty lonesome. Nothing up north except Interstate 80 and the Great Divide Basin, and nothing west until you reach Flaming Gorge, 100 miles (160 km) away. Craig, Colorado, is closer—only 40 miles (70 km) south—but there's nothing between Baggs and Craig. Baggs's isolation in the old days made it a favorite resort for bad guys. Butch Cassidy (as usual) came to Baggs to celebrate a $35,000 haul in Winnemucca, Nevada. He and his group took over the town, such as it was, and bullets and money flew around, much to the gratification of the inhabitants, who dodged the former and bagged the latter.

Nowadays, Baggs is a quiet little place, somewhat forlorn. Once a nice example of old-time, rustic, cow-town architecture, the sweeping highway improvement has totally destroyed its atmosphere, and most people wouldn't think of stopping except to get gas. The road that was supposed to bring visitors just takes them right through.

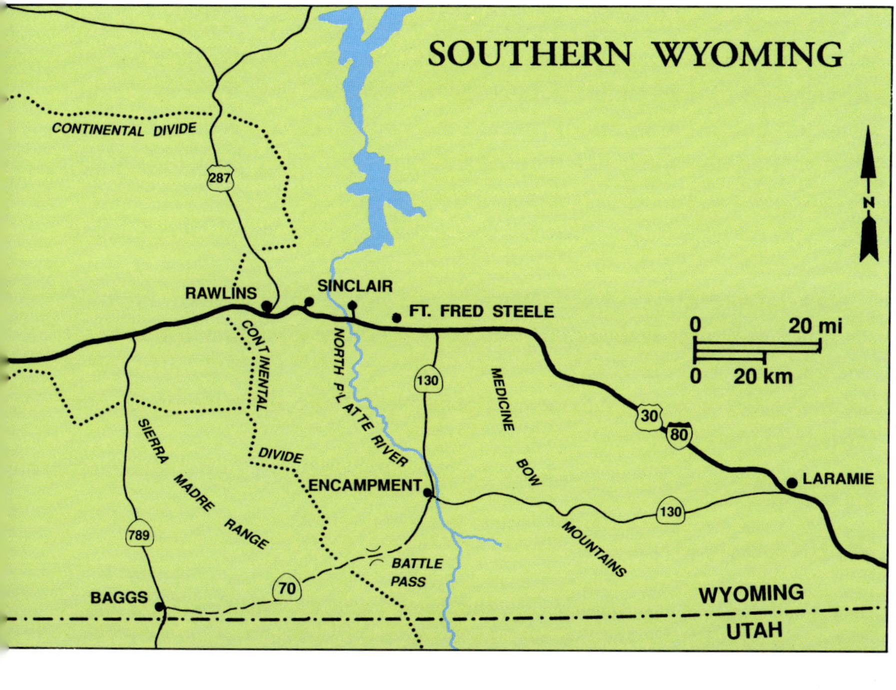

Wyoming State Highway 70 leaves Baggs to the east. Paved for the first 30 miles (50 km), it gradually rises to a pass across the Sierra Madre and on to the once-active copper-mining town of Encampment. It's surely one of the most handsome stretches of road in the state of Wyoming, but unfortunately, it's undergoing drastic rebuilding and "improvements" that will make it something of a problem for the next few years, and may ruin it permanently in the end. However, the present delays and roadside mess don't prevent the overall delight of the whole trip.

The first section east from Baggs to Savery, and then up into the foothills of the Sierra Madre, takes you along the beginnings of the Little Snake River (no kin to the big Snake), through an idyllic, green, remote valley of small ranches, with increasingly close views of the peaks to the south. These Sierra Madre (the only mountains with a Spanish name in the state) are shaped like Oriental pagoda roofs, exotic blue silhouettes that eventually disappear as the road climbs and enters an enormous forest of aspens. This fairy-tale forest, unbelievably colorful in fall, and the rising road itself culminate in a breathtaking viewpoint overlooking Battle Mountain and Battle Lake, and the valley below.

This region has, of course, its typically bloody Wyoming history. A group of trappers, led by Henry Fraeb, camped in the valley in 1841. A small party from the group, out to reconnoiter and look for furs, was attacked by Indians and saved in the nick of time by rescuers from the main camp. In revenge, the frustrated Indians set fire to the forest, which may possibly account for the great growth of aspen roundabout. (Aspens take over after a fire.)

Another story about Battle Lake tells how a visiting camper named Thomas Edison conceived the idea for the electric light bulb filament on that spot. Dubious.

After this spectacular viewpoint, the road goes on still higher in shaggy firs under the frown of Bridger Peak (11,007 feet/3,355 m) to the north, the highest in the Wyoming section of the range. Going over Battle Pass (9,915 feet/3,022 m), the road descends, paved once more, into the valley of the North Platte, and to the former boom town of Encampment.

■ ENCAMPMENT

Along with Centennial, Atlantic City, and South Pass City, Encampment is one of Wyoming's more famous "ghost towns." Unlike those others, Encampment has no remnant of ghostliness—that is, relics of past glory. Besides, it has a living population of about 600 people. It is a small, quite ordinary village on the lower slopes of the mountains, a bit above the valley floor, with a scattering of old houses and store buildings from its great days; but nothing conspicuously curious. Those great days were great indeed. Encampment once claimed to be Copper Capital of the United States, and the region was a scene of action and ecological destruction unmatched in the state until modern times.

Encampment derives its name from a rendezvous of trappers on the spot in 1851, but nothing much happened there until 1896, when Ed Haggerty found an outcrop of copper near Bridger Peak, in the northwest corner of the Sierra Madres. A mine was started the same year with the excruciating name of *Rudefeha*, derived from the names of the four original partners: (*Ru*msey, *De*al, *Fe*rris, and *Ha*ggerty). The Rudefeha was bought out in 1897 by Willis George Emmons, novelist, lawyer, politician, and promoter, who changed the name to the more sober North American Copper Company. He persuaded the Union Pacific to build a spur down from the main line at Walcott, and started a boom that riddled the mountains with mines, leaving the slopes gouged up to timberline.

By 1901, there were more than 260 companies at work in the area. Emmons and his attorney, Charles P. Winter (who has claims to being Wyoming's first native-born author), cashed in by writing half a dozen novels set in the area. Ten million dollars worth of ore was extracted, but the bubble burst in 1908 when the price of copper fell below the cost of mining it. The company was involved in scandal. Within a year, the population had emigrated, and the smelter was shipped to South America. Ranchers in the North Platte valley bought the railroad spur and then gave it back to the Union Pacific on condition that they keep it running.

The highway passes all this scene of short-lived riot, but everything is thoroughly overgrown now. One log building for years marked the site of Copperton, near Haggerty Gulch, where it all started. Of the town of Dillon, only the privies endured, built to withstand blizzards. Dillon was founded when the company town of Rudefeha banned saloons. Everyone deserted Rudefeha, tired of trying to pronounce the name, as well as thirsty, and moved the short distance to Dillon. A paper was founded there, the *Double Jack*. Rather like Laramie's Bill Nye and his *Boomerang*, this newspaper also had its nationally popular star, editor Grant Ives. Ives invented mythical monsters of the area, such as the Cogly Woo, the Backaboar, and the One-eyed Screaming Esu, which caught the fancy of the public and made the Sierra temporarily notorious. How-

(following pages) Moon rises over the Medicine Bow Mountains east of Encampment.

ever, Ives died shortly afer his arrival, in 1903. Now nothing remains except totally forest-hidden scars on the mountains. Surely one of the most peculiar aspects of this copper boom was its literary tinge.

Encampment keeps the memory of all this green with its mines, its towering smelter and a 16-mile (26-km) aerial tramway, largest in the world, that brought ore across the mountains. The marvelous **Grand Encampment Museum** stands on the southwest edge of the town's small gridiron, at Seventh and Barnett streets. It contains reminiscences of all this, and much more, around a grassy lawn with mountain views, where a row of old buildings was moved from elsewhere, preserved and refurnished. This includes the oldest building in town, a false-front store, and a rancher's log-cabin home filled with proper furniture and decoration. It's a special delight for sheer nostalgia's sake, and for a glimpse into the rather overwhelming past of this now retired village. Whatever the actual town may lack in atmosphere, the museum possesses.

From here on the route back to Laramie repeats in reverse the journey through Old Wyoming described in the beginning of this book.

GRAND ENCAMPMENT MUSEUM, ENCAMPMENT

The small logging and tourist town of Encampment lies in the foothills of the Sierra Madres, lovely country that was once home for thousands of copper miners. Today the area abounds in ghost towns from that era: Rudefeha, Dillon, Copperton, Rambler, Battle, and Elwood. The Grand Encampment Museum preserves artifacts from them all, including an historic stage station, ice cream parlor, school house, newspaper office, tiehack cabin, blacksmith shop, fire lookout tower, and seven other authentic buildings. Most unusual of all is the two-story outhouse. The lower level was used in summer, while the upper floor was reserved for when the snow drifts piled up. (The Australian term for outhouses, "long drop," has a special applicability here!) The museum also maintains pieces of the 16-mile (26-km) aerial tramway, the longest of its kind, which used to carry ore from surrounding mines.

—Don Pitcher

■ FINALE

This is really the proper Grand Finale to the whole great circle around the state of Wyoming. By itself, this last leg of the journey from Rawlins has plains and mountains, rivers and forests, and quite a bit of history—the essential ingredients of Wyoming's characteristic flavor. It ends at Laramie, like a snake biting its tail. After weaving around through all of the state's counties and countrysides, with their enormous distances and great variety, the persistent traveler arrives at the pleasurable starting point. It would be foolish to presume that anyone would actually follow the circle determinedly in one direction, from start to finish; but it could be done. The route does give a panorama of all the state's broader and more accessible beauties, and can serve at least as a foundation for travel; and above all as an introduction to the Equality State, Wonderful Wyoming.

> It would take thousands of words, hundreds of pictures, to tell about the rich variety of life in this river-bottom world along the Snake River, and still its spirit could not be captured. It is, so far, an area nearly untouched by man. For our small part of it we are so grateful that through all the years that it was a dude ranch Buster and Frances and their guests were careful never to disturb any wildlife, not even to pick many wild flowers.
>
> So that now, on an afternoon in May, Bob and Mickey and Olaus and I can make our way through the woods and come to a spot where we all kneel and look, and Olaus and Bob take some pictures. Fred, the young artist who lives in one of the cabins, has told us how to find this spot. Under the trees, in thick woods, on shaded mossy ground, a bed of calypso orchids. We count twenty-three: pink, exquisite, and quiet. It is most unusual to find this many in one spot. This is just one of thousands of memories of spring in the river bottom.
>
> —Margaret Murie, *Wapiti Wilderness*, 1966

PRACTICALITIES

How to Get There

The two principal conveyances into Wyoming nowadays are by car and by air. Transcontinental passenger trains have disappeared. Transcontinental buses exist for the adventurous, but are not preferred. The principal airports in Wyoming—Jackson, Casper, and Cheyenne—are served mostly from Salt Lake City and Denver.

Dress

If you care about how to dress (and unfortunately modern tourists don't seem to give a damn, particularly in Yellowstone Park, where the crowds can be a perambulating horror show), there is one basic uniform that fits Wyoming: blue denim riders. In the old days they were miscalled "overalls." They were called "Levi's" when Levi Strauss had a monopoly, and later "blue jeans," a more or less nautical term inappropriate to the Far West. "Riders" is a new term, but better. Local citizens, especially males, always wear them. They are practical, becoming (to all but the fat), and tough. Wyoming is a poor climate for shorts. Insects like legs. Woods scratch and prick, sun burns badly. Even in the summer, Wyoming can turn cold very quickly. Denim is proof against all of these; it wears well, and it looks western.

The big hat, however, is perhaps best left to natives. Somehow strangers don't seem to adjust.

Manners

Westerners, unlike Southerners, don't go in for elaborate politeness; but in general most Westerners don't show that they don't like strangers. A general geniality prevails. Don't be too sure that you are loved, however. Slobs and snobs are not appreciated. Gross, overfamiliar, loudmouthed joviality or snotty sneers get nowhere except into trouble. A sort of easygoing good humor is expected, and can lead to relaxed, happy, casual talk that can often reveal many interesting facts and stories. Take time. Westerners usually have lots of it.

(previous pages) A train rolls across the barren winter landscape near Kemmerer.

LODGING

The traveler's basic resort in Wyoming, as nearly everywhere else in the States, is the motel. All the principal chains are represented in every town of any size, and are proliferating in centers such as Cheyenne, Casper, and Jackson. They are not, however, what can be called indigenous, as non-chain motels sometimes are. But in the latter, of course, one might encounter faulty air conditioning, erratic plumbing, or other inconveniences.

There are two kinds of hotels: mostly modern ones that cater to conventioneers or business travelers, and mostly older ones that still retain a whiff of the old Wyoming grandeur and character. Among the latter are the Irma in Cody, the Plains in Cheyenne, the Wort in Jackson, the Virginian in Medicine Bow, the Wolf in Saratoga, and the magnificent Yellowstone hostelries—the Old Faithful Inn, the Lake and Mammoth hotels, and the Tower-Roosevelt Lodge.

Yet another delightful innovation is the bed-and-breakfast establishment. Way back before World War II, there used to be tourist homes, where the travelers slept in private houses, usually very plain, but pleasant. The modern bed-and-breakfast house is much more elegant. Some of the best can be found in Big Horn, Cody, Jackson, Rawlins, and Wheatland.

In Jackson Hole, some of the most popular accommodations are the hundreds of condominiums in the Teton Village area. The condos start with small studio units barely big enough for two very close friends, and go all the way up to full houses that could comfortably hold most of the population of Liechtenstein. Condominiums are especially popular with families and groups of skiers. For a listing of condo rental companies, phone the Jackson Hole Visitors Council at (800) 782-0011.

Probably the most attractive, intimate, and characteristic accommodations in Wyoming are guest ranches, which are concentrated in the northwest corner of the state, especially around Cody and Jackson. Some are real dude ranches, which never (or never used to) take anyone off the road without an introduction. Things have changed, however, and many dude (and all guest) ranches now offer overnight accommodations for tourists. All conform to the pattern of the dude ranch—a main log cabin for dining and socializing, and separate log cabins for sleeping. See the following section for more on dude ranches.

A serious problem in Wyoming is that accommodations are usually booked up pretty early in the day during the height of the tourist season. Without reservations, the weary motorist may be scrambling for a bed long after bedtime. A planned itinerary with reservations, or an early arrival, is essential.

For a complete listing of all motels and hotels in Wyoming (along with bed-and-breakfast houses, dude ranches, and campgrounds), request a copy of the free *Wyoming Vacation Guide* from the Wyoming Travel Commission in Cheyenne, at the corner of Interstate 25 and College Drive; phone (307) 777-7777. For a select list, see the "Backmatter" section of this book.

Dude Ranches

Dude ranches are the best way to get back into the country and the available fishing, game-spotting, and scenery. They are usually set in beautiful locations, and though not exactly luxurious, have a personal and genuinely Wyoming character that no mere motel or hotel can match.

At the turn of the century, the term "dude" was universal American slang for any dressed-up young man. In the West, it settled down to mean any newly arrived, unadjusted, and dressed-up Easterner. Nowadays, it is pretty much confined to guests at dude ranches. Contemporary dudes need not dress up. If anything, dudes tend to dress *down*, sometimes to the point of squalor. (Real Westerners don't dress dirty on purpose.)

Though Wyoming can honestly lay claim to the world's oldest dude ranch, the honorable tradition of regular catering to dudes actually started in North Dakota, where the hospitable Eaton brothers—Howard, Alden, and Willis—kept a horse ranch near Medora (they were neighbors of Theodore Roosevelt's). As more and more of their Eastern friends came to stay for the summer, the Eatons found that whatever money they were making on horses, they were losing on guests. The idea of charging guests for their board and keep was encouraged by the visitors themselves—and so the idea of the dude ranch was born.

In 1904 (two years after publication of *The Virginian*), the Eatons moved to Wolf Creek, on the edge of the Big Horn Mountains, west of Sheridan. Their ranch still continues under family auspices as the oldest surviving dude ranch in the world. It has served as a model for all the others: a family ranch, often actively engaged in cattle or horse raising, that takes in friends as paying guests for summer riding, fall hunting, and winter skiing. The idea of the dude ranch spread from Sheridan through Wyoming and the whole west. In the Big Horns, the Hortons' HF Bar Ranch, the Paradise Guest Ranch, and the Bones Brothers' Ranch near Birney, Montana, are almost as long-established as the Eatons'. In Jackson Hole, the JY Ranch began a few years after the Eaton Ranch, in the first decade of the twentieth century, and dude ranches have flourished there ever since.

Dude ranches are definitely not hotels or lodges. They are closer to sporting clubs—basically, a group of friends of the owner out for a holiday visit, in simple surroundings. Active outdoor participation in ranch life and a developing intimacy among the guests are the basis for this kind of community life.

This ideal of dude ranching was easy to maintain before the days of the automobile, when dudes perforce took a six-day train trip from the east, and a wagon or truck trip of a dozen or more hours from the nearest depot. In the twenties, as the automobile gradually made its way into Wyoming, a change began. Shorter stays were practicable. The dudes became less and less a close circle of friends of the family. Basically, however, the tradition of intimacy manages to persist. Families still come back year after year, and children grow up on the same ranch summer after summer.

The boom times of the 1920s were the golden age of dude ranching, when dudes were flush and automobiles were scarce. The depression of the thirties and the Second World War devastated the dude ranch business. Many ranches failed. After the war, the automobile and the plane changed their character. No one could pretend that most of the older establishments were really remote any more. The intimacy of dudes with the owner and one another came less naturally. The surrounding wilderness on which the ranches depended for riding, fishing, and camping became increasingly less wild. The small towns that provided weekend nightlife for dudes and hands became much less local and much more sophisticated.

The end result of these outside changes has caused a gradual blending of the dude ranches and the tourist courts. Some real old-line dude ranches now call themselves "guest ranches" and cater to drop-in travelers off the road. For these, introductions and friendship with the owners aren't necessary. Dude ranches that don't advertise would still require some sort of introduction. Your chances of just dropping in during the summer months at any of these places and getting a bed are minimal.

Food and Drink

Wyoming is not a state known for its haute cuisine or for snooty city-slicker soufflés. This is cattle country, the land of the free and the home on the range, where juicy steaks and the finest prime rib can be found in every podunk town in the state (the best steakhouse may well be in the don't-blink-or-you'll-miss-it town of Hudson, between Lander and Riverton). Or if you don't like that, try chicken-fried steak, the house specialty at every truckstop and greasy spoon. Wash it down with a beer, and then sit back for a big hunk of homemade (that's what the menu claims anyway) apple pie. For breakfast, it's pretty much standard all-American fare, accompanied by a dark brew that folks in these parts call coffee. Real cowboy coffee, made only over an smoky open fire and not available within 20 miles of any town, is a potent medicine, not advised for children and the weak-kneed. Check local outfitters for the prescription.

Actually, Wyoming food is not quite as uniformly meat-and-potatoes as might be imagined. The college town of Laramie has several creative and surprisingly reasonable restaurants, including vegetarian places. In southern Wyoming you'll find a number of authentic Mexican restaurants. As for other ethnic specialties, the choices are few and far between—an excellent Chinese place in Cheyenne, a German/Mexican restaurant in Green River, a soul-food eatery in Rock Springs, and nouvelle cuisine restaurants in Buffalo, Cheyenne, and Laramie.

The one glaring exception to this is Jackson Hole, a place packed to the gills with fancy restaurants (with prices to match). Wherever you wander, good restaurants await, offering hearty Austrian cuisine, macrobiotic vegetarian lunches, down-home cowboy grub, mesquite-grilled brook trout, or a steaming cup of espresso. (No wonder Jackson is viewed with such suspicion by the rest of Wyoming.)

There is only one brewery in the state of Wyoming, Otto Brothers Brewing Co. in Jackson Hole. They make Teton Ale and a number of other hearty beers. The brews are only available on tap, and currently only in Jackson Hole and Yellowstone.

Nightlife

In many Wyoming towns, drinking and carousing hold as much interest as eating, especially on Friday and Saturday nights. (This is less true in the Mormon-run towns of Afton and Lovell.) Every burg of any size has its resident country-western band, and saloon dance floors fill up with duded-up cowboys and cowgirls out for a night on the town. Many of these bands also play Eagles-style rock tunes for variety. The larger cities and tourist towns have several nightclubs, some with disc jockeys, others with basic rock and roll fare. Don't expect a steep cover charge to get in the door—most places are free.

Sports and Recreation

Wyoming is a mecca for sportsmen. Sports-minded people make up a large section of both the native and visiting populations. Hunters, fishermen, campers, hikers, riders, mountain climbers, and more recently, boaters and water-skiers—not to mention just plain sightseers—provide Wyoming with its most steady source of income.

Many of these sports, in fact, are just the modern versions of the ancient skills of survival in Wyoming. The Plains Indians lived by hunting. Somewhat the same was true for early white settlers. They shot and fished to eat, not just for fun. But when gentlemen sportsmen—like Francis Parkman, the German Prince of Wied, and various titled Englishmen—passed through, the tradition of hunting and fishing purely for pleasure was introduced.

In modern times, the boom in Wyoming sports has increased to the point of exploitation. The hunting of elk, deer, bear, moose, mountain sheep, and antelope has become almost an industry. The horseback pack trip, always a part of big-game hunting, has become an end in itself. In the old days, nobody ever walked, except fishermen along streambeds. Nowadays, the woods are full of backpackers. Roads, and unfortunately sometimes even trails, have bicyclists on them.

Winter sports are also an intrusion of modern times. Of course, everyone in the old days sleighed, skied, and snowshoed; they had to, just to get around. Today, Wyoming's mountains are full of ski lifts and their Swiss-Alpine appurtenances.

Another particularly modern aspect of Wyoming's sports scene is water recreation. For a state of which the larger part looks and acts like semidesert, Wyoming is surprisingly full of water. The sources of some of the greatest rivers of North America spring up in the state: the Yellowstone and the North Platte, tributaries of the Missouri; the Snake, tributary of the Columbia; and the Green, tributary of the Colorado. In olden days, except for local irrigation, stock watering, and some rafting, the only purpose of water in its natural state was fishing. Nowadays, on both natural lakes and reservoirs all over the state, motorboats, water-skiers, and sailboats preen and cavort under the frown of peaks and rim rocks. The most spectacular of these dams and their scenic

The one that didn't get away. (Photo by Mike McClure)

shores are those of the Flaming Gorge and Jackson Lake. Such reservoirs were built for irrigation, not fun; but they have adapted. Still, old-timers find it hard to adjust to wind surfers in the mountains.

Much more Old Wyoming is the art of horsemanship, particularly the "sport" of breaking horses. Cattle ranches and regional towns used to throw informal rodeos, and over the years some of these festivals of thrills and mayhem have become big-time amusements. They are no longer strictly native, however, as professional riders and ropers from all over compete for sizable sums of money.

Rodeo

It may come as a great revelation to many people, but rodeo is one of the most popular spectator sports in America; more people watch professional rodeos than go to NFL football games. In Wyoming, a state where even the license plate is graced with a cowboy astride a bucking bronc, it should come as no surprise that rodeo is king. Every small town in the state has a rodeo of some sort during the summer, and the larger cities

(opposite) Rodeo cowboys check to be sure the stirrups are exactly right before saddling up a bucking bronco at Cheyenne's Frontier Days.

have world-class rodeos that attract hundreds of riders and ropers from the Professional Rodeo Cowboys Association (PRCA).

Everyone argues over the official origins of rodeo, but credit is generally given to a bucking and roping competition between the Mill Iron and Hash Knife outfits who met near Deer Trail, Colorado, in 1869. They must have been a bit offended when a transplanted Englishman, Emilnie Gardenshire, won the contests. As the Wild West began to become fenced in, the various cowboy contests gradually moved into the nearby towns as organized "buckin' shows." Over the years, rodeo has gradually become more professional and less connected to the true cowboy. Many participants today come from cities and have never spent time herding cattle or working on a ranch.

The major rodeo events generally fall into two categories, riding and roping. In all the events, luck has much to do with who wins. Scoring is based on the difficulty of the ride (the toughest broncs or bulls are favorites, for they mean higher scores), and times for ropers are dependent upon the speed and behavior of the calf or steer they are trying to tackle.

The main events at a big rodeo include saddle and bareback bronc riding, bull riding, steer wrestling, calf roping, team roping, and in some places, steer roping. Women's barrel racing, clown bullfighting, and chuckwagon races complete the roundup of contests.

Steer wrestling, or bulldogging, involves leaping from a quarter horse onto the back of a 700-pound (300 kg) Mexican steer running at 25 miles an hour (40 kph), grabbing his horns and wrestling him to the ground. The event involves two men, a dogger and a hazer. When the steer hurtles into the arena, the two spur their horses in quick pursuit, with the hazer trying to force the steer to run straight ahead while the dogger gets into position to leap onto the steer's horns, wrestling him to the ground. Good doggers can get a steer down in less than seven seconds.

Calf roping originated in the old West when cowboys had to rope and tie calves for branding. This is the most competitive of all rodeo events today, and there is often big money for the winners. Time is of the essence, and the most valuable asset for a roper is his horse.

Probably the most controversial of all rodeo contests is steer roping, an event that has been banned from most rodeos because it is so hard on the animals, and is illegal in some states. Cheyenne Frontier Days is one place where it is still done. The procedure is essentially the same as calf roping, but with a much larger animal. When the 700-pound steer is jerked back by the rope and then thrown down with a thud, you can almost feel the impact.

When you say the word rodeo, many people immediately think of saddle bronc riding. The oldest of all rodeo sports, it originated from cowboys' efforts to train wild horses on the range. Rodeo saddle bronc riding is more complex than this, however, requiring a special "association" saddle, dulled spurs, and very precise rules. Broncs are saddled up in the chutes and riders climb on, grabbing a thick hemp rope in one hand and sinking their boots into the stirrups. When the gate opens, the bronc goes wild, trying to throw the rider off. To count as an official ride, the rider must hold his toes forward and out, with the spurs against the horse's shoulders for the first jump. Balance and rhythm are important, and only one hand can be used to hold on. The smooth back-and-forth motion of a good saddle bronc rider makes it look like he is atop a rocking chair. Rides last only eight seconds.

Bareback riding is a relatively recent rodeo sport, arriving on the scene in the 1920s. The rules are similar to saddle bronc riding, but the cowboy rides with only a minimum of equipment—no stirrups and no reins. The cowboy holds on with one hand, an effort akin to trying to juggle bowling pins while surfing on a big wave.

Bull riding is in a class of danger all its own. Unlike broncs, who just want that man off their backs, bulls want to get even. When a bull rider is thrown off (and this is most of the time, even with the best riders), the bull immediately goes on the attack, trying to gore or trample him. Many bull riders are seriously injured and some die when hit by 2,000 pounds (900 kg) of brute force. There are no saddles in bull riding, just a piece of thick rope wrapped around the bull's chest, with the free end wrapped tightly around the bull rider's hand. A cowbell hangs at the bottom of this contraption to annoy the bull even more. When the chute opens, all hell breaks loose as the bull does everything it possibly can to throw his rider off—spinning, kicking, jumping, and running against the fence. If the rider hangs on for the required eight seconds (style isn't very important in this event), the next battle begins—getting out of the way of one very angry bull. Here the rodeo clown comes in. Dressed in bright red-and-white shirts and baggy pants, they use every trick in the book to distract the bull away from the fallen bull rider: climbing inside padded barrels that the bull butts against, weaving across the arena, mocking the bull with matador capes, and simply running for their lives in an attempt to reach the fence ahead of the bull.

A title occasionally used for rodeo is "the suicide sport." It is, unfortunately, all too true. Accidents are very common and rodeos always have an emergency medical team ready to tend the inevitable smashed legs, kicked-in ribs, and broken collar bones. Many cowboys are crippled for life, and at least several die each year in the sport, including two at Cheyenne in the 1980s.

(top) The wild horse race at Frontier Days is one of the most chaotic of all rodeo events. (bottom) A night rodeo at the Cody Stampede.

Wyoming Events

During the summer months, every town in Wyoming has its own celebration, generally centered around a morning parade, an afternoon rodeo, and an evening of country music and dancing. Rodeos are the definitive Wyoming event, reflecting the enduring importance of cattle and cowboys, and on any given night between June and September there is probably a rodeo going on somewhere in the state.

By far the most famous Wyoming rodeo is the Cheyenne Frontier Days, a ten-day blowout at the end of July. Established in 1897, it is one of the top four rodeos in the world (the others being the Salinas California Rodeo, the Calgary Stampede, and the Pendleton Round-Up). With a purse of more than $400,000, Frontier Days attracts more than 1,000 contestants—so many that the timed events must begin at 7 a.m. daily. Of course, there are other events that bring people to Frontier Days—morning parades, nightly country-music concerts, square dances, Indian dancing, chili cookoffs, and free pancake feeds—but rodeo is the main attraction for the 300,000 visitors.

The Cody Stampede in early July is another very popular rodeo, parade, and all-round chance to party.

For something completely different, thousands of people flood the tiny settlement of Encampment for the Woodchopper's Jamboree in late June. Also in late June is the Chugwater Chili Cook-Off. (Bring along a bottle of Maalox.) Another big attraction is the Wyoming State Fair, held in Douglas in mid-August.

The famous legend of Rawhide, an outdoor play held each July since 1947, has a cast that seems to include half the town of Lusk. The story is based on the 1849 murder of a Sioux girl by a white gold-seeker, and the Indians' retaliatory skinning-alive of the protagonist (hence the name).

For a sanguine view of life in the early days, visit one of the many mountain men rendezvous held around the state. The biggest and best is the Fort Bridger Rendezvous, held each September. Participants dress up in handmade costumes, live in teepees and old tents, attempt to outshoot others with black-powder rifles, bake bread over a fire, and mug for the clicking cameras of tourists. A good time is had by all in an authentic and picturesque setting.

Jackson Hole has a number of popular events through the year. Especially worth noting are the Pole, Pedal, Paddle Race in April (a strenuous marathon of cross-country skiing, cycling, and kayaking), the highly-acclaimed Grand Teton Music Festival during July, and a fall arts festival that attracts entries from all over the world.

This is just a bare-bones sampling of the offerings. For a complete list with exact dates, contact the Wyoming Travel Commission in Cheyenne, at the corner of Interstate 25 and College Drive; telephone (307) 777-7777. Ask for their free Wyoming Summer Events and Wyoming Winter Activities brochures.

Getting into the Wilderness

To get a real feel for the natural beauty of Wyoming, you need to abandon your car, get away from the towns, away from Old Faithful, and out into the vast acreage of undeveloped public land. Wyoming's most popular backcountry areas are in the Wind River Mountains, the Medicine Bows, the Big Horn Mountains, and the entire northwest corner. Given the distances into some of these areas, many campers prefer to use horses for the longer trips, but backpacking is very popular on shorter trails, especially in the Wind Rivers and the national parks.

The largest public land agency, the Bureau of Land Management, owns nearly 18 million acres (7.2 million ha) in Wyoming, but most of this is leased to ranchers for cattle grazing, and has limited access. The bureau also manages a few patches of wilderness scattered around Wyoming. The U.S. Forest Service oversees 9.5 million acres (3.8 million ha), of which nearly a third is wilderness. The National Park Service has another 2.3 million acres (.9 million ha) divided between four national parks. Both Grand Teton and Yellowstone have extensive areas of undeveloped land that make for wonderful hiking and horseback riding. Despite the millions of visitors that both these parks attract each year, it is easy to escape the crowds by hiking a few miles out from the major roads.

For specific hiking information in the most popular areas, pick up a copy of the Sierra Club's pocket-sized guides: *Climbing and Hiking in the Wind River Range*, *Hiking the Yellowstone Backcountry*, and *Hiking the Teton Backcountry*. A good overall guide that lists addresses and general wilderness information is *The Sierra Club Guide to the Natural Areas of Idaho, Montana, and Wyoming*, by John Perry and Jane Greverus Perry (Sierra Club Books).

Although some people bring their own horses to Wyoming, most visitors leave the wrangling to an expert local outfitter. (If you've ever worked around horses in the backcountry, you'll understand why.) There are dozens of outfitters scattered across the state, especially in the Jackson Hole, Pinedale, and Cody areas. For an up-to-date listing of local outfitters in a given region, contact the local chamber of commerce; some are listed in "Backmatter."

Wyoming Wildlife

When the first mountain men and explorers wandered into the vast land that became Wyoming, they found an incredible abundance of wildlife: herds of bison that stretched to the horizon, antelope, elk, and deer grazing on the broad plains, and many grizzly bears. Today, while the populations of these animals are much reduced, and the grizzlies and bison survive in only the most remote areas, much of Wyoming remains undeveloped, and the chances to see wild animals are outstanding.

Get off the interstate highways, slow down, and keep your eyes open for herds of antelope, certainly the most abundant large mammal in Wyoming. You're guaranteed to see some at any time of year in a drive across the state. If you stop, get out of your car, and stand still, these inquisitive animals will sometimes come up to investigate.

Everyone's favorite place to see wildlife is Yellowstone Park. Bison and elk are the most commonly seen large mammals, creating long traffic jams as folks get out to take photographs, but visitors also frequently observe coyotes, moose, mule deer, and river otters. Other more secretive animals, such as black and grizzly bears, bighorn sheep, striped skunks, red foxes, bobcats, porcupines, and beaver, are sometimes seen. Ask where to look at the visitors centers.

More than 30,000 elk graze in Yellowstone alone, with many more in surrounding areas. Another extremely popular place to see them is the National Elk Refuge, just north of Jackson, the winter range of a herd of more than 7,500 elk. Visitors traveling by horse-drawn sleigh can actually ride through their midst. With bulls weighing up to 900 pounds (400 kg) and cows up to 600 pounds (275 kg), they are some of the largest antlered animals in the Americas. The bulls' massive antlers are also a favorite of collectors and of Asian aphrodisiac manufacturers. Local boy scouts collect the antlers, and an antler auction in Jackson each May attracts hundreds of buyers willing to pay more than $14 per pound.

Grizzly (or brown) bears once ringed the entire northern hemisphere. When Lewis and Clark crossed the Rocky Mountains in 1804, they found grizzlies common along the upper Missouri River, especially at Great Falls, where dozens congregated to fish. Unfortunately, as settlers arrived they quickly came to view these massive and powerful creatures as a threat to themselves and to their stock. They shot, trapped, and poisoned them, nearly to the brink of extinction outside of Alaska and western Canada. In the lower 48 states, they now exist in only the most remote parts of Montana, Wyoming, Idaho, and Washington. In Wyoming, perhaps only 200 grizzlies remain, all within

(following page) (top) A coyote hunts mice in Yellowstone National Park. (Photo by Mark Theken) (bottom) White-tailed deer near Devils Tower National Monument.

Yellowstone and the surrounding national forest lands. In recent years, the grizzly population seems to be increasing, with a gradual expansion of their range into previously occupied lands. Perhaps in the future, they will return to the Wind River Mountains to the south.

For many years both grizzly and black bears were common sights along Yellowstone's roads and at the garbage dumps, where grandstands were set up so that visitors could watch the bears. When the dumps were finally closed in the 1970s, the bears were suddenly forced to find more natural food sources. This sudden change led to a number of encounters between humans and bears, including maulings that killed two people. The incidents have declined as people have become more careful with their food and garbage, and as the bears have begun to relearn their old feeding patterns.

Grizzly encounters are rare and frightening experiences for most people. The adult males can weigh more than 500 pounds (225 kg). Surprising a bear, especially a sow with her cubs, is the last thing you want to do. When in bear country, talk loudly or sing, or carry bear bells to warn them of your presence. Most bears hear or smell you long before you know they are present, and hightail it away.

A good place to see the elusive bighorn sheep is in the aptly-named Bighorn Canyon National Recreation Area, northeast of Lovell. Herds of ewes and lambs are common along park roads here, while the more secretive rams hide in higher and steeper country for much of the year.

Wyoming is also home to one of the world's rarest mammals, the black-footed ferret, a small, sleek, black-masked creature related to the weasel. Long feared extinct, biologists discovered a small population living with a prairie dog colony near Meeteetse in 1972. Ferrets eat prairie dogs, and once lived among their colonies from Saskatchewan to Texas. The colonies were huge; one along the Cheyenne River in eastern Wyoming stretched for a hundred miles (160 km)! But as prairie dogs disappeared at the hands of the settler and the plow, so did the black-footed ferret. When the last colony seemed to be threatened by disease, it was captured and taken to the Wyoming Game and Fish Wildlife Research Unit at Sybille, southwest of Wheatland, where their numbers began to grow. There are plans to reintroduce the ferrets to a wild colony in Shirley Basin (south of Casper) in the near future, and to eventually have at least three wild populations of black-footed ferrets in Wyoming.

Bison are the veritable symbol of the old frontier. Often weighing up to 2,000 pounds (900 kg), they are also the largest land mammal in the New World. An outline of one graces Wyoming's state flag, and it was declared the state mammal in 1985. With

(previous page) (top) Bighorn sheep in Bighorn Canyon National Recreation Area.
(bottom) A young moose savors winter browse in Grand Teton National Park.

their massive heads, huge shoulder humps, heavy coats of fur, and oddly small posteriors, buffalo are certainly one of the strangest animals anywhere. They look so front-heavy as to seem unstable. This impression is, of course, false, for buffalo are remarkably well-adapted to life on the plains. They use their strong sense of smell to find grass buried in deep snowdrifts, which they sweep away with a sideways motion of their heads. They are also surprisingly fleet of foot, as many careless Yellowstone photographers have discovered. In addition, they are one very tough critter. In 1907 a buffalo was pitted against four of the meanest Mexican bulls at a Juarez, Mexico bullring. After knocking heads several times with the buffalo, the bulls fled and were saved only when bullfighters opened the chute gates to let them escape.

When whites first reached the New World, bison roamed across nearly all of North America, reaching east into New York and Virginia, south to Florida and Mexico, west to California and Oregon, and north into Canada and Alaska. The greatest concentrations lay in the plains and Rocky Mountain states: Kansas, Nebraska, the Dakotas, Montana, and of course, Wyoming. Two races of bison existed, the plains bison primarily east of the Rockies, and the mountain bison (sometimes called wood bison) in the higher elevations, such as in Yellowstone. Technically, these huge, hairy beasts are bison—the only true buffalo are the water buffalo of southeast Asia—but the name "buffalo" is used by nearly everyone.

The Lewis and Clark expedition of 1804-05 found the buffalo so plentiful that they "darkened the whole plains." As other explorers, mountain men, and the first tentative settlers reached into the "great American desert" of the plains, they were awestruck by the numbers. Travelers told of slowly moving masses of buffalo reaching to the horizon in all directions. They watched in astonishment as the herds stopped to drink at a river and literally drank it dry. A turn-of-the-century naturalist, Ernest Thompson Seton, estimated that the original population of buffalo in North America was 75 million.

Indian tribes that inhabited the vast interior of the North American continent depended heavily upon the buffalo for food. They used every part of the animal for one purpose or another. Hooves were carved into spoons, skins became buffalo robes and covers for boats and teepees, rawhide was used for drumheads, calf skins became storage sacks, hair was turned into earrings, and horns were formed into cups and arrow points. And this is just a small sampling of the ways the buffalo was used. Everything that remained—including the muzzle, penis, eyes, cartilage—was boiled down to use as glue for arrowheads. Even the ubiquitous buffalo chips burned easily and became a fuel on the treeless prairies. Later, when the U.S. government set out to subdue the Plains

Indians, politicians proposed that killing off the buffalo would starve the Indians into submission and force them to adopt a more "civilized" way of life.

A sudden international demand for buffalo robes and hides (the cattle from Argentina's pampas had been wiped out and tanneries needed a new source for leather), and the killing of bison for meat for the transcontinental railway construction workers, speeded up the slaughter. Once the railroads were completed, a new "sport" appeared, shooting buffalo from the moving railcars and leaving them to rot on the plains. Hundreds of people would climb aboard special excursion trains to join in the fun, leaving wounded and dead buffalo in their wake. In 1872, thousands of hunters spread through Kansas, Nebraska and Colorado in search of buffalo for the hide markets. During the next three years, they brought in more than three million buffalo hides to the railroad shipping stations, with Indians killing another 400,000 buffalo for meat and buffalo robes. Good hide hunters could kill 25 to 100 buffalo in a typical day, keeping five skinners busy from sun-up to sun-down; the record was more than 250 massacred in one day. Only the hides, cured hams, and buffalo tongues (which could be salted and shipped in barrels), were saved.

When General Dodge toured Kansas in the fall of 1873, he noted that, "The air was foul with a sickening stench, and the vast plain, which only a short twelvemonth before teemed with animal life, was a dead, solitary, putrid desert." Buffalo carcasses dotted the plains in such numbers that in later years bone pickers would collect massive piles of buffalo bones for shipment east where they were used for knife handles, combs, and buttons, or ground up to be used in sugar refining and for fertilizer and glue.

The first federal legislation protecting buffalo (only in Yellowstone park, however) did not pass until 1894. The following year, Ernest Thompson Seton estimated that only 800 buffalo remained in all of North America.

Despite this dismal picture, the population has rebounded dramatically in this century so that today there are an estimated 65,000 bison in the United States. The huge Durham Buffalo Ranch near Wright, Wyoming, has one of the largest private buffalo herds in the country: 2,500 head. In addition to various other private herds, there are small populations of buffalo in Hot Springs State Park, near Thermopolis, and in Grand Teton National Park. One of the few large wild populations is in Yellowstone. When the park was established in 1872, perhaps 1,000 mountain bison ranged across this high plateau. Sport and meat hunting (legal until 1894), along with later poaching, soon reduced this. By 1902, fewer than 50 remained. Plains bison were brought in from private ranches in Montana and Texas to help restore the Yellowstone herd, and eventually, the population of buffalo began to approach, and eventually exceed, its earlier levels. Today there are 2,600 buffalo in the park. Unfortunately, interbreeding between the mountain and plains bison means that the animals present in Yellowstone today differ from the original inhabitants.

Museums

Although Wyoming is a young state—it only reached the age of 100 in 1990—it seems to have more history per square inch than just about any other place in America. This history is a mixture of cowboys and Indians, of settlers and outlaws, of schemers and dreamers, of railroad magnates and cattle barons, and of just plain folks clinging to a plot of marginal farmland despite unbelievable odds. This rich treasure trove from the past is stored in the more than 60 museums scattered in towns across the state. Although nearly all contain something of interest, many are primarily old collections of stuff that gramps and grandma kept in the attic or barn—horse-drawn farm implements, long lacy dresses, mounted moose heads, collections of arrowheads dug up by the kids, sheepherder wagons, World War I uniforms. The finest large museums—Cody's Buffalo Bill Historical Center and Cheyenne's Frontier Days Old West Museum—should not be missed, but a visit to the smaller and less-known museums is also worthwhile. Check the index or "Backmatter" for specific museums.

Shopping

Wyoming has never claimed to be a shopper's paradise, but it has its moments. At the top of the list are Western clothes and accessories. Every town of any size provides big hats, boots, riding pants and shirts, bandanas, belts and so forth. If a person is built for this kind of thing, they would be done up proud. Most travelers might not be interested in real stockmen's gear—saddles, ropes, and so forth—but stores full of them are characteristic of Wyoming and worth visiting. Probably the most famous of these is King's, in Sheridan.

Wyoming has masses of handmade art and souvenir objects on view at the better stores: Indian and local pottery, leather goods, wood carvings, handmade rugs, "rustic" furniture, all sorts of jewelry, even some excellent artwork—for those who take the trouble to look around. There are some beautiful Indian handicrafts on sale at St. Stephen's mission on the Wind River Indian Reservation. Jackson in particular is overrun by sellers of this kind of thing, bad and good.

LOST DOG

DINO

FARSON MERC.
PEPSI
GENERAL STORE
POST OFFICE
STORE
HOTEL
phone
phone
Cream o'Weber

BOOKSTORES

There are fewer than a score of real bookstores in the state, not including stationery stores and racks of paperbacks. Jackson has three, notably the Teton Bookshop, which publishes a beautifully illustrated annual, *Teton Magazine.* The national parks, most museums, and many chamber of commerce bureaus sell useful and ornamental pamphlets or books about local and state subjects. The products of the various western university presses also get around.

RECOMMENDED READING

Among the great mass of literature on Wyoming, first and foremost is the WPA-written *Wyoming: A Guide to Its History, Highways, and People* (University of Nebraska Press), with an instructive preface by T.A. Larson. As an actual guide, it's half a century out-of-date; but as a depository of fact and myth it remains invaluable. Oddly enough the basic road structure of Wyoming has not changed, except for the intrusion of Interstates 80, 25, and 90. No other main routes have been added. Flaming Gorge has been created, Grand Teton Park has been extended, various historical sites have been refurbished, and towns have grown—but that's about it. If you buy one book about Wyoming, this should be the one. It's now a classic, albeit an anonymous one.

Another bible is the *History of Wyoming* by T.A. Larson (University of Nebraska). Larson's bicentennial *Wyoming History*, part of a series of state historical works under the auspices of the American Association of State and Local History, is a condensation of his monumental work. The shorter version is more convenient and up-to-date for the average traveler. It tells you all you want to know about the whole span of Wyoming's past, from prehistoric days to the height of the energy boom, with plenty of picturesque detail. Larson, however, is one for the facts, not myths, and you won't get much of the latter. Without such myths, Wyoming loses a lot of its special character.

Powder River (Farrar and Rinehart, 1938), by Struthers Burt, a volume in the voluminous Rivers of America series, gives you all the mythology Larson eschews. It is no longer in print, but every Wyoming public library will have it. The book cultivates the colorful aspects of Wyoming's history, based on the activities along the Powder River and gives you all the stories that Larson doesn't.

Not to be missed is Francis Parkman's *The California and Oregon Trail,* published in 1849 (Corner House, 1980). This first and most vivid account of Wyoming, when nobody knew about it except Indians, trappers, soldiers, and a few adventurers like young Parkman, is the classic account of that early time.

Theodore Roosevelt's *Ranch Life and the Hunting Trail (Hippocrene Books, 1985)*, from 1896 is the rather detailed and sobersided, but still romantic, account of his ranch life in the Dakotas during the great cattle days of the 1880s. The illustrations are by Frederic Remington. This is not quite Wyoming, of course, but might as well be.

The Virginian (Penguin, 1988), by Owen Wister, is a novel. Still, it fits right in with the Roosevelt-Remington picture of the Far West of that same period.

A 1947 classic is Bernard deVoto's *Across the Wide Missouri (American Heritage Library, 1980)*, the most famous modern account of the trappers and their Far West. It won the Pulitzer Prize and remains the best account of that epic.

John McPhee's *Rising from the Plains* (Farrar-Straus-Giroux) provides a contemporary picture of the state, based on what was basically a trek across the state on Interstate 80. It describes the geology and modern energy development en route, with many picturesque diversions into other eras and areas. Some of the rock-work, however, is fairly dense for non-rock-lovers. It is too young to be a "classic" like the others so far mentioned; but it may well be, later on.

David Saylor's *Jackson Hole, Wyoming* (Oklahoma University Press) is a thorough, rather detailed account of the history of the valley, from trapper to tourist, and as such representative of the history of the state as a whole.

In *Wapiti Wilderness* (Knopf), Margaret E. Murie and her late husband, Olaus, present a charming autobiographical account of a woman's life and experiences in the Hole, winter and summer, that is as personal and intimate as Saylor is objective and factual.

Struthers Burt's *Diary of a Dude Wrangler* (Scribner's) is the earliest autobiographical and local account of Jackson Hole, the dude ranch business, and the stories that accumulated about both. Taking off from where it ends is Nathaniel Burt's *Jackson Hole Journal* (University of Oklahoma Press), reminiscences of 60-odd years of the valley's lives and times.

Roadside Geology, by David R. Lageson and Darwin R. Spearing (Mountain Press), handily takes you along the major roads of the state, with geological explanations of what you see. Designed not for experts but for average travelers, the book can be enormously rewarding.

Other specialized surveys include *Fossils of Wyoming* by Michael W. Hager (Wyoming Geological Survey, Bulletin 67), a concise, illustrated digest of the state's long paleontological past; and the *Traveler's Guide to the Geology of Wyoming*, by D. L. Blackstone, Jr. (Geological Survey of Wyoming, Bulletin 67).

BACKMATTER

Additional information is available from the Wyoming Tourism Association.

Wyoming State Information Centers

Cheyenne; 1-25 at College Dr.; (800) 225-5996 (out of state), (307) 777-7777 (in state); open daily, year-round

Evanston; 1-80 East at Exit 6; (307) 789-6540; open daily, year-round

Jackson; 532 N. Cache; (307) 733-3316; open daily, year-round

Laramie; 9 miles east on I-80, Happy Jack exit; Laramie Chamber of Commerce, (307) 745-7339; May to mid-October

Pine Bluffs; I-80 at Pine Bluffs exit; May to mid-October

Sheridan; I-90 at 5th St. exit; (307) 672-2485; open daily (weekdays in winter); I-90 at Port-of-Entry; (307) 283-2440; May to mid-October

Federal and State Resource Agencies

Archives, Museums, and Historical (State Historic Sites); Barrett Building, 2301 Central Ave., Cheyenne, 82002; (307) 777-7014

Bureau of Land Management; Box 1828, Cheyenne, 82003; (307) 772-2334

Wyoming Game and Fish Commission; 5400 Bishop Blvd., Cheyenne, 82002; (307) 777-7735

Wyoming Geological Survey; Box 3008, University Station, University of Wyoming, Laramie, 82071; (307) 766-2286

Wyoming Recreation Commission (State Parks); Herschler Building, 2 West, 122 West 25th St., Cheyenne, 82002; (307) 777-7695

National Forests

Big Horn National Forest; 1969 S. Sheridan Ave., Sheridan, 82801; (307) 672-0751

Black Hills National Forest; Bearlodge Ranger District, Box 680, Sundance, 82729; (307) 283-13611

Bridger-Teton National Forest; Box 1888, Jackson, 83001; (307) 733-2752

(previous pages) Sunlight streams through storm clouds over Grand Teton National Park.

Medicine Bow National Forest; 605 Skyline Dr., Laramie, 82070; (307) 745-8971
Shoshone National Forest; Box 2140, Cody, 82414; (307) 527-6241

NATIONAL PARKS, MONUMENTS, AND RECREATION AREAS

Bighorn Canyon National Recreation Area; Box 487, Lovell, 82431; (307) 548-2251
Devils Tower National Monument; Devils Tower, 82714; (307) 467-5370
Wyoming Gorge National Recreation Area; Green River, 82935; (307) 875-2871
Grand Teton National Park; Moose, 83012; (307) 733-2880 or 733-2220 (recording)
Yellowstone National Park; Box 168, Yellowstone, 82190; (307) 344-7381

EVENTS

JANUARY

Jackson: Cutter Races
Lander: Wyoming State Winter Fair
Thayne: Cutter Races

FEBRUARY

Alpine: Winterfest
Jackson: Teton Winterfest; Powder Eight Championships
Riverton: Wild West Winter Carnival
Saratoga: Sierra Madre Winter Carnival
Thayne: Cutter Races

MARCH

Torrington: Shriners Invitational Chariot Races

APRIL

Jackson: Pole, Pedal, Paddle Race; Championship Snowmobile Hill Climb

M A Y

Casper: Wyoming Rodeo Association Rodeo
Jackson: Elk Antler Auction; Old West Days
Rock Springs: Flaming Gorge Fishing Derby
Shoshoni: Old Time Fiddle Contest

J U N E

Casper: Casper Air Show
Cheyenne: Summer Music Festival
Chugwater: Chugwater Chili Cook-Off
Cody: Frontier Festival
Douglas: Ft. Fetterman Days; Jackalope Days
Encampment: Woodchopper's Jamboree
Evanston: Chili Cook-Off
Ft. Washakie: Eastern Shoshone Indian Days Pow Wow
Greybull: Days of '49
Hulett: Hulett Rodeo
Kemmerer: Lake Viva Naughton Fishing Derby
Laramie: Black Powder Rendezvous
Lovell: Mustang Days Celebration
Pinedale: Roundup Rodeo
Shoshoni: Boysen State Park Fishing Derby

J U L Y

Afton: Parade and Night Rodeo
Casper: Casper Classic Bicycle Race
Cheyenne: Cheyenne Frontier Days; Warren Air Force Base Air Show; Open Golf Tourney
Cody: Cody Stampede Rodeo
Curt Gowdy State Park: Happy Jack Mountain Music Festival
Ethete: Arapaho Sundance
Evanston: Uinta County Fair
Ft. Bridger: Living History and July 4th Celebration
Ft. Casper: Platte Bridge Encampment
Ft. Laramie: Fourth of July Celebration
Gillette: Old Timers Rodeo

Green River: Flaming Gorge Days
Jackson: Cowboy Poetry Gathering; Grand Teton Music Festival; Mountain Arts Rendezvous; Teton County Fair; Teton County Fiddle Contest
Kemmerer: Turn of the Century Days
Lander: Pioneer Days Parade and Rodeo
Laramie: Laramie Jubilee Days; Summer Music Festival
Lusk: Legend of Rawhide
Medicine Bow: Medicine Bow Days
Pinedale: Green River Rendezvous
Powder River: Sheepherder's Fair
Powell: Homesteader Days
Riverton: Hot Air Balloon Rally
Rock Springs: Red Desert Rodeo; Sweetwater County Fair
Saratoga: Saratoga Craft Fair
Sheridan: Sheridan County Fair; Sheridan Rodeo
Sundance: Memorial Youth Rodeo
Ten Sleep: Ten Sleep Celebration
Wright: Wright Roundup & Rodeo

AUGUST
Alta: Grand Targhee Music Festival
Big Piney: Sublette County Fair
Buffalo: Johnson County Fair and Rodeo
Casper: Central Wyoming Fair and Rodeo
Douglas: Wyoming State Fair
Dubois: Whiskey Mountain Buckskinners Rendezvous
Evanston: Bear Claw Mountain Man Rendezvous
Ft. Laramie: Military Encampment
Gillette: Campbell County Fair
Jackson: Old Timer's Rodeo
Kemmerer: Turn of the Century Days
Lander: Apple Festival
Laramie: Albany County Fair
Lusk: Niobrara County Fair
Moorcroft: Keyhole Expo

Pine Bluffs: Trail Days
Rawlins: Carbon County Fair
Riverton: Fremont County Fair
Sheridan/Buffalo: Bozeman Trail Days
Sundance: Crook County Fair
Torrington: Goshen County Fair
Wheatland: Platte County Fair
Worland: Washakie County Fair
Thermopolis: Gift of the Waters Pageant

SEPTEMBER
Cheyenne: Cowboy Allweather 1000
Curt Gowdy State Park: Mountain Man Rendezvous
Ethete: Labor Day Pow Wow
Evanston: Cowboy Days Rodeo
Ft. Bridger: Mountain Man Rendezvous
Jackson: Jackson Hole Fall Arts Festival
Lander: One Shot Antelope Hunt
Lusk: Oktoberfest
Meeteetse: Labor Day Rodeo
Worland: Oktoberfest (in September!)

OCTOBER
Casper: PRCA Rodeo
Gillette: Oktoberfest
Rock Springs: Oktoberfest

NOVEMBER
Casper: Ski Sports Show
Lovell: Christmas Parade and Craft Fair
Riverton: Veteran's Day Parade

DECEMBER
Alta: Torchlight Ski Parade, Sleigh Rides
Jackson: Torchlight Ski Parade
Thayne: Cutter Races

■ ACCOMMODATIONS

Listed below is a choice selection of Wyoming's better hotels, motels, and bed-and-breakfast houses. For a complete listing, see the Wyoming Vacation Guide, available from the Wyoming Travel Commission, I-25 at College Dr., Cheyenne, 82002; phone (800) 225-5996 out of state, or (307) 777-7777 in state. For all phone numbers listed below, use area code 307.

B = Budget (under $20) **M** = Moderate ($20-40) **L** = Luxury (above $40)

BIG HORN

Spahn's Bed & Breakfast; 9 miles west of Big Horn; 674-8150; L

BUFFALO

Best Western Cross Roads Inn; on U.S. 16; 684-2256; M

CASPER

Casper Hilton Inn; 800 N. Poplar; 266-6000; L
Downtowner Motor Hotel; I-25 and Center; 235-2531; L
Holiday Inn; 300 West F St.; 235-2531; L

CHEYENNE

Hitching Post Inn, 1700 W. Lincolnway; 638-3301; L
Holding's Little America; 2800 W. Lincolnway; 634-2771; L
Holiday Inn; 204 W. Fox Farm Rd.; 638-4466; L
Plains Hotel; 1600 Central Ave.; 639-3311; M

CODY

Best Western Sunset; 1601 Eighth St.; 587-4265; L
Holiday Inn; 1701 Sheridan Ave.; 587-5555; L
Irma Hotel; 1192 Sheridan Ave.; 587-4221 (Buffalo Bill's hotel, named for his daughter); M-L
The Lockhart Bed & Breakfast Inn; 109 W. Yellowstone Ave.; 587-6074 (long the home of the flamboyant and controversial author, Caroline Lockhart); M

DOUGLAS

Holiday Inn; 1450 Riverbend Dr.; 358-9790; M-L

DUBOIS

Geyser Creek Bed & Breakfast; 4 miles west; 455-2702; L

EVANSTON

Dunmar Inn; 1019 Lombard; 789-3770; L
Pine Gables Lodge Bed & Breakfast; 1049 Center St.; 789-2069; M

GILLETTE

Best Western Tower West Lodge; 109 N. Hwy 14-16; 686-2210; L

GRAND TETON NATIONAL PARK

Jackson Lake Lodge; 5 miles NW of Moran Jct. on Hwy 89-287; 543-2855 (famed historic building); L
Jenny Lake Lodge, Jenny Lake; 733-4647 (log cabins with spectacular vistas); L
Signal Mountain Lodge; 4 miles NW of Moran Jct.; 543-2831; L

JACKSON AREA

Alpenhof, Teton Village; 733-3242; L
Big Mountain Inn Bed & Breakfast; Wilson; 733-1981; L
Heidelberg Bed & Breakfast; Wilson; 733-2462; L
The Inn at Jackson Hole; Teton Village; 733-2311; L
Spring Creek Resort; two miles NW of Jackson on Spring Gulch Rd.; 733-8833; L
Teton Tree House Bed & Breakfast; Wilson; 733-3233; L
Wort Hotel; Broadway and Glenwood, Jackson; 733-2190; L

LARAMIE

Annie Moore's Guest House; 819 University; 721-4177; L
Best Western Gas Lite; 960 N. Third; 742-6616; M

LITTLE AMERICA

Holding's Little America; I-80, Exit 68; 875-2400 (luxury in the middle of nowhere!); M-L

LUSK

Covered Wagon Motel; 1/2 mile S on U.S. 20/85; 334-2836; M

MEDICINE BOW

Virginian Hotel; 404 Lincoln Hwy; 379-2377 (restored old classic); L

R A W L I N S

Best Western Bel Air Inn; Spruce at 23rd St.; 324-2737; L
Ferris Mansion Bed & Breakfast; 607 W. Maple; 324-3961; M

R O C K S P R I N G S

Comfort Inn; 1670 Sunset Dr.; 382-9490; M-L

S A R A T O G A

Hood House Bed & Breakfast; 214 N. Third St.; 326-8901; M
Wolf Hotel; 101 E. Bridge Ave.; 326-5525 (nicely restored); B-M

S H E R I D A N

Holiday Inn; 1809 Sugarland Dr.; 672-8931; L

T H E R M O P O L I S

Holiday Inn; Hot Springs State Park; 864-3131; L
Plaza Inn; Hot Springs State Park; 864-2251 (mineral baths and massage; funky but friendly); B-L

W H E A T L A N D

Blackbird Inn Bed & Breakfast; 1101 11th St.; 322-4540 (lovely old Victorian home; very friendly); B

Y E L L O W S T O N E N A T I O N A L P A R K

Lake Yellowstone Hotel; 344-7311 (summers only); M-L
Mammoth Hot Springs Hotel; Mammoth Hot Springs; 344-7311; M-L
Old Faithful Inn; Old Faithful; 344-7311 (incredible 3-story log building, summers only); M-L

Dude Ranches

B I G H O R N M O U N T A I N S

Deer Haven Lodge; Box 76, Ten Sleep; 366-2449
Eaton's Ranch; Wolf; 655-9285
HF Bar Ranch; Saddlestring; 684-2487

Kedesh Ranch; 1940 Shell Route (Highway 14), Shell; 765-2791
Meadowlark Resort; P.O. Box 86, Ten Sleep; 366-2424
Paintrock Outfitters; Box 509, Greybull; 765-2556
Paradise Guest Ranch; Box 790, Buffalo; 684-7876
TX Ranch; Box 453, Lovell; 484-2583

CODY AND WAPITI VALLEY

Absaroka Mountain Lodge; Box 168, Wapiti; 587-3963
Bill Cody's Ranch Resort; Box 1390-T, Cody; 587-2097
Castle Rock Ranch; 412 Road 6NS, Cody; 587-2076
Crossed Sabres Ranch; Box WTC, Wapiti; 587-3750
Grizzly Ranch; North Fork Route, Cody; 587-3966
Hunter Peak Ranch; Box 1731, Cody; 587-3711
Pahaska Tepee Resort; 50 miles west on U.S. 14-16-20; 527-7701 (Buffalo Bill's old hunting lodge)
7D Ranch; Box 100, Cody; 587-9885
Shoshone Lodge; Box 790WT, Cody; 587-4044

DOUGLAS

Pellatz Ranch; 1031 Steinle Rd., Rt. 2, Douglas; 358-2380

DUBOIS

Absaroka Ranch; Dubois; 455-2275
CM Ranch; Rt. 60, Box 1601A, Dubois; 455-3415
Lazy L & B Ranch; Dubois; 455-2839
Ram's Horn Guest Ranch; Box 564, Dubois; 82513
Triangle C; Box 691, Dubois; 455-2225

GRAND TETON NATIONAL PARK

Flagg Ranch; Box 187, Moran; 543-2861 or (800) 443-2311
Heart Six Guest Ranch; Moran; 543-2477;
Lost Creek Ranch; Box 95, Moose; 733-3435
Moose Head Ranch; Box 214, Moose
R Lazy S Ranch; Box 308, Teton Village; 733-2655
Togwotee Mountain Lodge; Box 91, Moran; 543-2847
Triangle X Ranch; Moose; 733-5500
Turpin Meadow Ranch; Box 48, Moran; 733-6521

J A C K S O N   A R E A

Darwin Ranch; Box 511, Jackson; 733-5588

Diamond R Ranch and Outfitters; Box 211, Moran; 543-2479

L A R A M I E   M O U N T A I N S

Flying X Ranch; 799 Halleck Canyon Road, Wheatland; 322-9626

M E D I C I N E   B O W   N A T I O N A L   F O R E S T

Boyer YL Ranch; Box 24, Savery; 383-7840

Medicine Bow Guest Ranch and Lodge; Box 752, Saratoga; 326-5439

Moore Guest Ranch; Box 604C, Encampment; 327-5574

Mountain Meadow Guest Ranch; Box 203, Centennial; 742-6042 (national historic place)

P I N E D A L E

Big Sandy Lodge; Box 223-W, Boulder; 332-6782

David Ranch; Box 5, Daniel; 859-8228

Green River Guest Ranch; Box 176, Cora; 367-2314

Spring Creek Ranch; Box 33, Bondurant; 733-1184

T H E R M O P O L I S

High Island Guest Ranch; Hamilton Dome; 867-2374 or (800) 624-4188

■ RESTAURANTS

The restaurants and cafes listed below include an eclectic group of Wyoming eateries. Some are the fanciest and most expensive steak and seafood houses in town, while others offer a distinctive local ambiance and honest home-cooked food. All are strongly recommended by locals; use area code 307.

B = Budget (under $10)   **M** = Moderate ($10-20)   **L** = Luxury (above $20)

A F T O N

Homestead Restaurant; Hwy 89 S. of Afton; 886-3878; B-M

A L P I N E

Bette's Coffee Shop; 654-7536; B-M

ATLANTIC CITY
Atlantic City Mercantile; 332-5143; M

BASIN
Outpost Restaurant & Lounge; 151 N. Fourth St.; 568-2134; M

BUFFALO
Steve's Restaurant; 820 N. Main; 684-5111; M

CASPER
Anthony's Restaurant; 241 S. Center St.; 234-3071; M
Benham's; 739 N. Center; 234-4531; L
El Jarro's Mexican Restaurant; 500 W. F St.; 577-0538; B-M
South Sea Chinese Restaurant; 2025 E. Second St.; 237-4777; M

CHEYENNE
Emanuel's; 222 W. 16th; 632-1744; B
Luxury Diner; 1401 W. Lincolnway; 638-8712; B
Owl Inn; 3919 Central Ave.; 638-8578; B
Twin Dragon; 1809 Carey Ave.; 637-6622; B-M
Whipple House; 300 E. 17th St.; 638-1883; M

CODY
Cassie's Supper Club; 214 Yellowstone Ave.; 587-3383; M
Tranca's Italian Dining; 1374 Rumsey Ave.; 587-5354; M

DAYTON
Dayton Mercantile; 655-2214; B

DIAMONDVILLE
Luigi's; 819 Susie Ave.; 877-6221; M

EVANSTON
Legal Tender Restaurant; 1601 Harrison Dr.; 789-3770; M

GILLETTE
Bailey's Bar & Grill; 301 S. Gillette Ave.; 686-7667; M
Bazels Restaurant; 408 Douglas Hwy.; 582-9322; B-M

Boothill Night Club; 910 N. Gurley Ave.; 682-1600; M
Ole's Pizza; 114 N. Hwy. 14-16; 682-8484; B-M

GREEN RIVER

Trudel's Restaurante; 3 E. Flaming Gorge Way; 875-8040; M

HUDSON

Club El Toro; 132 S. Main; 332-4627; M
Svilar's; 173 Main; 332-4516; M

JACKSON HOLE

The Alpenhof Dining Room; Teton Village; 733-3462; L
Anthony's Italian Restaurant; 50 S. Glenwood; 733-3717; M
Billy's Giant Hamburgers; 55 N. Cache; 733-3279; B-M
Bubba's Bar-B-Que Restaurant; 515 W. Broadway; 733-2288; B-M
The Bunnery; 130 N. Cache; 733-5474; B
Cafe Montana; 750 W. Broadway; 733-9194; M
The Granary; Spring Creek Ranch; 733-8833; L
La Chispa Mexican Restaurant; 25 N. Cache; 733-4790; B-M
The Lame Duck; 680 E. Broadway; 733-4311; M
Nora's Fish Creek Inn; Wilson; 733-8288; B-M
Shades Cafe; 82 S. King; 733-2015; lunch B, dinner L
Stiegler's Restaurant; The Aspens; 733-1071; L
Sweetwater Restaurant; 85 King St.; 733-3553; M

KEMMERER

Lake Viva-Naughton Marina Restaurant; 15 miles north; 877-9669; M

LANDER

The Hitching Rack; Hwy. 287 South; 332-4322; M

LARAMIE

Cafe Jacques; 216 Grand Ave.; 742-5522; M-L
The Cavalryman; 4425 S. Third; 745-5551; L
Cowboy Bar & Grill; 309 S. Third; 742-3141; M
Giorgio's Supper Club; 2312 Grand Ave.; 745-7676; M
Jeffrey's Bistro; 123 Ivinson Ave.; 742-7046; M

The Mandarin; 360 N. Fifth; 742-8822; B-M
The Overland; 100 Ivinson Ave.; 721-2800; M

LINGLE

Lira's Mexican Food; 837-2826; B-M

MORAN

Togwotee Mountain Lodge; 16 miles east of Moran; 543-2847; M

NEWCASTLE

Flying V-Cambria Inn; 8 miles north on Hwy 85; 746-2096; M-L
Hi-16 Drive In; 2951 W. Main; 746-4055; B
Old Mill Inn; 500 W. Main; 746-4608; M
Slatewood Inn; 66 Old Hwy E.; 746-4688; M

PINEDALE

McGregor's Pub; 21 N. Franklin St.; 367-4443; L

POWELL

Munchies; 333 E. Second; 754-2683; B-M

RANCHESTER

B J Pizza; 655-9315; B-M

RAWLINS

Rose's Lariat; 410 E. Cedar; 324-5261; B-M

ROCK SPRINGS

Ted's Supper Club; 3 miles west on I-80; 362-7323; M

SARATOGA

Wolf Hotel Restaurant; 101 E. Bridge Ave.; 326-5525; M

SHERIDAN

Silver Spur; 832 N. Main; 672-2749; B-M
Spotted Horse Cafe; 120 N. Main; 672-2838; B-M
Sugarland Mining Co.; 1809 Sugarland Dr.; 672-8931; M

S T O R Y

Lodore Supper Club; 6 N. Piney Rd.; 683-2455; M
Tunnel Inn; 683-9921; M

T H A Y N E

Dad's; 883-2300; B-M
Star Valley Cheese Cafe; 883-2446; B

T H E R M O P O L I S

Pumpernick's; 512 Broadway; 864-5151; M

W H E A T L A N D

J.J.'s Brown Derby; 1707 N. Ninth St.; 322-4257; M

W O R L A N D

Antone's Supper Club; Hwy 16 West; 347-2301; M
Coffee Cup Cafe; 1010 Big Horn; 347-8501; B

Y E L L O W S T O N E   N A T I O N A L   P A R K

Old Faithful Inn; 344-7311; M-L
Lake Yellowstone Hotel; 344-7311; M-L
Mammoth Hot Springs Hotel; 344-7311; M-L

■ Wyoming Museums and Historic Sites

Nearly every town in Wyoming has a museum of one type or another. Here is a list of the largest and most interesting. Use area code 307.

Anna Miller Museum; Delaware-Washington Park, Newcastle; 746-4188
Bradford Brinton Memorial Museum; Big Horn; 672-3173
Buffalo Bill Historical Center; 720 Sheridan Ave., Cody; 587-4771
Campbell County Rockpile Museum; Hwy 14-16 W., Gillette; 682-5723
Carbon County Museum; Ninth and Walnut, Rawlins; 324-9611
Cheyenne Frontier Days Old West Museum; Frontier Park, Cheyenne; 778-7290
Dubois Museum; Ramshorn St., Dubois; 455-2284
Nici Self Museum; Centennial; 742-7158

Fort Bridger State Historic Site; Fort Bridger; 782-3842
Crook County Museum; Crook County Courthouse, Sundance; 283-3666
Fort Caspar Museum; 4001 Fort Caspar Rd., Casper; 235-8462
Fort Fetterman State Museum; NW of Douglas; 358-2864
Fort Laramie National Historic Site; Fort Laramie; 837-2221
Fort Phil Kearny; near Story; 684-7629
Fossil Country Frontier Museum; 400 Pine Ave., Kemmerer; 877-6551
Frontier Prison; 5th and Walnut, Rawlins; 324-4111
Grand Encampment Museum; Encampment; 327-5205
Grant Village Visitor Center; Yellowstone National Park; 344-7381
Greybull Museum; 325 Greybull Ave., Greybull; 765-2444
Guernsey State Park Museum; Guernsey; 836-2900
Historic Governor's Mansion; 300 E. 21st St., Laramie; 777-7878
Homestead Museum; S. Hwy. 85, Torrington; 532-5612
Homesteader's Museum; 133 S. Clark, Powell; 754-9481
Hot Springs Historical Museum; 700 Broadway, Thermopolis; 864-5183
Indian Arts Museum; Colter Bay, Grand Teton National Park; 543-2467
J.C. Penny Home; Kemmerer
Jackson Hole Museum; 105 N. Glenwood, Jackson; 733-2414
Jim Gatchell Museum; 100 Fort, Buffalo; 684-9331
Laramie Plains Museum; 603 Ivinson Ave., Laramie; 742-4448
Medicine Bow Museum; Medicine Bow; 379-2383
Museum of the Mountain Men; 700 E. Hennick St., Pinedale; 367-4101
National First Day Cover Museum; 702 Randall Blvd., Cheyenne; 634-5911
Nicolaysen Art Museum; 104 N. Poplar, Casper; 235-5247
North American Indian Heritage Center; St. Stephens; 856-4330
Old Trail Town; 1831 Demaris Dr., Cody; 587-5302
Pioneer Museum; 630 Lincoln St., Lander; 332-4137
Pioneer Museum; Fifth St., Afton; 886-3667
Riverton Museum; 700 E. Park Ave., Riverton; 856-2665
Rock Springs Museum; 1897 Dewar Dr., Rock Springs; 362-3771
South Pass City State Historic Site; South Pass City; Meeteetse; 868-2423
Stagecoach Museum; 322 S. Main, Lusk; 334-3444
Sweetwater County Historical Museum; 80 W. Flaming Gorge Way, Green River; 362-7870

Tate Mineralogical Museum; Casper College, 125 College Dr., Casper; 268-2310
Ten Sleep Museum; Ten Sleep; 366-2265
Teton County Historical Center; 105 Mercill Ave., Jackson; 733-9605
Trail End Historic Center; 400 Clarendon Ave., Sheridan; 674-4589
Uinta County Historical Museum; 36 Tenth St., Evanston; 789-2757
University of Wyoming Anthropology Museum; Anthropology Building, Laramie; 766-5310
University of Wyoming Art Museum; Fine Arts Center, Laramie; 766-6622
University of Wyoming Geological Museum; Geology Building, Laramie; 766-4218
Warm Valley Arts & Crafts; North Fork Rd., Ft. Washakie; 332-7330
Washakie County Museum and Cultural Center; 1115 Obie Sue Ave., Worland; 347-4102
Werner Wildlife Museum; 405 E. 15th St., Casper; 235-2108
Wildlife of the American West Art Museum; 110 N. Center St., Jackson; 733-5771
Wyoming Game and Fish Visitors Center; 5400 Bishop Blvd., Cheyenne; 777-7735
Wyoming Pioneer Museum; 1700 Fairgrounds Rd., Douglas; 358-9288
Albright Visitor Center; Mammoth Hot Springs, Yellowstone National Park; 344-7381
Wyoming State Museum; State Office Building; 22nd St. and Central Ave., Cheyenne; 777-7024

Definition: Jackalope—an unusual mammal that moves by bounding, found originally in Converse County, Wyoming, but now distributed throughout the Western United States. It has the horns of an antelope and the body of a jackrabbit. First observed by trapper Roy Ball in 1829, and later noted by cowboys and others after too little sleep, too many days in the saddle, and too much cheap whiskey. A nocturnal animal, Jackalopes are never seen during the day. They are reputed to obtain speeds of up to 90 miles an hour and known to sing just before thunderstorms. Powerful and vicious when attacked. The hornless does are commonly seen by tourists, while the federal government is hushing up the true story of these dangerous critters to make cowboys look like liars.

I N D E X

■ About the Author

Nathaniel Burt was born on a kitchen table in a log cabin during a blizzard on the Bar BC Ranch, in Moose, Wyoming. Son of Struthers and Katherine Burt, themselves famous authors—he the author of *Diary of a Dude Wrangler* and *Powder River* and she the author of many romantic novels on the West—Burt grew up in the truly American Shangri-la of Jackson Hole in the shadow of the Grand Teton. In his earlier book, *Jackson Hole Journal,* he tells a story of life surrounded by his parent's eccentric Eastern friends who came to ride, fish, sing Western songs and write poetry to each other. In this guide he shares the secrets of a state he has known since childhood, helping us understand why its citizens are proud to call Wyoming home.

Burt is a composer and writer whose many published works include poetry, fiction, and non-fiction. His musical compositions have been performed at the Teton Village Music Festival.

■ About the Photographer

Don Pitcher's travel photography and writing grew out of his interest in the natural world. While working for the National Park Service in Alaska, he picked up a copy of the *Alaska-Yukon Handbook* (Moon Publications), and his long letter of feedback to the author led to his writing a section of the new edition. He has also written the *Wyoming Handbook* for Moon.

Pitcher received an M.S. in Wildland Resource Science from UC Berkeley. Since graduating, he has worked on bear and owl studies, forest fire research, and as a wilderness ranger in Alaska, Wyoming, and California. His photographs have appeared in a wide variety of books, calendars, and magazines. He is also author of the guidebook *Berkeley Inside/Out* (Heyday Books).